LINCOLN CHRISTIAN COLLEGE AI

D0986371

IRISH JESUS, ROMAN JESUS

IRISH JESUS, ROMAN JESUS

THE FORMATION OF EARLY IRISH CHRISTIANIITY

Graydon F. Snyder

TRINITY PRESS INTERNATIONAL
Harrisburg, Pennsylvania

Copyright © 2002 Graydon F. Snyder

All rights reserved. No part of this book may be reproduced, stored in a retrieval system, or transmitted, in any form or by any means, electronic, mechanical, including photocopying, recording, or otherwise, without the written permission of the publisher, Trinity Press International.

Trinity Press International, P.O. Box 1321, Harrisburg, PA 17105
Trinity Press International is a division of The Morehouse Group.

Cover art: Christ Pantocrator, Byzantine mosaic, copyright Scala/Art Resource, NY. Crucifixion monasterboice SW, photograph by Graydon F. Snyder.

Cover design: Wesley Hoke

Library of Congress Cataloging-in-Publication Data
Snyder, Graydon F.
    Irish Jesus, Roman Jesus : the formation of early Irish Christianity /
Graydon F. Snyder.
        p. cm.
    Includes bibliographical references and index.
    ISBN 1-56338-385-3 (pbk.)
        1. Celts – Religion. 2. Celtic Church – History. 3. Church
history – Primitive and early church, ca. 30–600. I. Title.
BR737.C4 S69 2002
274.15 – dc21

                                            2002009362

Printed in the United States of America

02   03   04   05   06   07   10 9 8 7 6 5 4 3 2 1

Contents

104631

Preface

This study began in 1967 when I first analyzed the impact of the Jesus tradition on Roman culture, especially on non-verbal materials. Since that time I have often wondered what would have happened if the Jesus tradition had infiltrated a culture other than the Roman. That pondering has led to this book.

In a preface, of course, the author ought to thank those people who inspired him to produce such a tome. Though I have many friends who have expressed interest in the Irish Jesus, I must say that the thesis expressed here is not theirs. I alone bear that responsibility.

However, I will thank Henry Carrigan and Laura Hudson, editors at Trinity Press International, for their considerable encouragement and assistance. Therese Boyd and John Eagleson labored much to make the text comprehensible. To all of them and the staff at Trinity I want to express appreciation.

All the photographs have been enhanced by either me or my son Jon Snyder. Some of the photos were taken by my wife, Lois Snyder, and some by photographer Jeanine Wine.

It should be clear to the reader that this study would have been impossible without access to a great library. Use of the University of Chicago's Regenstein Library has been a great gift. In fact, at this stage of my life the entire project feels like a remarkable gift.

Introduction

This is not another book about the Irish. There are many fine works on the Celts and the Irish.[1] This study will need them, because I am a New Testament scholar with absolutely no background on the Irish. Strange as it may seem, our purpose is to better understand the nature and power of the Jesus tradition. The impact of the Jesus tradition on Roman culture created Western Christianity. The impact of the Jesus tradition on Celtic culture eventually resulted in a Christianity demonstrably different from its Roman counterpart. On this there is no disagreement.

That resultant Celtic Christianity is, of course, Irish Christianity. Although the Celts consisted of a high-level culture stretching from Turkey to Spain, generally in middle Europe, eventually they were either destroyed, assimilated, or pressed to the farthest reaches of the known world, known today as Ireland and Scotland (north of Hadrian's Wall).[2] That area was only slightly touched by the Roman culture, and the Irish Celts bitterly opposed any attempt by Romans to conquer them or alter their culture. Consequently they make a nearly perfect test case: What would happen when the Jesus tradition affected a culture other than the Mediterranean culture?[3]

The differences between Irish Christianity and Roman Christianity are self-evident. How the differences occurred is problematic. When and how did the Jesus tradition first have an impact on Celtic culture? How did that Palestinian tradition spread to western Europe, especially Gaul and Iberia? What are the differences between British Celtic Christianity and Irish Celtic Christianity, and why did those differences arise? How and when did the Jesus tradition reach the western isles? How did the Irish Celtic culture and the Jesus tradition so interact as to create what is called Irish Christianity? Why is Christianity, as Westerners know it, Roman rather

1

than Irish? Is Roman Christianity the best and only way to convey the Jesus tradition to other cultures?

These questions are nearly impossible to answer, yet they are critically important to a Christian world seeking new life and new forms. How is Irish Christianity related to the Jesus tradition?

The problem of inculturation and assimilation may involve theology, philosophy, and ideology, but for the most part it is considered a sociohistorical issue. In part I adopt sociohistorical methods because culture involves popular life more than rational thought. In Celtic culture I will look at their political organizations, economic policies, morality or ethics, art, architecture, symbols, commensality, religion, language, writing, rituals for death and dying, calendar, community, and cultural expansion. Then I will ask how the Jesus tradition was inculturated in Celtic Ireland.

Notes

1. To mention only a few: Thomas Cahill, *How the Irish Saved Civilization: The Untold Story of Ireland's Heroic Role from the Fall of Rome to the Rise of Medieval Europe* (New York: Doubleday, 1995); Norman Davies, *The Isles: A History* (Oxford: Oxford University Press, 1999); Gerhard Herm, *The Celts: The People Who Came Out of the Darkness* (New York: St. Martin's Press, 1977); Simon James, *The Atlantic Celts: Ancient Peoples or Modern Invention* (London: British Museum Press, 1999), and *The World of the Celts* (London: Thames and Hudson, 1993); Thomas M. Charles-Edwards, *Early Christian Ireland* (Cambridge: Cambridge University Press, 2000); and Peter Berresford Ellis, *The Ancient World of the Celts* (New York: Barnes and Noble, 1999).

2. James, in *The Atlantic Celts*, refers to these supposed remaining areas — Galicia, Brittany, Wales, Scotland, Cornwall, Ireland and Isle of Man — as the Atlantic Celts (see 16–19).

3. The Celts are not the only potential test case. The Goths, Anglo-Saxons, and Picts were also untouched by Romans in certain areas. We will use that fact in this study. On the other side of the Mediterranean, Ethiopian Christianity also was untouched by Roman culture. Doing a similar study there would be extremely useful — especially if Ethiopian Christianity could be considered the origin of precolonial African Christianity. On the deleterious effect of the hellenization and romanization on the Jesus tradition, and the escapement of Ethiopian Christianity, see J. N. K. Mugambi, *African Heritage and Contemporary Christianity* (Nairobi: Longman Kenya, 1989), 1–13.

Chapter 1

The Celts

Origins

Before the Greeks and Romans developed their respective cultures another culture whose origin is much debated was forming in northcentral Europe. Some historians would like to connect them with the Indo-Europeans who may have immigrated from the East around 2000 B.C.E. From the Indo-Europeans would have come, among others, the various European languages, with the exception of Finnish, Estonian, and Hungarian, or, better stated, people similar to the Indo-Europeans began to appear in Europe, particularly in the Balkans, Austria, Switzerland, France, and Spain (using modern terms).[1] These new people were not involved in a forceful takeover of the land. They were content with local tribal formations rather than the creation of an empire. Such local tribes were often transient or nomadic. When they did become stationary, they developed farms where they cultivated livestock perhaps even more than produce. They did not develop towns or cities. Those in political leadership led a cultivated life, as did their priests (later Druids) who organized religious ceremonies involving the sun god, and their poets (later *filidh*) who formed and transmitted the tribal traditions. These Indo-Europeans settled in a variety of areas already occupied by other tribes. They may have brought their own cultural characteristics but also were assimilated by the various continental groups and tribes. While these differing tribes were not Celts, perhaps not even proto-Celts, the stage was set for the appearance in middle Europe of a culture that clearly differed from the developing Roman and Greek.

However plausible the theory of an Indo-European migration, and however likely the probability of an ancient common source for the languages of Europe and Asia, it will not explain the origin of what are called the Celts. Many of those characteristics called Celtic are older than the date used to identify the Indo-European migration, making it difficult to pin down a specific date. One thinks of the circular edifices such as Newgrange and Stonehenge, stone tombs in Ireland and Brittany, ringforts, and ornamentation like spirals, circles, and chevrons, but these existed long before the migration occurred. Still, there must be some type of continuity between the third-millennium people of Ireland and the Celts that emerged in the first millennium. This continuity became Celtic by accretion; perhaps a better term might be gradual "celticization."[2]

Evidence of proto-Celtic social practices dates back to about 1300 B.C.E. with burying after cremation. The ashes were placed in pots made of sheet bronze and interred in flat fields. Other bronze items, like shields, also appeared at the same time.

A more precise archaeological date for the appearance of the Celts, however, would be about 600 B.C.E. In 1846 in a cemetery near Hallstatt, a town in the Upper Austrian Salzkammergut, a mining inspector discovered some ancient graves, eventually 193 altogether. In all, 3,000 objects such as pins, brooches, belts, torcs, earrings, daggers, spearheads, axes, pots, bowls, and dishes were uncovered. The Hallstatt finds enabled scholars to realize, because of similar artifacts elsewhere, that throughout much of Europe there had been "another" culture that eventually became what is now called Celtic. Remains found throughout middle Europe included hillforts and the artifacts of burial mounds of a Hallstatt culture that existed about 1200 to 475 B.C.E.[3]

The isles remain a serious question, though. There older artifacts and artistic designs that resemble early continental proto-Celtic remains exist. The language of the isles resembles what would eventually be called Gaelic. But there is no sign of a massive Indo-European immigration into Ireland that brought with it specific designs and language. It does appear that the original Indo-European language shifted into a variety of languages and dialects, most of which were latinized. However, Gaelic kept retreating to the West until it finally reached the end of Europe in Ireland, where it was not romanized or latinized. Surprisingly then, there is a close linguistic connection between Sanskrit and Old Irish.[4]

In 1857 at the northern end of Lake Neuchâtel in Switzerland, at a place called La Tène, an amateur archaeologist discovered a huge cache of ancient swords, spears, fibulae, and tools. The lush, finely tooled decorations had no counterpart in Roman or Greek art. While Greeks and Romans tended to portray vines and plants in a static way, La Tène art portrayed vegetation in a vibrant, even abstract manner.[5] Furthermore the decorations contained finely detailed animal and human figures, with little empty space left. Scholars dated the find at La Tène about 450 B.C.E. The discovery of similar artifacts throughout most of Europe north of the Alps made it clear that La Tène was a subsequent development of the Hallstatt culture.[6]

The remaining history of the Celts is somewhat better known, thanks to the writings of Julius Caesar, Polybius, and other Romans. Earlier, it was the Greeks (ca. 500 B.C.E.) who first spoke of the people of middle Europe as Keltoi (Celts). Various Keltoi tribes were found from northern Turkey across to Spain. For reasons not always clear or even rational, the Romans constantly attempted to subdue the Celtic tribes. Admittedly, the Celts occasionally made serious forays against Rome. At the beginning of the fourth century B.C.E. Celtic tribes crossed over the Alps into northern Italy. The Romans thought these Gallic barbarians could be easily crushed. They were wrong. The Celts defeated the Romans at the battle of Allia (a tributary of the Tiber) and Rome was sacked. Although the Celts were fierce, heroic warriors, they lacked the professional military discipline of the Roman armies. The Romans often suffered serious losses, but eventually brought the Celts under their control.

Under pressure from the Romans, Celtic types continued to move westward. The Celts of Gaul crossed over the channel to England, where they continued to be romanized until the Romans left Britain in 410 C.E. Some of the Celts of Spain, however, following long-established travel and trade routes, likely crossed over to Ireland to become the Irish Celts. This group, whose language and culture differed from the British Celts, vehemently resisted any romanization, either from the British or from the Romans themselves. Eventually Ireland and Britain north of Hadrian's Wall became an isolated pocket of non-Romans.[7] While this book will concentrate on Irish Celts, it is best here to summarize some of the particular cultural practices that characterized Celts as a whole.

Political Organization

Much like the original emigrés from the East, the western Celts were itinerant. When they finally reached a satisfactory location, they tended not to build towns. As farmers they preferred to live on the land itself or in small settlements (e.g., hillforts), raising grains and cattle, pigs, sheep, and horses. The importance of animal husbandry to the culture can be seen in the striking roles domestic animals played in Celtic mythology (e.g., Táin Bó Cúailnge or Brown Bull of Cúailnge).[8] There was no overall central organization of the Celts, so, in contrast to the Romans and Greeks, there was never a Celtic empire. Instead, the Celts remained tribal in nature, with a propensity to intertwine culturally with those who had previously lived on the land. Consequently, they became a multifaceted culture, unified by a relatively common language.

One result of cultural assimilation was the development of towns about the end of the La Tène period (ca. 50 B.C.E.). For the most part these towns were circular structures built on the top of hills, referred to as hillforts by the Celts, but called *oppida* by Caesar. Outstanding warrior leaders were able to create enough unity among some tribes to take over other tribes, defend against the Romans, or even attack Roman positions. But there never emerged a leader of such magnitude that a single Celtic culture could appear.

According to Caesar, who was after all only an outside observer speaking of Celts in Gaul and Britain, three classes of society existed below the king: druides, equites, and plebs. The higher class, which Caesar called druides, included intelligentsia and professionals like bards, jurists, physicians, historians, and skilled craftsmen. The equites, or knights, included warriors, landowners, and wealthy patrons. In addition there was a class of mercenary-type warriors called Gaesatae by the Romans. They were not a tribe, as the Romans thought, but professional fighters; according to the Romans, they apparently fought naked for religious reasons.[9] The plebs were freemen, commoners, small landholders, and less-skilled craftsmen. Little is known about the slaves. Among the Celts there was little individualism since everyone belonged to an extended family or kindred, called the *fines*. For example, any penalty levied against an individual would be handled by the total fines. The larger social structure, a *tuath*, would be ruled by a king.

Economic Policies

As capitalists, the Celts were interested in acquiring wealth and then displaying it through lavish banquets and feasting. One suspects, from reading Irish legends, that wealth was measured by the number of cattle a family possessed. Early Irish units for barter were based on a séd, the value of a milk cow.[10] In the legendary Cattle Raid of Cooley, Medb, the queen of Connacht, debated heatedly with her husband, Ailill, about their respective wealth. At the end of the debate Ailill was acknowledged to be wealthier because he owned the great White-Horned Bull (Fionbanach). In her fury Medb organized the famous cattle raid of Cooley to gain an even greater bull, the Brown Bull.

Another major source of income was the export of metal. Some hillforts or oppida had foundries, and some hill sites were entirely given over to mining, smelting, and blacksmithing. In 1955 a huge oppidum was discovered near Ingolstadt, north of Munich. Its wall was four miles long. Inside were places for smiths, foundries, iron and glassworks, potteries and trading posts. Obviously Celts of the second century B.C.E. had shifted from husbandry to metalwork and arts. The Celts turned out remarkably well-decorated weapons and ornaments, as well as quite functional tools and containers.[11] Their wagons and chariots were unmatched in the ancient world.

The Celts were interested in acquiring things and not always honestly. While their sack of Rome in 390 B.C.E. may have been instigated by Roman improprieties, it resulted in their seizing considerable booty. This was also true for their foray into Delphi,

Greece, where they did not seek to conquer, to expand, or convert, but rather to plunder.

Determining the Celtic infrastructure for trading and barter is no longer possible, but evidently not everything was barter since the Celts were minting coins by the third century B.C.E. Striking coins was probably initiated by the arrival in Gaul of coins called staters, brought from Greece and Galatia by mercenary Celts.[12]

Identifying specific trade routes is a very important aspect of any study of the Celts. Given their nomadic origins, interest in acquiring, and prevalence of wagons, it is evident that the tribes of Celts participated in regular, organized trading trips. The Celts of Galatia corresponded with the Celts of Spain in an exchange of ideas as well as of goods, artistic symbols, and designs.[13] The connection between the Celts of Spain and the Celts of Ireland is clear and the route west from Spain to Ireland seems undeniable. In a recent study, the DNA of the ancient (pre-Celtic) Spanish people was found far more in Irish people today than in any other European people.[14]

What is more difficult is to explain the origin of African symbols in Irish and Pict art. It is likely that people from the south Mediterranean came as far north as the region of Galatia and there inserted artistic materials, among other things, into the Celtic trade route. The art they brought with them may have included those fantasy tropical symbols such as elephants and lions that appear in Pictish art especially. To move ahead briefly, if southern Mediterranean people were in Galatia, and they surely were (Antiochus I of Syria conquered the Galatian Celts in the famous Elephant Battle, 275 B.C.E.), then this would also help explain why Paul traveled through Galatia in the first place. It would also explain how the southern oral Jesus tradition, by word of mouth, by wagon train, and by boat, reached the Atlantic Celts.

Morality or Ethics

Of course, morality is relative to a particular culture so that any discussion of ethics reflects the nature of the culture but does not necessarily measure what is called civilized. The Romans, who tended to support the cultural systems of people they conquered, were not so broadminded in their estimation of the Celts. For them the Celts were barbarians. First, the Celts were known as head-hunters. It is difficult to determine whether this was true, why they did it and how often, but the Romans said that Celtic warriors carried skulls of their victims on their belts. It is fact that some oppida and permanent Celtic homes had skulls built into the walls (e.g., Entremont, in Provence, southern France). Whether they came from the dead or the living cannot be established, but the conclusion must be drawn that they did cut off their enemies' heads. There can be little doubt that this was more than an arrogant show of military skill. In Celtic anthropology the head was the seat of the person. Somehow preserving the heads of enemies impeded their psyche and enhanced the psyche of the victors.[15]

The second barbaric act was human sacrifice. Again apart from apparently prejudicial Roman literature, the extent of such sacrifices would be hard to determine. Religious exercises were supposedly performed in what was known in Galatia as a Drunemeton (possibly an oak temple) in an oak grove. According to Strabo the Galatian tribes also used the Drunemeton as a gathering place for tribal decisionmaking. At these places the Celts would dig deep pits into which were thrown or placed sacrificial items such as metal items, cauldrons, and cattle. Human remains have occasionally been found as well. In some instances the method of death can only be explained as a ritual killing.[16]

The third barbarism was the Celtic way of warfare. The Celts did not practice a disciplined means of fighting. In sharp contrast to the rows of Roman soldiers protected by conjoined shields, Celt warriors started with shouts, often stripped off their clothes, and then viciously attacked without regard for their own lives. The mercenary Gaesatae would often strip naked. The Romans considered such irrational behavior barbaric because it showed more of a disregard for life than did their own culture. Again, though, this is a matter of cultural relativity since the Celts did not consider death the end of life.

The so-called fourth mark of barbarism was far more peaceful. It appeared to the Romans that the Celts were illiterate because they had no writings. To a Roman culture that put everything in written form, this was clearly barbaric. The Romans were wrong but apparently could not see their error. Celtic inscriptions appear in many various alphabets. More important, the Celts had a great oral tradition, as the many rich Irish legends prove. Exactly what those oral legends and narratives contained may never be known and what elements of extant insular legends actually reflect the earlier continental Celts may never be determined. Whatever the case, a rich oral tradition was passed on by the trained narrators, filidh or *vates* (Latin).[17] These associates of the Druid priests were responsible for the corporate memory of the Celtic tribes, religious, legal, and mythical. Oral repetition of the memory allowed for constant adjustments, and during the Christian era, even prior to writing, Christianizing of the oral material must have occurred. Still, there are memories in the stories that surely reflect the La Tène period (450 B.C.E.) and later.

Roman writers insist that Celtic men, perhaps warriors in particular, stressed male bonding and preferred sleeping with other men to sleeping with women. Outside this Roman observation there is little proof of the accusation. If it were true, then sexual relations with women would have served primarily for propagation. Again this cannot be proven. Since the Romans would hardly be in a position to accuse the Celts of denigrating their women, one suspects an ulterior motive for the observation. Irish legends abound with strong, even fierce, women, some even rulers. Goddesses are well represented in the Celtic pantheon. In contrast with the Roman rumors, the Irish/Celtic culture valued highly the role of women.[18]

Despite the constant treachery expressed in the Irish sagas, ultimately integrity is valued above clever trickery. In the seminal *Táin Bó Cúailnge,* the hero of the story, Cú Chulainn, otherwise indestructible and a master of headhunting, makes a wager with a ghost that he can cut off his head. When the ghost's head grows back, Cú has to allow the ghost to cut off his head. Though indestructible, Cú submits to his own destruction because he cannot violate the word he has given. The integrity of mythical figures like Cú probably served as a model for Irish Christianity, that is, saints like Columba as well as literary figures like Parsifal (Perceval) or King Arthur.

Symbols

While one seldom finds a symbol that belongs solely to one culture, nevertheless most cultures have symbols that are repeated often enough to be considered specific marks. In what little Jewish art and architecture exists, the menorah, shofar, ethrog, lulab, and torah shrine are unmistakable. In Greco-Roman architecture the egg and dart motif is nearly standard, and columns with Doric, Ionic, and Corinthian capitals invariably mark a Greco-Roman origin. Symbols that would identify the source as uniquely Roman are not so obvious. Perhaps the ubiquitous SPQR, or the toga, or the DM on gravestones comes closest to signaling "Roman."

Celtic art has two basic symbols: the chevron and the spiral. The chevron is nearly universal from Hallstatt on, though found much earlier in Ireland. In its simplest form it is a V, open at the bottom or the top. The open side can be closed to create a triangle. The two open sides can be joined to create what might be called a diamond. Or two open chevrons may be joined to form a VV. From these basic forms the Celts created an infinite number of variations — and surely one mark of the Celtic artist was to be creative.[19] It would be presumptuous to say that every artist who uses a symbol reflects on its meaning — if, indeed, it has one. Yet, at the same time cultural symbols have deep-seated meanings, perhaps more unconscious than not. The American flag or Big Ben comes to mind. Given the warrior mentality of the Celtic men, the chevron probably reflects the sharpness of a sword or the point of a spear.

The other symbol, the spiral, is far more definitive of Celtic culture. It appeared early in Celtic history and throughout the Christian era. At first it may have been a simple spiral, but in most extant examples several spirals are attached in what seems like a maze. The famous proto-Celtic stone in front of the Newgrange mound stands as a classic example of the intertwining spiral (plate 1). An amazing variety of finely worked spirals appeared on mirrors, torcs, and other metal ornaments and instruments. In the Christian era the spiral appeared plaited or knotted, as seen in the Pictish Aberlemno Cross (plate 2). Often, as seen in this example, the spirals not only intertwined but the ends became mythical animals much like dragons. This remarkable symbol system became the basis for the extravagant borders and capital letters of the famous Irish manuscripts and illuminated gospels.

Primary geometric shapes reflect aesthetic values, as well as philosophical and theological positions. The rectangular religious builtform indicates a faith that requires a person to move forward toward the presence of God. Often the move forward includes a community hierarchy. The square builtform reflects a strong emphasis on the community itself with no hierarchy, a community that knows God is present. The circle implies the use of rituals to find the presence of God. Dancing in a circle would be the most obvious ritual. The circular builtform is capped by a dome where God can be reached by upward prayer and ritual fervor.[20]

In contrast to the longitudinal Romans, the Celts were pre-eminently circular. Hillforts or oppida were circular. Remains of thousands of ringforts, from pre-Christian times, circular, of course, can be seen in Ireland. Private settlement or homes called crannogs were circular man-made islands in lakes or wet places. The Celts were so circular that some scholars say that the presence of a rectangular building points to Romano-British construction instead of Irish Celt.[21] Early pre-Celtic religious mounds like Newgrange and the extant remains in the Boyne Valley were precisely circular in order to follow the sun.

The circle appeared early in Irish Christianity. The Christian ringforts, or monasteries, were round, though some buildings in the compound were rectangular.[22] And, of course, the absolute mark of Irish Christianity is a circle on the cross, circles that do not always portray the crucifixion but often include other scenes.

The circle signifies a community aware of God's presence "above" them, not "beyond" them. The spiral signifies the spiritual ascent to that close presence. Celtic mythology and Irish Christianity have places and times where one can easily ascend into the other world. The Drunemeton in Galatia, or its western equivalent, was such a place. The distinction between human and divine was a very thin line. Early Christian saints experienced the same thin relationship with God and even shape-shifting could occur. Modern Irish Christians speak of such occasions and locations as "thin places." One could reasonably argue that the symbol of the spiral defines the Celtic experience and Irish Christianity.

Art

Art in the Hallstatt period centered on the chevron and spiral designs. These figures appeared primarily on finely tooled metal objects such as mirrors, swords, torcs, and cauldrons. In the La Tène period, influences from the East and from Etruscan art brought a shift toward pictorial representations, primarily in stone sculpture. The first representations were gods and goddesses with animal characteristics or even monstrous distortions. These stone sculptures can be found in museums all over temperate middle Europe.

Eventually metalwork artisans also shifted to pictorial representations. One of the best examples can be seen on the Gundestrup cauldron, found in 1880 in Denmark. Well represented is the god Cernunnos, who always appears with a set of antlers (note the La Tène–style torc on the neck of Cernunnos and in his right hand). Elsewhere on the cauldron are many other extravagant mythical animals. Fighting is a main theme on this cauldron, with both clashing animals and warriors using La Tène–style weapons.

With the increasing presence of the Roman Empire, Celtic art shifted more toward a classical style. God and goddess began to look anthropomorphic rather than theriomorphic. In fact, in late La Tène it became difficult to distinguish Celtic deities from their Roman counterparts. Nevertheless, Celtic art lacked the Roman interest in accurate representation of the human figure, or even the hint of narrative movement.

Irish Celtic art is primarily decorative (for example, the Turoe stone, or the Pictish slab, plate 3), but when Irish Christian art appeared in the sixth century, it had preserved much of the La Tène style.

Architecture

Few examples of pre-Roman private dwellings remain. Most were made of wood and have long since disappeared.[23] From what

evidence exists, it is evident that southern families built rectangular single dwellings. Because the foundation remains of private
dwellings in Britain and Ireland are circular, one may suppose the
Celts of middle Europe also built circular dwellings. Later in Ireland
the Celts built circular crannogs on artificial islands near lakes. Remains of circular stone domestic structures called "hut circles" can
be found where stone was available. The circular private dwelling
may have even preceded the formal Celtic immigration. Ringforts
or cashels consisted of stone or earthen banks and ditches that protected a dwelling and farm buildings. The foundations of thousands
of these buildings still exist throughout Ireland.[24]

The early Celts seemed not to care for urban life, so we do not
often find Mediterranean-type towns, built in attractive flat areas.
What would most closely resemble urban settlements are the hillforts or oppida. Hillforts were constructed for defensive purposes.
One unique element of the few remaining pre-Roman Celtic towns,
like Entremont, Roquepertuse, and Nages in southern Gaul, is the
presence of shrines exhibiting the actual heads of defeated victims
and severed heads built into decorations and statuary. Diffidence
toward towns and cities changed about the second century B.C.E.,
when continental Celts began to form towns of major consequence.
Caesar mentions a number of these oppida, forerunners of some
modern cities like Paris, Reims and Bourges.[25] There is no record
of such towns in Ireland or Scotland.

Regarding early Celtic religious gatherings, except for posts and
pits, there are few extant remains. Some groves became more permanent and identifiable through a square earthwork surrounding the
posts, pits, and burials. In Ireland such earthworks surrounded pre-
Celtic monuments like those at Tara and Emain Macha. In Britain
the same is true of Stonehenge and Avebury. Under the influence of
the Romans the Celts built some permanent temples. Though these
temples honor Roman deities, they have sufficient Celtic elements to
identify them as a religious amalgamation. They are usually square,
with a raised cella that may enclose a pit or burial.

When Christianity first came to Ireland, it continued the circular domestic architecture of the Celtic world, like those in Skellig
Michael. Other early religious buildings looked more like an ark.

The earliest extant example occurs in County Kerry, the Gallerus oratory.

Religion

The pre-Celtic world revered the sun and tracked its movement as diligently as any ancient culture (Newgrange, Stonehenge, and the Trundholm Chariot). This interest in the sun continued into the culture of insular Celts to the point that the distinguishing mark of an Irish cross is the circle (sun) around the crossbars or spokes. The Celts had as many as sixty-seven major gods and goddesses. As the Roman world encroached on the Celtic world, some Celtic divinities coalesced with their Roman counterpart, as commonly seen in statuary.[26] Jupiter had several Celtic equivalents, the most obvious being Taranis, who is pictured on the interior of the Gundestrup cauldron holding a wheel. The wheel may signify Taranis as the one who drove the sun chariot, or the wheel may be the sun itself. In any case, the large number of wheels in Celtic inscriptions and art signify the role of Taranis as the sun god. In addition, Taranis was a warrior, as most Celtic gods were, and a god of healing.[27]

Despite the frequency of the wheel in archaeological material (e.g., the Jupiter crosses), there is very little in the sagas of the Celts to indicate actual worship of a sun god. However, Saint Patrick condemned the worship of the sun god because Christ is the true Sun, so the Irish Celts must have been using the sun in some form of religious exercise.[28] The sun wheel, with its spiritual meaning, was eventually absorbed into the four-spoked Celtic cross.

The sacred place of the Celts was the oak groves. The leaders or priests were called Druids (oak persons). They were highly educated and lived in the highest class of Celtic society. As such they oversaw religious rites and directed religious and political decision-making. The bards and filidh (sing. *fili*), associates of the Druids, were responsible for the recitation and transmission of Celtic sagas. Eventually Irish Christianity assimilated the Druids and the bard. The filidh, or Christian equivalents, remained key members of the educated community until the seventeenth century.

Unlike the proto-Celtic cultures who practiced cremation, the

Celts buried their dead. Extant graves show that they prepared their dead well for the journey to the next life. Aristocratic graves might contain a body placed in a chariot. Other graves included weapons and ornaments. The dead were also furnished with drink and food for the journey.

There is little evidence of an extensive grieving process in Celtic death rituals. Celtic warriors notoriously fought with abandon, perhaps because there was no higher honor than to be a great warrior and that sometimes entailed death. But sheer heroics do not seem a sufficient explanation for this lack of a grieving process. The Celts must have believed that they would return after death. Roman writers stated that the Celts believed in some form of transmigration. Julius Caesar said the Druids taught that "souls do not disappear but wander from one body to the other." Lucan, in *Pharsalia*, spoke to the Celts with these words, "If we understand you aright, death is only a pause in a long life."[29] So understood, perhaps some of the artifacts have been misread. Perhaps the wheel refers as much to rebirth as to the sun. Perhaps the purpose of headhunting was to assure the victor that the victim could not return for another challenge.

For the Celts there was a very thin line between animal/human and the divine. Gods and goddesses became animals or humans. Humans could enter the divine world. The transfer was especially potent on the night before the festival Samhain, which marked the shift from summer to winter, from life to death. On this night spirits could easily leave their *sidhe* (spirit mound) and become animals or enter the human world. According to the sagas the sidhe, or otherworld, was an extraordinary place filled with beautiful people, great food, and music. Any human would desire it.

Language

From the original language of the Indo-European people came the language of the Celts, closely related to Sanskrit and derivative European tongues. This proto-Celtic, Indo-European language developed into the universal Celtic language known as Gaelic. Sometime before the La Tène era linguistic changes gave rise to a separate, simplified dialect of Gaelic called brythonic or P-Celtic.[30] An earlier dialect, called goidelic or Q-Celtic, appeared in the Irish, Scottish, and Manx languages. P-Celtic, on the other hand, was spoken by Celts in Gaul and on the continent. Before the La Tène era the Q-Celtic speakers were forced from the continent by the P-Celtic speakers. They must have gone through Spain to the back side of the British Isles. According to the *Book of Invasions,* the *Leabhar Gabhála Éireann,* the final invasion was made by the Sons of Mil, the Gaels or Celts. Their father was Míl Espáine, a soldier of Spain, and they first landed in the southwest corner of Ireland. From there they defeated the Tuatha Dé, a divine race that had conquered Ireland before the Celts arrived. Eventually an agreement was made that the Tuatha Dé would inhabit the underworld or Ireland and the Celts could have the island itself.[31] However mythical the tradition, at least it was stated that the Celts and Goidelic came from Spain.

Apparently the brythonic speakers expanded later, at the beginning of the La Tène period, into Britain proper — a migration noted by Roman writers. Traces of P-Celtic can be found in the Welsh, Cornish, and Breton languages.[32]

Writing

The Celts, with a culture very rich in oral tradition, left few written records or written literature. The first Celtic written documents in Ireland were recorded in the fourth century in an unusual alphabet that represented letters by means of dashes and dots. Such dots and dashes were often placed in vertical lines on gravestones and other markers.

The first Irish writings can be traced to Saint Patrick's *Confession* and his *Letter to the Soldiers of Coroticus* in the fifth century. By the sixth century monks were copying many manuscripts from continental Europe in part in an effort to save them from the destruction that swept the Roman world. Students from all over Europe came to these monasteries for an education and to keep alive the Western heritage. Had the Celts not copied this material, much of what we now know as Western civilization would have been lost.[33]

Before the rise of the Caesars, the Celts had been the most powerful people in Europe. Eventually the Romans pushed them to the westernmost part of the empire, where they defended themselves from Roman incursions and even refused to interact with the Romano-Celts in Britain. Furthermore, since they possessed an oral tradition, they did not avidly scour the written literature of Rome. Consequently, Roman literature had no significant effect on the Celts' culture. They were isolated geographically, temperamentally, and linguistically.

Calendar

The discovery of a first-century B.C.E. bronze tablet in Coligny, Burgundy, gave scholars both increased knowledge of the Gaelic language and some minimal knowledge about the Celtic calendar. The Coligny calendar belonged to the Druids and therefore registered their schedule for rituals and appropriate times. It is obvious from this calendar that the Celts followed the rotation of the sun, as did most cultures. The smaller units were dictated more or less by the waning and fullness of the moon. So the solar year was divided into units of twenty-nine days and thirty days — six each. Of course, six thirties make 180 days, and six twenty-nines total 174 days (354 in toto). That leaves eleven extra days each year. As is true in every culture, an intercalation was necessary. The Celts solved it by adding two more months every five years (a sixty-two-month, five-year cycle).

The solar year was divided into four seasons: Samhain, Imbolc, Beltene, and Lughnasad. Passage from one season to the other was celebrated by a great festival. Most important was Samhain, which marked the end of the year. Cattle were brought in for the winter and sacrifices were made. The festival occurred on November 1 and was preceded by a spirit night when spirits left their sidhe and transmutation could occur. Imbolc occurred on February 1. The festival was dedicated to the goddess Brigid and may have marked the lactation of the ewes. Beltene (presumably associated with the god Belenus, a sun and healing deity) was celebrated on May 1 and marked the season when the cattle went out to open grazing. Bonfires were lit to celebrate the return of the sun's warmth. Lughnasad came on August 1. Sacrifices were made to the high god Lugh to celebrate harvest time.

The Celts were an ancient, powerful people. They migrated from the East sometime in the second millennium B.C.E. Eventually they covered most of Middle Europe, that is, north of the Alps and south of the Teutonic regions. It wasn't until 1846, at Hallstatt, that archaeological discoveries made known the high quality of that Celtic culture. It has been assumed the Hallstatt culture existed for the first half of the first century B.C.E. The finds at La Tène, in 1857, produced materials more like what is known to us as specifically Celtic (450–50 B.C.E.). These finds show a culture deeply interested in material things, highly skilled in metallurgy, and unmatched in decorative artistry.

Celts first appeared in written history when they were described by Roman writers such as Julius Caesar and Strabo. The life of the Celts as portrayed by the Romans differed radically from that of the classical world. Though the Celts had kings, they were led by wise priests or Druids. Their laws and traditions were kept orally by the Druids and bards, so we have very few written records. They organized by tribes that individually infiltrated various areas of Middle Europe. One cannot speak of a Celtic empire, for unlike the Romans they had no desire to conquer and rule. They can be identified as a culture because of a relatively common language (known now as Gaelic and Welsh) and a common artistic or decorative style. They counted wealth in terms of cattle and lived on the top of hills in ringforts. Like the Romans they were polytheistic. Their gods are known to us through many legends passed on by the bards. Because these gods were functionally determined (weather, fertility), they could easily correspond to Roman gods, so the earliest artistic portrayals often combine Roman and Celtic divinities. Various seasons of the year marked the divine functions. In no way did these celebrations correspond with the Roman solar year. Instead, they commemorated important events, such as when the cattle were shifted from place to place. The festivals were times for sacrifices and for thin places with the other world to appear.

Eventually the Romans pushed the Celts to the far reaches of western Europe (northern Spain and Portugal, Brittany, Cornwall, Ireland, northern Britain, and the Isle of Man). From there the Celts still impacted the western world, but they never became the dominant force. Historians realized that the predecessors of the Celts in western Europe were much like the Celts just described. Remains like Newgrange with its sun orientation, with spiral artistry and chevron markings, point to the existence of a Celtic culture centuries before the Hallstatt era. These proto-Celts had shifted easily into the emerging Celtic world of the first millennium B.C.E. The process has been called celticization.

After 32 C.E. the Jesus tradition entered the hellenistic world rather quickly, perhaps first in Philippi. Even before that Paul had carried the Jesus tradition to the far western Celts in North Galatia. From there the history of Irish Christianity begins.

Notes

1. Pierre-Yves Lambert, *La langue gauloise: Description linguistique, commentaire d'inscriptions choises* (Paris: Editions Errance, 1995), 13; Peter Berresford Ellis, *The Ancient World of the Celts* (New York: Barnes and Noble, 1999), 16–26; Herm, *The Celts*, 68–84.

2. For how the term is used in this study, see Miranda Green, *The Gods of the Celts* (Gloucester: Alan Sutton, 1986), 1–6.

3. Herm, *The Celts*, 102; James, *World of the Celts*, 20.

4. Myles Dillon, *Celts and Aryans: Survivals of Indo-European Speech and Society* (Simla, India: Indian Institute of Advanced Studies, 1975), 32–51. Dillon speaks of this phenomenon as a striking example of lateral survival.

5. Bieler notes the distinction and states that later early Irish Christian art, independent of Rome, was the first abstract Christian art; Ludwig Bieler, *Ireland: Harbinger of the Middle Ages* (New York: Oxford University Press, 1963), 2. See also James, *World of the Celts*, 106–15.

6. James, *World of the Celts*, 15.

7. Ibid., 128–29.

8. Ellis, *Ancient World of the Celts*, 101–10.

9. Caesar, *Gallic War*, 6.13–15.

10. Peter S. Wells, "Resources and Industry," in *The Celtic World*, ed. Miranda J. Green (London: Routledge, 1995), 216–29.

11. Ellis, *Ancient World of Celts*, 107.

12. Daphne Nash Briggs, "Coinage," in *The Celtic World*, ed. Green, 246–49.

13. The lack of extensive archaeological investigations in Galatia leaves this assumption even more problematic. Recent discoveries in Gordium of Phrygia

demonstrate the presence of Celts in Galatia, but does not prove trade connections with the westerns Celts. See John Noble Wilford, "Archaeologists Find Celts in Unlikely Spot: Turkey," *New York Times*, 25 December 2001. For a more complete report, see Jeremiah R. Dandoy, Page Selinsky, and Mary M. Voight, "Celtic Sacrifice," *Archaeology* 55 (2002): 44–49.

14. Emmeline W. Hill, Mark A. Jobling, and Daniel G. Bradley, "Y-chromosome Variation and Irish Origins," *Nature* 404 (2000): 351–52. For the function of navigation in the formation of the pre-Christian Atlantic community, see Barry Cunliffe, *Facing the Ocean: The Atlantic and Its People, 8000 B.C.–A.D. 1500* (Oxford: Oxford University Press, 2001), esp. 109–212.

15. Barry Cunliffe, *The Ancient Celts* (Oxford: Oxford University Press, 1997), 127–28, 209–10.

16. Strabo, *Geography* 12.5.1; Miranda J. Green, *Dictionary of Celtic Myth and Legend* (London: Thames and Hudson, 1992), 183–84.

17. Ellis, *Ancient World of the Celts*, 27–36; Green, *Dictionary of Celtic Myth and Legend*, 98.

18. Ellis, *Ancient World of the Celts*, 87–100; James, *World of the Celts*, 66–69; Herm, *The Celts*, 246.

19. Laurence Flanagan, *Ancient Ireland: Life Before the Celts* (New York: St. Martin's Press, 1998), 68–69.

20. See my "Aesthetic Origins of Early Christian Architecture," in *Text and Artifact: Judaism and Christianity in the Ancient Mediterranean World*, ed. Stephen G. Wilson and Michel Desjardins (Waterloo, Ontario: Wilfrid Laurier University Press, 2000), 289–307.

21. Lloyd Laing and Jennifer Laing, *Celtic Britain and Ireland: Art and Society* (New York: St. Martin's Press, 1995), 73; James, *World of the Celts*, 57–59.

22. Kathleen Hughes and Ann Hamlin, *The Modern Traveller to the Early Irish Church* (1977; Dublin: Four Courts Press, 1997), 54–55.

23. Laing and Laing, *Celtic Britain and Ireland*, 11.

24. Nancy Edwards, *The Archaeology of Early Medieval Ireland* (Philadelphia: University of Pennsylvania Press, 1990), 7–33.

25. John Collis, "The First Towns," in *The Celtic World*, ed. Green, 159–75. See also his *Oppida: Earliest Towns North of the Alps* (Sheffield: Department of Prehistory and Archaeology, University of Sheffield, 1984), and Françoise Audouze and Oliver Büchsenschütz, *Towns, Villages, and Countryside of Celtic Europe: From the Beginning of the Second Millennium to the End of the First Century B.C.*, trans. Henry Cleere (London: Batsford, 1992), 240–43.

26. An inscription on an altar in Chester reads: "To Jupiter Best and Greatest Tanarus" in Green, *Dictionary of Celtic Myth and Legend*, 206.

27. Miranda J. Green, *The Wheel as a Cult-Symbol in the Romano-Celtic World* (Bruxelles: Latomus Revue d'Etudes Latines, 1984), 162; Green, *Dictionary of Celtic Myth and Legend*, 197.

28. *Confession*, 20, 59, and esp. 60.

29. Caesar, *Gallic War* 6.14; Lucan, *Pharsalia* 1.457–58; Herm, *The Celts*, 152.

30. Ellis, *Ancient World of the Celts*, 16–18; Dillon, *Celts and Aryans*, 32–51. Brythonic used a *p* for the *q* in goidelic.

31. Proinsias MacCana, *Celtic Mythology* (London: Hamlyn Publishing, 1970), 64–66. The Spanish connection is assumed as accurate by writers like Timothy J. Joyce, *Celtic Christianity: A Sacred Tradition, a Vision of Hope* (Maryknoll, N.Y.: Orbis Books, 1998), 6.

32. André Cherpillod, *La langue gauloise* (Courgenard: Autoédition, 1998), 3–13; Herm, *The Celts,* 204.

33. Cahill, *How the Irish Saved Civilization.*

Chapter 2

Paul and the Galatians

The Celts in Galatia

While much of the Celts' story involves their migration west to Ireland, actually the tale begins not in the West, but in the East. In the fourth century the Celts moved into the Balkans. They paused for a time on the northern edge of Greece but eventually moved south into Greece. The key moment (279 B.C.E.) was the defeat of the Greeks at the famed narrow mountain pass called Thermopylae. At that point the Celtic forces split, possibly because of internal conflicts. Leotarios and Leonto took 20,000 warriors, the Tolistobogii, Tectosages, and Trocmii tribes, toward modern Turkey, while Acichorios and Brennus with their Celts moved on toward the shrine at Delphi, the place of the Pythian oracle.[1] They ransacked the temple complex, killed the elderly Pythia herself, and apparently made off with the great temple treasures.[2] Following heavy losses and probably the death of Brennus, the remaining Celts retreated back north.[3]

Shortly after the sack of Delphi, Antigonus Gonatus, the general of Macedonia, defeated the invading Celtic army. Nicomedes of Bithynia then recruited the defeated Celts as his mercenaries. In 278 B.C.E. the 20,000 Celtic warriors and their families crossed the Bosphorus and settled in central Asia Minor.[4] They formed the first Celtic state, issued coins, and set up a loose central government. They remained rural, built hillforts rather than towns, and organized around a Drunemeton. Their language, common to all three tribes and derived from earlier Gaulish, remained in use possibly until the eighth but at least to the end of the fourth century C.E.[5] The Celts, or Galatians in Latin, learned Greek as a second language (sometimes they were known as Gallogrecians), though

23

later they appear to have preferred Roman customs and perhaps even the Latin language.

The Celts assimilated the Phrygians of the area, although, as was usual for the Celts, they retained some Phrygian influence. One primary Phrygian element would be the worship of the Great Mother Goddess, Cybele, whose central temple was located in Pessinus, a chief town in the Tolistobogii area. It is not clear when and to what extent the Celts first met the Jews. There are a few Jewish inscriptions in Galatia, but no known synagogues.[6] The Jesus tradition, and its form of Judaism, most likely first came to the Celtic world through the missionary efforts of the Apostle Paul.

Paul in Galatia According to Acts

Paul, Barnabas, and their companions were commissioned by the church at Antioch to carry the gospel to Asia Minor. They went first to Cyprus and then sailed to Perga in Pamphlyia. Their missionary journey included the towns of Pisidian Antioch, Iconium, Lystra, and Derbe, all located in the southernmost part of the Roman province, also called Galatia. In the first century B.C.E., with the death of the Celtic leader Deiotarus II, the Romans had formed the province of Galatia, which included the territory of Galatia.

In Antioch and Iconium Paul entered the synagogue where he first addressed the Jews (and God-fearers? [Acts 13:13–14:7]). In Lystra no synagogue is mentioned and the missioners were hampered by translation problems (14:8–20). In every town Paul and his companions formed churches and appointed elders (14:23). These towns, though belonging to the province of Galatia, were not near the territory of Galatia where the three tribes had settled three centuries earlier. So there were two Galatias in the New Testament. One is the Roman province and the other is a Celtic territory that is included in the Roman province. Scholars refer to that part of the province that is not Celtic as south Galatia and the section that is Celtic, the territory, as north Galatia.

After his first visit to south Galatia, Paul returned in order to encourage the new Jesus converts and inform them of decisions made by the Jerusalem Council (16:1–5). Instead of returning to

Antioch, however, the team went through the region of Phrygia and Galatia (16:6). Since Phrygia was not a province, one suspects the Galatia mentioned also was the territory, not the province. Paul's team went on to the west side of Asia Minor, opposite Mysia. They tried to move into the province of Bithynia, just north of the Celtic territory, but, held back by the Spirit, it was not to be. At that point the Greek mission began (16:9–10). Following the mission to Greece, Paul returned to Antioch and Jerusalem before going once more to the churches in the territory of Phrygia and Galatia (18:23).

Attempting to correlate the missionary journeys of Paul in Acts with the actual Letter to the Galatians has proven extraordinarily difficult, if not impossible. Over the years scholars have not been able to decide whether Paul wrote his letter to the churches of the province (south Galatia) or the churches of the territory (north Galatia). Regardless of the destination, the letter requires two visits: one to establish the churches (Gal. 1:6, 11–12), and one to discover relapses from his first visit (1:7–9, 3:1). If the letter was written to the southern churches after Paul's second visit (15:36–16:5), then that letter was likely Paul's first letter written about 49 C.E.[7] If the letter was written to the Galatians of the Celtic territory, since he first went to north Galatia on his second visit to Asia Minor, then it had to be written after the third missionary journey (probably 53 or 54 C.E.; 18:23). If those who insist that Paul wrote to south Galatia are correct, then nothing is known of Paul's encounter with the Celts. If those who insist that Paul wrote to north Galatia are correct, then it was surely Paul who first brought the Jesus tradition to the Celtic world. That is the starting point for our thesis.

According to Acts, when Paul entered a town he first went to a synagogue to speak to the Jews and any Gentiles who might have gathered with them. His initial contact was with members of the Jewish faith. Paul's letters to Thessalonica, Corinth, and Philippi reflect those Jewish encounters. Paul also spoke in synagogues in southern Galatia. As in his other writings, his Letter to the Galatians reflects a serious discussion with persons who are at least somewhat familiar with Judaism. Nothing is known of Paul's missionary approach in north Galatia, but it is a fact that there were

no synagogues for Paul to enter. In terms of Paul's usual missionary procedure as recorded in Acts, the south Galatia thesis fits the
pattern. The north does not.

While the Letter to the Galatians contains much that escapes easy
explanation, it does reflect the problems facing a congregation with
a Jewish background. In fact, the letter closely parallels the Letter
to the Romans with its intense reflection on the Jewish Law and the
justification given by God in Jesus Christ. Galatians belongs to the
same time in Paul's thought as Romans — about 55 C.E. It does not
at all appear to be a letter written early in Paul's life as a missioner.
The Letter to the Thessalonians, with its interest in the end-time,
more accurately typifies the early Paul, prior to his growing conviction about the cross of Christ. It seems nearly impossible that
Paul could write Galatians and then revert to Thessalonians. So the
south theory seems highly improbable if it entails making Galatians
the first letter.

At the same time, the presence of such intensely Jewish arguments in a letter addressed to the Celts leaves much to be explained.
Perhaps it does help to remember that Paul wrote the parallel Letter
to the Romans without having spoken to anyone in Rome. That is,
what is in Romans and Galatians reflects more the maturation of
Paul's thought than it does a message to a specific audience.[8]

Paul's First Visit

The church at Antioch commissioned Paul and his team to make
missionary visits that presumably led to the towns of south Galatia.
According to Acts, it was the first missionary journey and it marked
the inclusion of Gentiles in the Jewish-based faith. It would seem
that such an important enterprise would necessarily be mentioned
in a letter to the Galatians. It is not. Quite the contrary: the occasion
for Paul's visit was a health problem:

> You know that it was because of a physical infirmity that I
> first announced the gospel to you; though my condition put
> you to the test, you did not scorn [me] or [spit at] me, but
> welcomed me as an angel of God, as Christ Jesus. What has

become of the good will you felt? For I testify that, had it been possible, you would have torn out your eyes and given them to me. (Gal. 4:13–15)

There is no reason to suppose from this letter that Paul had been on a mission to the Galatian tribes. His stay in Galatia was a historical accident. While on the way to Mysia he became ill and had to stop in the territory of the Celts.[9] His memory of that welcome evoked considerable warmth. Something about the illness could have repulsed the Celts, but Paul expressed appreciation that it did not. Though the nature of the potential repulsion remains uncertain, the illness must have involved his eyes, perhaps an obnoxious abscess, since, in reflecting on their very gracious hospitality, he noted they would have torn out their eyes to give him a new pair.[10] While all Near Eastern cultures had places of healing, the Celtic spas were especially well known. Whether Paul would have stopped in north Galatia and visited a Celtic hot spring to heal his eyes remains a mystery, though it was certainly possible.

Direct Evidence That Celts Are the Addressed

While there is no direct evidence that the churches of south Galatia were the recipients of the letter, neither is there absolute evidence for Celtic recipients. Paul does exclaim:

You foolish Celts! Who has given you the evil eye? It was before your eyes that Jesus Christ appeared as crucified! (Gal. 3:1; author's translation)

It can be plausibly argued that "O foolish Celts" is simply a Greek rhetorical exclamation like "O foolish man" (*Shepherd of Hermas, Vis.* 3.8.9).[11] On the other hand, it could also be a cynical, even angry address from a Greco-Roman who knows the reputation of the illiterate Celts as barbarians.

Indirect evidence for Celtic recipients exists, but there is little linguistic evidence for either the north or south thesis. For example, Paul was born in Tarsus, just south of the province of Galatia. Livy wrote that Tarsus did fall in the province. Would the young

Paul have known some Celtic phrases from north Galatia? Or did he learn some Celtic while his eyes were being healed? Or was all business, visiting, and speaking, whether province or territory, done in Greek? If Paul knew some Celtic, why doesn't it appear, even as a courtesy, in this letter written to persuade? "O foolish Galatians" stands, with its Latin form of the word *Celts,* as the only direct reference to the Celts.

Indirect Evidence That the Celts Are Addressed

While there is little, if any, direct evidence that the Letter to the Galatians was addressed to Celts, there is considerable circumstantial evidence.

Galatians 1:2

To the churches of Galatia

Galatia is a territory or province, not a city. This is the only letter Paul addressed to the churches of a region. All the others are addressed to cities like Thessalonica, Corinth, Philippi, and Rome (secondarily Ephesus and Colossae). Paul may have addressed multiple house churches, but all in one city. If Paul was writing to the churches in a southern province, one would have expected him to name the receiving town and ask the initial recipients to pass the letter on to other house churches and cities (Col. 4:15–16). So it can reasonably be assumed that the letter is addressed to a group of house churches in the north located near the road toward Pessinus and Ancyra.[12] There is no city to name because all the house churches existed in a nonurban area, such as the Celts were known to inhabit. The churches would have met in homes substantial enough to house the new faith communities and to serve their communal needs, and Paul's emissary would have taken the letter from one house church to another. Since these house churches were in close proximity, "mailing" directions were unnecessary.

Galatians 1:6

> I am astonished that you are so quickly deserting the one who called you in the grace of Christ and are turning to a different gospel.

Paul is amazed that only four years after receiving the Good News from him they have already shifted to something else. It is not certain who caused them to shift or to what they shifted. The Celts were known to assimilate other cultures. As the Indo-Europeans swept west into Europe they settled among the local tribes, assimilated some of their characteristics, and eventually created the variety of middle European cultures known today. Likewise when the Hallstatt Celts moved west into Gaul they permeated the local groups in such a way that countless tribes of Celts resulted. When some Celts from Gaul moved into Asia Minor, they absorbed cultures such as the Phrygians'. In order to understand the slow, peaceful inculturation of the Jesus tradition into the Irish Celtic world, one must take seriously this assimilative characteristic. In Galatia they assimilated Paul's Jesus tradition and then either reverted to their Celtic beliefs or assimilated some other version of the Jesus tradition.

Without written traditions the Celts' culture was always open to the processes associated with storytelling: adaptation, expansion, and addition. The rhetor had the option of adapting the older tradition to the cultural situation in which the Celts found themselves. Apparently the rhetor or Druid did not carry a codified tradition. If adaptation involved the inclusion of a new group, the rhetor could alter the new tradition to fit into the received Celtic culture. The same rhetor could take the Celtic tradition and, in homiletical fashion, expand it in appropriate places to include materials from the new tradition. Or the rhetor might simply at some point add new material to his recitation. Such an oral society can be very assimilative because there are no written materials against which the rhetor can be judged.[13] Through their Druids, bards, and brehons (lawyers), the Celts easily adapted to other cultures.

The elders of the churches in Galatia, or perhaps the rhetors, did not fall back into their previous Celtic belief system but, under the influence of other Celtic leaders, readapted what Paul had offered them. Coming as he did from a written or at least codified tradition, Paul was astounded that they could so easily alter what he had taught them.

Galatians 1:12

> for I did not receive it from a human source, nor was I taught it, but I received it through a revelation of Jesus Christ.

Paul responds sharply to the assimilative nature of Celtic oral tradition. What Paul had taught them was not to be altered. He was not a rhetor with skills to persuade (1:10; note 1 Cor. 10:10). His gospel could not be assimilated or adapted. It was not even a human tradition but an apocalypse or revelation of God through Jesus Christ. The conflict between Paul and the Celts set for the first time issues that would never go away. The Jesus tradition and the kerygma are a revelation, not a human tradition. Yet the revelation can function only if it can be inculturated. In that process adaptation and assimilation must occur.

In the Celtic religion the religious actor or person honored the gods and sought their favor (healing, fertility, military prowess). Narratives carried the ancient myths and the ritual procedures, but the narration was not a revelation and certainly was not exempt from the rules of orality. Paul apparently was mystified by this aspect of Celtic culture. His letter was written in part to clarify the distinction between divine revelation and human tradition. Presumably the storytelling Celts did not catch the distinction. It is possible that the Celtic converts never heard why Paul was mystified.

It is indeed confusing. Paul himself was not a literalist. As a Pharisee he knew that the Torah would be adapted for succeeding generations (the Mishnah and the Talmud, at least). In his letters, even in this letter, Paul adapted the Septuagint to suit his purposes. Paul encourages the Galatians to live by the Spirit (3:3). For Paul the function of the Spirit is to create spontaneity and purpose within the body of Christ. Then what was absolute revelation for Paul? It is not the Torah, nor is it the Hebrew Scriptures. From this letter it is clear that the immutable revelation is the gospel of Christ (1:7). While it is not certain, it appears that Paul's gospel as he had given it to the Celts is: (1) Christ crucified; (2) faith in Jesus Christ; and (3) right relationships through faith. A part of the mystery for scholars today, as well as for the first Celtic recipients, is to identify the disastrous adaptation of which Paul spoke. Paul continues his argument for revelation over against human tradition through to 2:10, where he shifts to the Agape meal.

Galatians 2:12

> for until certain people came from James, he used to eat with the Gentiles. But after they came, he drew back and kept himself separate for fear of the circumcision faction.

At 2:11 Paul shifts briefly to the encounter with Peter (Cephas) at Antioch. Peter and Paul had eaten together with Gentiles at Antioch. At an unspecified special occasion some Jerusalem disciples joined the Antioch fellowship at mealtime. The Jerusalem group withdrew to their own tables for fear of defilement. Peter then joined them. Paul was infuriated. That occasion, which led to Paul's powerful discussion of justification by faith (2:15–3:21), has rightly been the center of scholarly debate for over a century. The problem is not made any easier by assuming the text has significant meaning for the new Celtic disciples. First, to state the obvious: the incident at Antioch with Peter does not directly involve the Galatians, whether south or north. This is clearly Paul writing to state his faith and by analogy addressing the Galatians. The incident serves as a pedagogical illustration. For what purpose? The Antioch illustration follows well the argument of the preceding paragraphs. If Paul was following human tradition (the Jerusalem congregation), then his eating with the Celts, sharing the Agape with them, and passing on the eucharistic tradition would have been in vain. Commensality could be quickly altered by the customs of any given culture as, for example, the Jewish kashrut laws. It is not easy to tell now whether the Jerusalem disciples reacted to nonkosher food, to nonkosher wine, to eating at the same table with non-Jews, or to eating in the same room with non-Jews.[14] But for the Celtic recipients, these are nonissues. One absolute of Paul's gospel is the transcultural unity of the body of Christ through faith. Like the rest of the Mediterranean world, the Celts were remarkably hospitable. It would bring shame on a family or village to turn away a stranger. So at first glance they would not understand how different members of the body of Christ could not eat at the same table. Paul's reaction to the Peter incident would have resonated well with Celtic culture. At that point he is at one with them and their hospitable culture. The Jesus tradition and Paul agree that the faith community is formed by eating together — even across cultural and racial lines. Though Jesus did not establish table fellowship with Gentiles, he too had communion across clean and unclean lines:

> When the scribes of the Pharisees saw that he was eating with sinners and tax collectors, they said to his disciples, "Why does he eat with tax collectors and sinners?"
> When Jesus heard this, he said to them, "Those who are well have no need of a physician, but those who are sick; I have come to call not the righteous but sinners." (Mark 2:16–17)

Following the Jesus tradition, Paul, too, insists on the unity of eating together. Not only does the remarkable Antioch incident appear in Gal. 2:11–14, but in Corinth Paul excoriates those who fail to eat the Agape as a communal meal (1 Cor. 11:17–22). Because they fail to recognize the function of a common meal, some of the Corinthian community have become sick (1 Cor. 11:29).

Why was this illustration necessary for the north Galatians? Something apparently had gone wrong. Paul did teach that the Agape and the Eucharist were for the disciples and not for sinners:

> Clean out the old yeast so that you may be a new batch, as you really are unleavened. For our paschal lamb, Christ, has been sacrificed. Therefore, let us celebrate the festival, not with the old yeast, the yeast of malice and evil, but with the unleavened bread of sincerity and truth. (1 Cor. 5:7–8)

> Whoever, therefore, eats the bread or drinks the cup of the
> Lord in an unworthy manner will be answerable for the body
> and blood of the Lord. (1 Cor. 11:27)

After Paul's eyes were healed and he left the Galatian house
churches, the Celts fell into a pattern both alien to their own culture and contradictory to what Paul had taught. They interpreted
his warnings as mandates to be exclusive. In contrast to the Jesus
tradition and Paul's sense of the common meal, they, as congregations, began to decide who could and who could not participate
in the life of the congregation. From Paul's perspective these congregations had shifted to a faith determined by law. He used the
Antioch narrative as a negative example of commensal legalism.

Galatians 3:1–3

> You foolish Celts! Who has bewitched you? It was before your
> eyes that Jesus Christ was publicly exhibited as crucified! The
> only thing I want to learn from you is this: Did you receive
> the Spirit by doing the works of the law or by believing what
> you heard? Are you so foolish? Having started with the Spirit,
> are you now ending with the flesh?

The most apparent direct evidence for assuming the recipients are
Celtic is the ejaculation by Paul, "O foolish Celts." Paul repeats
the same demeaning accusation in 3:3. The use of the adjective
here in an absolute sense does not echo the possible Greek rhetorical style of "*You* foolish Celts." One must assume he does indeed
address them as barbarians. His address may have been more cynical than vituperative. That is, why didn't they trust their own Celtic
experience?

In 3:1b Paul enters into the Celtic thought world in a unique
way. The Celtic Jesus converts had seen Christ crucified. For Paul
the Agape and Eucharist formed and celebrated the faith community's *koinonia*. In 1 Corinthians 10 Paul speaks of the Agape and
Eucharist as a celebration of the koinonia.

The cup of blessing that we bless, is it not a sharing in the blood of Christ? The bread that we break, is it not a sharing in the body of Christ? (1 Cor. 10:16)

Drinking the cup of wine celebrates the blood of Christ and invokes the gift of the Spirit given to the community. The breaking of the bread together creates and celebrates the historical reality of the body of Christ. The Agape and Eucharist mark the presence of the expected end-time community. Surely Paul taught the Celts about this transcultural body of Christ and the meal that created it.

Paul also presented a form of the Eucharist that enabled the participants to partake in the death and resurrection of Jesus:

and when he had given thanks, he broke it and said, "This is my body that is for you. Do this in remembrance of me." In the same way he took the cup also, after supper, saying, "This cup is the new covenant in my blood. Do this, as often as you drink it, in remembrance of me." (1 Cor. 11:24–25)

Remembrance means far more than simply a memory. Remembrance means reenactment of the saving event, participation in the event itself.[15] Paul surely taught the Celts that the Eucharist would enable them to participate in this saving event. But something more happened in these Celtic churches. Shape-shifting! Transmogrification! And Paul recognized it. Because of the thin line between historical reality and mythical reality, the Celts not only participated in the death of Jesus, they could actually see the crucifixion of Jesus.[16] These were not individual apparitions, but an event experienced by the entire assembled community. Only here does Paul speak of the visible nature of Jesus on the cross as seen when the cup was drunk and the bread was broken. Such an amazing experience would have occurred only in the Celtic thought world.

Galatians 3:6–18

Just as Abraham "believed God, and it was reckoned to him as righteousness," so, you see, those who believe are the descendants of Abraham. And the scripture, foreseeing that God would justify the Gentiles by faith, declared the gospel before-hand to Abraham, saying, "All the Gentiles shall be blessed in you." For this reason, those who believe are blessed with Abraham who believed.

For all who rely on the works of the law are under a curse; for it is written, "Cursed is everyone who does not observe and obey all the things written in the book of the law." Now it is evident that no one is justified before God by the law; for "The one who is righteous will live by faith." But the law does not rest on faith; on the contrary, "Whoever does the works of the law will live by them." Christ redeemed us from the curse of the law by becoming a curse for us — for it is written, "Cursed is everyone who hangs on a tree" in order that in Christ Jesus the blessing of Abraham might come to the Gentiles, so that we might receive the promise of the Spirit through faith.

Brothers and sisters, I give an example from daily life: once a person's will has been ratified, no one adds to it or annuls it. Now the promises were made to Abraham and to his off-spring; it does not say, "And to offsprings," as of many; but it says, "And to your offspring," that is, to one person, who is Christ. My point is this: the law, which came 430 years later, does not annul a covenant previously ratified by God, so as to nullify the promise. For if the inheritance comes from the law, it no longer comes from the promise; but God granted it to Abraham through the promise.

If this passage reflects an understanding of the Law as the Jewish basis for works righteousness, then it hardly speaks to the Celts of Galatia. Since the Celts had no laws that could justify them be-fore their gods, they would have hardly recognized Paul's argument. This much-debated passage is indeed a critical moment in the argu-ment. What did Paul tell the Celts about the Law? Did he tell them there was a divine Law which, if not obeyed, would become a curse to those who lived under it? Did he tell them (the Celts) that Christ came to redeem them from the curse of their (Celtic) rigid law? Or is he speaking to the nonexistent Jews of north Galatia?

Or had Paul described the Law in quite a different way? Had he told them the Law was subordinate to the promise, a promise that Gentiles such as the Celts would also receive God's blessing. In that case, was the Law to which Paul objected the cultural law that separated Jew from Gentile and prevented the fulfillment of the promise? The structure of Galatians is built on these three laws: the problem of clean and unclean food (2:11–14), calendar (4:8–11), and circumcision (5:2–12).[17] If Paul did indeed speak of Laws that identified the Jew, then the Celts would have understood his argument.[18] They too had marks of identification that involved food, calendar, and sexuality. If, then, Paul addresses that kind of Law in 3:6–18, recent exegetical proposals can be very helpful. E. P. Sanders has rejected the works righteousness definition of the Jewish Law for what he called "covenant nomism."[19] God made a covenant with the Jewish people, and the Law described their proper response. It was not possible to gain favor with God by works. In the case of improper response, the covenant relationship provided the opportunity for repentance.

Once free of works righteousness exegesis, Dunn and others described the Law in quite a different way. The laws against which Paul struggled were laws that prevented the gentile mission. Dunn and others have spoken of this new understanding of Law as the "New Perspective on Paul."[20] If Paul had presented the Law this way, the Galatians would have understood how and why they could participate in God's blessing (for the Gentiles). They would have understood how Jesus, by abrogating the cultural laws, became one of them. Further, they would have understood that they too could violate the Jesus mission by ossifying their own (new?) marks of identity.[21]

Galatians 3:24–25

> Therefore the law was our disciplinarian until Christ came, so that we might be justified by faith. But now that faith has come, we are no longer subject to a disciplinarian.

With arguments based on the Hebrew Scriptures Paul continues to maintain that God's promise and God's covenant precede the coming of human tradition and laws. To be sure laws were an aid to keeping the covenant and following God's promise. But now that faith in Christ has come, law is no longer needed. In these verses Paul uses a synonym for *law* with an audience that would not understand his argument. He tells them law is a teacher or disciplinarian. The disciplinarian was necessary for a time, and useful, but with the coming of Christ it was no longer needed. While the Celts would not have understood the meaning of an impersonal, revealed Torah, they did understand the teaching and legal function of Druids and brehons in their corporate life. Aware of the power of the Druids, Paul uses the term *pedagogue* to clarify the function of the Law in terms of their prior Celtic structure. As the Jewish Law was the pedagogue for Paul, so the codes of the Druids and brehons were the pedagogue for the Celts. Now that they know Christ, the druidic pedagogue is no longer necessary. In essence, the Celtic code had been a custodian, even warden, until such a time as faith had been established.[22] The use of the term still leaves the impression that some in the Celtic congregations were making divisive rule decisions that destroyed the power of the Spirit. Some of them had adapted the gospel to what must have seemed to them to be a historical cultural necessity.

Galatians 4:8

> Formerly, when you did not know God, you were enslaved to beings that by nature are not gods.

While the comment about many gods would have applied to a few recipients in south Galatia (Acts 14:12), it applies specifically to the Celts with their massive pantheon of gods spread throughout the multiplicity of tribes. It certainly does not apply to possible Jewish readers.[23] In fact, it is a typical mission attack by Jews toward Gentiles (1 Cor. 8:4–6; Isa. 46:1–2). Paul stays with his prior argument even though he has changed the subject. The Celts knew no gods who made covenantal revelations. They only knew gods who had to be served in order to achieve particular effects. For Celts the shift to monotheism with a revelatory God would have been a monumental task, as Paul now articulates.

Galatians 4:10

> You are observing special days, and months, and seasons, and years.

The shift from Celtic culture to nascent Christianity, from multiple divinities to monotheism, required considerable effort and determination. Surely a major problem was the calendar. The Celtic tribes followed a specific calendar with seasons based on agricultural cycles (a sixty-two-month, five-year cycle), and special days to celebrate the beginning of each period (Samhain, Imbolc, Beltene, Lughnasad).[24] Changing calendars required breaking with one's cultural context, failing to follow accepted time sequences, and otherwise visibly becoming deviant. It had to be a social disaster for anyone who tried to live by some other calendar. Some of the recipients of this letter were continuing to use the calendar that organized the world in which they lived. They may have had no other choice. For the Galatians that meant accommodating the new faith to their Celtic culture. It meant celebrating Celtic feast days; it meant adhering to the Celtic calendar; it meant revering the Celtic gods, the elemental spirits (4:9) of the Celts (e.g., honoring Lugh on Lughnasad). People who also live in multicultural situations might be more understanding than Paul was. Christmas, Easter, and Sunday laws make life nearly impossible for our Jewish or Muslim population. For a very small minority group to follow their own deviant calendar would have been almost unthinkable. They must have followed the Celtic calendar to some extent.

That is not the worst problem with this verse. The fact is Paul had no "Jesus" deviant calendar to suggest. In 53 C.E. the first communities who followed Jesus still lived by the Jewish calendar. To be sure there is a slight hint in 1 Cor. 16:2 that the first day of the week was taking on importance:

> On the first day of every week, each of you is to put aside and save whatever extra you earn, so that collections need not be taken when I come.

Even if the first day is becoming special, the words "on the first day of every week" indicate Paul is operating on a Jewish calendar rather than a Roman system or even something he has newly created. It was Paul then who offered the Celts a Jewish calendar, not the supposed Judaizing opponents.[25] Several decades would pass before a calendar change would be spoken of positively (on the Lord's Day, Rev. 1:9). In order for the Jesus tradition to make sense and in order to differentiate new disciples of Jesus from non-Jews, Paul must have imposed a Jewish calendar on the Celts, who later reverted to the Celtic calendar of their immediate culture. This is a critical point. If Paul was not changing the non-Jewish (Celtic) calendar to a Jewish one, then what does he mean here? If Paul was writing to the south Galatians, did he call on the Jews there to shift to a nonexistent "Christian" calendar? Or did he ask them to become time/calendar anarchists?

Paul does not advocate a new culture. That will come later. Rather he wants to make all cultural values relative. One may participate in cultural norms and events without giving them ultimate significance. While his cultural relativity is evident throughout, the clearest statement came in Paul's advice to suspend marriage practices:

> I mean, brothers and sisters, the appointed time has grown short; from now on, let even those who have wives be as though they had none, and those who mourn as though they were not mourning, and those who rejoice as though they were not rejoicing, and those who buy as though they had no possessions, and those who deal with the world as though they had no dealings with it. For the present form of this world is passing away. (1 Cor. 7:29–31)

Paul speaks of marriage, race, and social class as irrelevant for those in Christ. He makes the same statement to the Celts. Normal cultural distinctions are irrelevant:

> for in Christ Jesus you are all children of God through faith. As many of you as were baptized into Christ have clothed yourselves with Christ. There is no longer Jew or Greek, there is no longer slave or free, there is no longer male and female; for all of you are one in Christ Jesus. (Gal. 3:26–28)

Given the fact there is no specifically "Christian" calendar for the Celts and that Paul considers cultural norms something to be endured, it can be assumed that the Celts, lacking strong pressure to be Jewish at this point, must have reverted in a significant way to the Celtic calendar.

Galatians 4:24–26

> Now this is an allegory: these women are two covenants. One woman, in fact, is Hagar, from Mount Sinai, bearing children for slavery. Now Hagar is Mount Sinai in Arabia and corresponds to the present Jerusalem, for she is in slavery with her children. But the other woman corresponds to the Jerusalem above; she is free, and she is our mother.

All allegories are complex for readers who enjoy historical research. Paul's two allegories, 1 Cor. 10:1–5 and Gal. 4:21–5:1, are no exception. In one sense this allegory is clear. Hagar is the slave mother and Sarah is the free mother. Following Paul's argument up to this point, Hagar is the mother of that which enslaves us, the Law, while Sarah is the mother of that which frees us. Indeed, Hagar was a slave woman whose son by Abraham, Ishmael, was not the son of the promise. Sarah was the legitimate wife of Abraham, and her son, Isaac, was the son of the promise. From that point on, the biblical narrative in Genesis has been jettisoned. Hagar had nothing to do with the Law. She was simply the maid of Sarah who gave birth to Ishmael after Abraham began to doubt the fecundity of Sarah. Though the procedure followed by Abraham and Hagar was legitimate in that society, Hagar and Ishmael were inappropriately abandoned after the birth of Isaac.

Paul's allegory intends to place Hagar on Mount Sinai, the origin of the Law. That associates her enslavement with the giving of the Law that defines boundaries and the exclusive Judaism found in Jerusalem. For her part the allegory associates Sarah with Jerusalem above — a transcultural Judaism free of a Law that creates boundaries.

While the allegory does state Paul's thesis about enslavement and freedom, the details are otherwise inexplicable. It may be that here is a connection with the Celtic culture. While the Celts have no reason to attach Hagar to a mountain, they did absorb some mountain elements from the Phrygian culture. One major religious tradition was the mountain mother of Gods, whose major temple was to be found in Pessinus, an Anatolian city near where Paul must have stopped for his eye treatment. As he adapted transmogrification in 3:1, Paul may have borrowed enough parts of the myth of the Phrygian mountain goddess to show how Hagar the mountain mother brought Law rather than the transcendent freedom of Christ.[26]

Galatians 5:12

I wish those who unsettle you would castrate themselves!

In 5:2–12 Paul shifts to the third Jewish cultural law that has prevented the Jews from becoming the people of the promise (the first was kashrut, and the second was calendar). The presence of the circumcision argument in the Letter to the Galatians has puzzled every reader. It would be tempting to say that he had dealt with clean/unclean food laws and the Sabbath law, and now, as a matter of course, was simply compelled to mention the third delimiting law, circumcision. That argument will not do, however. There is a problem among the recipients of this letter to the Galatians that involves circumcision in some way, or, at least, involves proponents of circumcision. Because this is true, it would be reasonable to assume, as most have, that the churches addressed included members who were circumcised Jews or God-fearers. It would be reasonable to assume those followers of Jesus not circumcised are being pressured by those Jews who believe all new Christians should be circumcised (like the Judaizers of Gal. 2:3–5). The churches in south Galatia would meet this criterion. Or perhaps the churches have been invaded by opponents of Paul who have unsettled the faithful — even persuaded some.[27] All of these options have been suggested, though no consensus has been established.

There are some other possibilities. In his initial preaching and teaching Paul may have triggered an interest in circumcision. He surely dealt with the issue on that first visit. In 5:11 he says that he is still preaching circumcision.[28] Despite his insistence on the priority of God's promise, he still holds the Law in high regard. To non-Jews the Jewish Law must have appeared primarily as food regulations, Sabbath observance, and circumcision. After Paul left some leaders tended to limit commensality to the faithful and to practice the new worship cycle on dates set by the Celtic calendar. Is it possible some of them, aware of the third Law, also advocated circumcision? It seems unlikely. There is nothing in the Celtic culture to point toward the idea that they would be willing to accept the — to them — barbaric custom of circumcision.

Another possibility may fit better in the north Galatian theory. Assuming Paul was willing to enter the Celtic thought world, Gal. 5:12 takes on a different meaning. In the Phrygian mother-of-the-mountain cult the male religious actor might, while experiencing intense ecstasy, cut off his genitals, race through the street with the parts in his hand, and then take on female clothes.[29] If Paul stopped anywhere near Pessinus, these *galli,* as they were called, would have been known to him. Presumably the galli were also honored and admired by local Celts, including the new Jesus converts. There is no reason to suppose the castration of the galli would have been called circumcision, but one could easily assume the same leaders who adapted the new faith to the Celtic calendar might also have advocated castration for certain Spirit-led members. Paul refutes the value of circumcision, the castration of the galli, and in anger says he wishes these misguided charismatics would castrate themselves instead of misleading the faithful. The irony does reflect more the Phrygian custom than the Jewish one.

Paul made the "human" Law subordinate to the promise of God. The Law of which he spoke consisted of the three Jewish regulations that made the promise of universal blessing through the Jews impossible: kashrut (2:11–14), Sabbath observance (4:8–11), and circumcision (5:2–12, 6:13–15). Overriding these three regulations, Paul argues that right relationships and freedom come from faith in Christ, not obedience to the Law. Furthermore, while human traditions (the Law) might be adapted, the revelation of God in Christ cannot be altered.

Paul's Letter to the Galatians follows the organization of the three "laws." He used the "law" of food even if it did not directly apply. The problem in Galatia was the calendar, not the Sabbath. The problem in Galatia was castration, not circumcision. Let us make it clear, with some whimsy. If there was a culture that refused table fellowship with anyone who ate dog meat, made Wednesday a sacred day, and mandated the piercing of ears fourteen days after birth, then Paul would speak to them about kashrut, Sabbath observance, and circumcision. Structurally speaking, how could he do otherwise?

Galatians 5:19–21

> Now the works of the flesh are obvious: fornication, impurity, licentiousness, idolatry, sorcery, enmities, strife, jealousy, anger, quarrels, dissensions, factions, envy, drunkenness, carousing, and things like these. I am warning you, as I warned you before: those who do such things will not inherit the kingdom of God.

Near the end of a letter Paul, or secondary Paul, would often include a vice list and a virtue list (Eph. 4:31–32; Col. 3:5–17; see 1 Cor. 5:9–12). The lists normally condemn sins of a sexual nature, idolatry, and drunkenness. The list here in Galatians contains the usual sins of the flesh, but adds some sins unique to this letter: sorcery, enmities, and dissensions. Sorcery and vicious fighting would mark the Celtic culture. There is no known reason for Paul to have added these elements for the south Galatians. Nor is there any reason to suppose the northern Celtic churches were still involved in superstitious practices or vicious fighting.[30] But Paul knew the Celtic culture, so he included these particular sins as past problems (1 Cor. 1:26).

Notes

1. Pausanias, *Description of Greece,* 10.19
2. Some Greek historians would have us believe otherwise. See Stephen Mitchell, *Anatolia: Land, Men and Gods in Asia Minor* (Oxford: Clarendon Press, 1993), 13.
3. James, *World of the Celts,* 39.
4. Wilford, "Archaeologists Find Celts in Unlikely Spot: Turkey." A more extensive report was made by Jeremiah R. Dandoy, Page Selinsky, and Mary M. Voight, "Celtic Sacrifice," 44–49.
5. Philip Freeman, *The Galatian Language: A Comprehensive Survey of the Language of the Ancient Celts in Greco-Roman Asia Minor* (Lewiston, N.Y.: Mellen Press, 2001), 1–4. Jerome, *Comm. In. ep. Ad Galatas* 2, 3, writes, "The Galatians, except for Greek words, that are spoken by everyone, have nearly the same language as Treviros." See Cunliffe, *The Ancient Celts,* 85, and Mitchell, *Anatolia,* 50.
6. J. Louis Martyn, *Galatians* (New York: Doubleday, 1977), 16 n. 11.
7. Hans Dieter Betz, *Galatians* (Philadelphia: Fortress Press, 1979), 11–12.
8. See Peter Stuhlmacher, *Paul's Letter to the Romans: A Commentary,* trans. S. J. Hafemann (Louisville, Ky.: Westminster/John Knox, 1994), 4–5.
9. So Dieter Lührmann, *Der Brief an die Galater* (Zürich: Theologische Verlag, 1978), 10.
10. Martyn, *Galatians.* Martyn also assumes Paul stopped in Galatia because of illness, but reads the reference to eyes as simply a standard way of expressing care (15, 421). Given the thought world of the first century C.E., it is possible the implication may be that a Jewish opponent gave him "the evil eye" while he was in south Galatia and the eye was cured by the Celts in north Galatia. See Rivka Ulmer, *The Evil Eye in the Bible and in Rabbinic Literature* (Hoboken, N.J.: KTAV, 1994), 5. Among other things the evil eye could be cured by water and spit (189–90). Pheme Perkins, in *Abraham's Divided Children* (Harrisburg, Pa.: Trinity Press International, 2001), 1–3, also suspects the eye problem may have been an "evil eye" that was cured by spit (83). For an analysis of the Greek see John H. Elliott, "Paul, Galatians, and the Evil Eye," *Currents in Theology and Mission* 17 (1990): 262–73.
11. Betz, *Galatians,* 130, argues for the rhetorical use, but Martyn argues that the appellation "Galatians" should be understood as "Celts" (16).
12. Martyn, *Galatians,* 85–86; so Philip F. Esler, *Galatians* (New York: Routledge, 1998), 29–30, 32–33.
13. Carolyn Osiek, *Shepherd of Hermas* (Minneapolis: Fortress Press, 1999), 14–15.
14. Graydon F. Snyder, *Inculturation of the Jesus Tradition: The Impact of Jesus on Jewish and Roman Cultures* (Harrisburg, Pa.: Trinity Press International, 1999), 151–57.
15. On anamnesis as reenactment see Nils Alstrup Dahl, *Jesus in the Memory of the Early Church* (Minneapolis: Augsburg, 1976), 11–29.
16. The Greek word *proegraphe* probably refers more to a vivid description than to an inscription or placard. See Gerhard Ebeling, *The Truth of the Gos-*

pel: An Exposition of Galatians, trans. David Green (1981; Philadelphia: Fortress Press, 1985), 156. Burton, on the contrary, shows that Greek writers used the term to mean "write ahead of time." He doubts that Paul did write in advance, so he settles for a placard. Ernest de Witt Burton, *The Epistles to the Galatians* (1921; Edinburgh: T. & T. Clark, 1971), 144–45.

17. With J. D. G. Dunn, *Jesus, Paul, and the Law: Studies in Mark and Galatians* (Louisville, Ky.: Westminster/John Knox, 1990), 194.

18. Dunn speaks of them as badges in ibid., 194.

19. E. P. Sanders, *Paul and Palestinian Judaism* (Philadelphia: Fortress Press, 1977), 45–48, 75, 154–60.

20. J. D. G. Dunn, "Works of the Law and the Curse of the Law (Gal. 3:10–14)," in *Jesus, Paul and the Law*, 215–41 and 183–214.

21. For a defense of the traditional view see Seyoon Kim, *Paul and the New Perspective: Second Thoughts on the Origin of Paul's Gospel* (Grand Rapids, Mich.: Eerdmans, 2002).

22. Taking the Greek word *eis* to mean "until" rather than "preparing for." See Ebeling, *Truth of the Gospel*, 195.

23. Martyn, *Galatians*, 410. Lührmann, *Der Brief an die Galater*, 71.

24. Though Martyn assumes the Galatians are Celts, he reads the holy times as aberrations of the Jewish calendar rather than the Celtic calendar (414–18). Troy Martin argues that the calendar can't be Jewish in "Pagan and Judeo-Christian Time-Keeping Schemes in Gal. 4:10 and Col. 2:16," *NTS* 42 (1996): 111–19. See also Dieter Lührmann, "Tage, Monate, Jahreszeiten, Jahre (Gal 4:10)," in *Wirken und Werden des Alten Testament,* ed. R. Albertz et al. (Göttingen: Vandenhoeck & Ruprecht, 1980), 430–31.

25. Troy Martin, *By Philosophy and Empty Deceit: Colossians as Response to a Cynic Critique* (Sheffield: Sheffield Academic Press, 1996), 128–30.

26. Susan Margaret Elliott, "Choose Your Mother, Choose Your Master: Galatians 4:21–5:1 in the Shadow of the Anatolian Mother of the Gods," *JBL* 118 (1999): 661–83.

27. Lührmann, *Der Brief an die Galater*, 49. He believes the "Gegner versprachen den Galatern den Geist als Folge den Werke des Gesetzes." Mark Nanos argues that the "influencers" were some representatives of Jewish communities who had assumed the Pauline converts had been God-fearers who were now persuading them that they should follow normal Jewish procedures and become proselytes. Nanos, *The Irony of Galatians: Paul's Letter in First-Century Context* (Minneapolis: Fortress Press, 2002), 317–18.

28. Peder Borgen argues that Paul was misunderstood as he tried to replace physical circumcision with spiritual circumcision. See his *Paul Preaches Circumcision and Pleases Men: and Other Essays on Christian Origins* (Trondheim: Tapir, 1983), 33–42.

29. Susan Margaret Elliott, "The Rhetorical Strategy of Paul's Letter to the Galatians in its Anatolian Cultic Context: Circumcision and the Castration of the *Galli* of the Mother of the Gods," Ph.D. diss., Loyola University, Chicago, 1997.

30. Martyn also supposes these are special Celtic problems: *Galatians*, 497.

Chapter 3

Intimations of Culture
in the Jesus Tradition

If the Jesus tradition entered the Celtic world through Paul's mission to Galatia, what traditions about Jesus would have been current about the time Paul was preaching and teaching (for our purposes, 49–56 C.E.)? What elements of the Jesus tradition were present in Paul's actual oral message? That message, though hardly the entire Jesus tradition, must have been made known to the Celts of Galatia.

Sources of the Jesus Tradition

In a deep sense, as far as culture is concerned, Paul came to the Galatians empty-handed. There was no "Christian" culture. There was no culture based on the Jesus tradition. When the Jesus tradition affected a given culture, such as the Romans, it did create cultural expressions (inculturation), but it did not bring with it self-evident cultural expressions. The same would have been true for the Celtic culture. From the beginning the Jesus tradition was encapsulated in the Jewish tradition. While there were surely hellenistic elements in the tradition as Paul knew it, there was not yet a Roman Jesus tradition. Available sources for that pre–Roman Jesus tradition are the sayings source, Q; its parallel, the Gospel of Thomas; and the Gospel of Mark. Helpful as it would be, it is not possible to distinguish clearly between the oral stage of the Jesus tradition and the written stage. When Paul spoke in Galatia he would not have had access to a written Gospel of Mark or a written Gospel of Thomas. Since Q does not exist as a document, it is not possible to state for certain how it was circulated.[1] So here I will summarize the earliest Jesus tradition available to Paul.

Language

Jesus spoke and taught in Aramaic, so his words have come not only through secondary sources but also as a Greek translation, even in the oral stage.[2] The translation nature of the tradition can be easily seen in the narrative of Mark:[3]

> He proclaimed [saying], "The one who is more powerful than I is coming after me; I am not worthy to stoop down and untie the thong of his sandals." (Mark 1:7)

The "and" translates the frequently used Aramaic connective *w,* while the use of the participle to repeat and strengthen the verb reflects a common Semitic style. In the words of Jesus, the Semitic habit of repeating can be seen in such phrases translated as "measuring" or "hearing:"

> "Let anyone with ears to hear listen!" And he said to them, "Pay attention to what you hear; the measure you give will be the measure you get, and still more will be given you." (Mark 4:23–24)

Another well-known mark of Hebrew/Aramaic expression is parallelism, where one line or strophe will be repeated in a different way by a second line or strophe. *Parallelismus membrorum* occurs throughout the early Jesus tradition. An example would be:

> For there is nothing hidden, except to be disclosed; nor is anything secret, except to come to light. (Mark 4:22)

A more direct indication of the original language would be the use of untranslated Aramaic. Unfortunately there is little evidence. In the prayer of Gethsemane (Mark 14:36) Jesus invokes God: "and he said, 'Abba, Father.'" Paul must have used the same appellation in his preaching (Gal. 4:6; Rom. 8:15).[4] Other examples would be the words of Jesus to the presumed dead little girl: he said to her, "Talitha cum," which means, "Little girl, get up!" (Mark 5:41), or the deaf man, "Ephphatha," that is, "Be opened" (Mark 7:32). Some Aramaicisms entered the mainstream Jesus tradition, but then were dropped because they became incomprehensible, for example, the use of *bar* to express intensification. "Son of God" remained a significant appellation because of the use of the term *filius dei* for the emperor and early Christian affirmations of the divinity of Jesus. But *barnasha,* or "Son of man," the intensification of humanness (see Ezek. 2:1), though a primary nomenclature for Jesus, had no significance in Greek. It was not perpetuated after the New Testament period.

The original Jesus tradition most likely circulated in Aramaic, though some scholars would insist that Hebrew was a viable possibility.[5] When and how it was translated into koine Greek cannot be ascertained. The issue is not unimportant but evidence is lacking. There is no compelling reason to suppose any part of the tradition was written down in Aramaic. Early Christian communities needed a Greek tradition rather than Aramaic; Antioch or Caesarea are early examples. Bilingual community rhetors must have translated the Aramaic into Greek for the benefit of those who had no Aramaic background. Their oral translation into Greek kept elements of the Aramaic original. Eventually the Aramaic tradition was dropped and only the Greek remained. Unless one accepts a proto-Mark theory, the Jesus narrative was not written down before 65 C.E. Since Q first appears in Matthew and Luke, it would not be necessary for the sayings tradition to have been written down until after the appearance of Mark. That determination depends on whether Mark was aware of Q. Even so, no one would place the formation of a written Q or Mark before Paul made his first trip into north Galatia. Admittedly it would be somewhat disastrous for my thesis to discover that Paul carried in his tentmaking toolbox written copies of Q and proto-Mark, copies from which he read and which he shared with the Celts. The assumption here is that Paul carried in his mind the Jesus tradition; he shared that orally with the Celts; and the Celts, having translated the Jesus tradition into a Celtic dialect, added it to their own oral tradition. Of course, while the Jesus tradition in Greek would have been understood by the north Galatians, it was probably not first carried to Galicia or Ireland in that language.

While in oral form, the Jesus tradition was performed, not transmitted. It was the intent of the rhetor to convince the listener by dramatic means. Of course, the dramatic quality has been much debated. Some consider oral tradition a nearly precise transmission.[6] Others assume a loose, homiletical use of the tradition. Probably both are correct. In the oral tradition, community-forming data was transmitted accurately, while details could be altered for persuasive purposes. Bailey makes the distinction between formal controlled tradition that passes from generation to generation with precision, on the one hand, and informal uncontrolled oral tradition that has no memory requirements, on the other. A given culture could have both styles or even a combination (informal controlled oral tradition).[7] The Druids passed on accurately the sayings of the master Jesus but did not convey precisely the expositions made by Paul.

Ultimate Authority

In the Jesus tradition there is no question about authority. The words of Jesus make that clear from the very beginning: The kingdom of God is at hand. In the political world imperial authority cannot override divine authority, the kingdom of God.[8] To be sure, the ultimacy of divine authority does not abnegate political authority. Though never satisfactorily understood, Mark 12:17 expresses legitimization for political authority, although not its ultimacy:

> Give to the emperor the things that are the emperor's, and to God the things that are God's. (Mark 12:17)

This important tradition continues in Matthew (22:15–22) and Luke (20:19–26), and in an attenuated form in Egerton Gospel 3:1–6. Surprisingly enough, the rather early Gospel of Thomas adds the authority of Jesus to the saying:

> Give the emperor what belongs to the emperor, give God what belongs to God, and give me what is mine. (100:2b–4)

Jesus criticized the way the rulers of the non-Jews exercised their authority. They tyrannized their subjects. In the Jesus tradition, that is, in the theocracy, political leaders would act as servants:

So Jesus called them and said to them, "You know that among the Gentiles those whom they recognize as their rulers lord it over them, and their great ones are tyrants over them. But it is not so among you; but whoever wishes to become great among you must be your servant." (Mark 10:42–43)

Jesus assumed the servanthood of authorities. When he was brought before the Roman authorities, the servants of God, he did not act in a rebellious manner, but at the same time he did not cooperate (Mark 15:2). Despite the ambiguity of the coin saying, the Jesus tradition offers a clear attitude toward civil authorities. The sovereignty of God is primary and political leaders function as servants of that God. The Jesus tradition sharply criticizes the style of Roman political leadership but does not advocate civil disobedience or revolution.

Nevertheless, the Jesus tradition, while tolerant of political authorities, sharply undermined any type of national allegiance. Expanding on QS 9 and QS 58, the call to love your enemy found in Matthew renders useless any kind of defensive nationalism.[9]

You have heard that it was said, "You shall love your neighbor and hate your enemy." But I say to you, Love your enemies and pray for those who persecute you, so that you may be children of your Father in heaven; for he makes his sun rise on the evil and on the good, and sends rain on the righteous and on the unrighteous. For if you love those who love you, what reward do you have? Do not even the tax collectors do the same? And if you greet only your brothers and sisters, what more are you doing than others? Do not even the Gentiles do the same? Be perfect [mature], therefore, as your heavenly Father is perfect [mature]. (Matt. 5:43–48)

Religious Leadership

The attitude of the Jesus tradition toward dominant religious authority does not differ greatly from its attitude toward civil authority. After Jesus healed the leper, he himself did not attempt to return the man to his appropriate social context. He recognized that as the legitimate function of the priest (Mark 1:40–44). Standing before the high priest, Jesus was noncooperative, but he did not attack the high priest and his council, nor did he incite his own followers, who were in a volatile state of mind in any case, to some sort of sectarian revolt (14:60–62).

Religious authorities were not to be considered ultimate, especially in their interpretation of God's will. Jesus questioned their understanding of divine forgiveness (2:7–10). He attacked their position on table fellowship (2:15–17). He cast suspicion on their right to interpret the Sabbath (2:23–28). He had harsh words for the scribes and Pharisees who insisted on clean/unclean regulations (7:1–23). He warned the disciples about the improper influence of religious and political leaders (8:15), especially the religious practices of the scribes (12:38–40 and Q parallels). He attacked the abuse of the temple by priests and moneychangers (11:15–19). He even threatened to destroy the temple so completely that it could not be rebuilt (GT 71), or at least not as a material structure (Mark 14:58).

Just as the Jesus tradition respected the authority of political leaders, so it respected the authority of religious leaders. But Jesus was very quick to chastise and criticize leaders who placed their authority over divine authority. The Jesus tradition was not anarchical. Civil and religious leaders were subsets of divine authority, but they could abuse that fact by insisting on human laws and interpretations that thwarted the intent of God. For that reason their authority was severely impaired among those who followed the Jesus tradition.

Calendar

There is no reason to suppose the Jewish calendar had been jettisoned. No non-Jewish calendar can be perceived, and there is no sign of a new Jesus tradition calendar. Jesus kept the Sabbath (Mark 3:1–6), but he insisted it was intended for the good of humankind, not a calendar law to be obeyed:

One sabbath he was going through the grainfields; and as they made their way his disciples began to pluck heads of grain.

The Pharisees said to him, "Look, why are they doing what is not lawful on the sabbath?"

And he said to them, "Have you never read what David did when he and his companions were hungry and in need of food? He entered the house of God, when Abiathar was high priest, and ate the bread of the Presence, which it is not lawful for any but the priests to eat, and he gave some to his companions." Then he said to them, "The sabbath was made for humankind, and not humankind for the sabbath; so the Son of Man [Jesus tradition?] is lord even of the sabbath." (Mark 2:23–28)

Even if the narrative means that the new community now controls the Sabbath, the calendar itself has not been altered. It is true that the women followers of Jesus discovered the resurrection very early on the first day of the week, Mark 16:2, but there is no hint of a celebrative day that has replaced the Sabbath. In fact, such intimations come very late in the New Testament tradition (Rev. 1:10 may be the first, though see 1 Cor. 16:2; John 20:19 might also be included).

There is a problem in Mark 14:1:

It was two days before the Passover and the festival of Unleavened Bread. The chief priests and the scribes were looking for a way to arrest Jesus by stealth and kill him.

This may not reflect a calendar issue, though eventually the appropriate date for Easter did divide the church (especially the Celtic Irish). For the later tradition in John, the final supper occurred twenty-four hours before the Passover. It would appear from Mark 14:1 that the Markan tradition also knew that. If that is true, the correlation of the Last Supper with the Passover would be a theological/liturgical emendation rather than a calendar issue. In the Synoptics, the Last Supper was identified with the Passover meal in order to make the Eucharist an *anamnesis* (remembrance) event. There is not really an alteration of the Jewish calendar here. If the events recounted in the Synoptics could not have occurred on the Passover (Jesus before the Sanhedrin; Simon of Cyrene on a journey; the crucifixion itself; and the burial), the dating in John actually seems more plausible. There had to have been some manipulation of the calendar, but Mark's attempts to identify the Last Supper with the Passover only affirms the use of the Jewish calendar in the Jesus tradition.

Time

The time system of Jews had circular elements such as annual enthronement celebrations (Ps. 24:7–10), fertility rites (Gen. 38:20–23), and mountain divinities (Ps. 121:1). For faith reasons the Jews struggled hard to develop a linear view of time. It is known as end-time thinking — God's people will eventually be a blessing to all the world (Gen. 12:1–3). This simple eschatology, promise and fulfillment, makes the Jewish time system linear. Eventually the promise-fulfillment system failed so that radical divine intervention became necessary (Isa. 27:12–13). Radical intervention called *apocalypticism* nevertheless was in linear time. It was still end-time thinking. At the time of the Jesus tradition, some elements of Judaism had turned to apocalypticism as a worldview. Whether or not Jesus thought this way has been the subject of hot debate.

If Jesus was strictly a wisdom teacher, the apocalyptic time frame would not have been appropriate.[10] Wisdom teachers, especially peripatetic Cynics, tended to undermine the time system accepted by the dominant culture. There is little indication of that in the earliest Jesus tradition. To the contrary, the earliest Jesus tradition is driven by a vision of the end. Disciples are chosen (Mark 1:16–20). Missionary activity occurs (1:38, 3:14, 6:6b–13). Goals and visions are set and articulated (8:34–9:1).

Despite the overwhelming evidence for linear time in the Jesus tradition, some who stress the teaching of Jesus have insisted that the time in the Jesus tradition is only relative to transcendent truth. The phrase in Mark 1:15 means the sovereignty of God has touched our present situation. The sovereignty of God does not refer to the linear end of time, but the presence of the transcendent ultimate.

Apart from Mark 1:15 there are a few other intimations of "realized eschatology" in the Jesus tradition: the end-time becomes present when Jesus heals (1:40–45) or when Jesus forgives sin (2:8–10).[11]

Cosmological Good and Evil

The genius of monotheism lies in its monistic view of good and evil. Consequently, the existence of evil must somehow be derived from the faith that God is one and God is good. A monistic view of cosmology stretches one's religious imagination. Most cultures prefer the simpler dualism: good and evil are both ontological powers.

Disobedience

In the Hebrew Scriptures evil does not derive from a created dualism, but from the disobedience of humankind (Genesis 3; Jer. 5:24–25). For the most part that understanding of evil continues through the biblical material even into the Jesus tradition. Even so, disobedience or sin does not figure in the Jesus tradition as much as one would expect. John the Baptist baptized persons who confessed their sins (Mark 1:5). Jesus continued John's mission with a call to repent (1:15). While the key kerygma involves sin and repentance, that theme does not occur often in the earliest Jesus tradition. The primary topos for forgiveness of sins occurs as a controversy story inserted into the healing of the paralytic narrative (2:5b–10a). Before Jewish leaders Jesus says, "Son, your sins are forgiven." Other than this unique narrative, personal sin or disobedience does not play a significant role. Far more important as an act of alienation is to cause someone else to fall. The Law has been summarized as love of God and love of each other (12:29–31). Failing to love the other creates evil. Causing one of the little ones to sin ("stumble," 9:42–48) will bring harsh punishment. The "little ones" are new in the faith or not yet central to the community. The disciples discouraged the presence of children near Jesus, but he scolded them because they failed to care for those not yet mature in faith (10:13–16). The rich man was a perfect Jew, but he could not follow Jesus — he lacked love for the poor (10:17–22). In the earliest

Jesus tradition the act of disobedience was more failing to love than it was breaking the Law. Jesus had stern words for the scribes who acted piously (but they devour widows' houses: 12:40). Evil was caused by noncaring.

In the Jesus tradition there are two other causes for evil: the Near Eastern combat myth and demonic power.

The Combat Myth

In the Babylonian and/or Canaanite mythology the world was created by the divine struggle with the sea and sea monsters. The covenant theology of the Jewish people can hardly incorporate the combat myth of the ancient Near East. At the same time there are clear elements of the myth throughout the Hebrew Scriptures.[12] Three such monsters exist in the Jewish tradition — Leviathan, Rahab, and Tannin — all of which from time to time reflect the combat myth. In some passages Leviathan clearly appears as an enemy to be destroyed:

> You crushed the heads of Leviathan; you gave him as food for the creatures of the wilderness. (Ps. 74:14)

> On that day the LORD with his cruel and great and strong sword will punish Leviathan the fleeing serpent, Leviathan the twisting serpent, and he will kill the dragon [*tannin*] that is in the sea [*yam*]. (Isa. 27:1)

Rahab, on the other hand, seldom appears neutral. In Isa. 51:9–10 the Lord not only fought Rahab, but in so doing enabled the Jews to cross dry shod through the sea (Exodus):

> Awake, awake, put on strength, O arm of the LORD! Awake, as in days of old, the generations of long ago! Was it not you who cut Rahab in pieces, who pierced the dragon [*tannin*]? Was it not you who dried up the sea [*yam*], the waters of the great deep [*tehom rabah*]; who made the depths of the sea [*yam*] a way for the redeemed to cross over?

The term *tannin* may be closest to describing a dragon. Ezekiel calls the Pharaoh a tannin with scales:

> speak, and say, Thus says the Lord GOD: I am against you, Pharaoh king of Egypt, the great dragon [*tannin*] sprawling in the midst of its channels, saying, "My Nile is my own; I made it for myself."
> I will put hooks in your jaws, and make the fish of your channels stick to your scales. (Ezek. 29:3–4)

Leviathan, or its sea-monster equivalent, occurs in the New Testament only as the dragon of Revelation 12–17. Actually the dragon itself does not appear as a sea monster, but does give its power to two beasts, the first of which arose from the sea. However, there is also the sea monster in the sign of Jonah to consider. Although Mark does not mention Jonah as the sign given to "this generation" (Mark 8:11–12), Q (QS 32) identifies the probable sign as that of Jonah (Matt. 12:38–40; Luke 11:29–30). Matthew more explicitly identifies the sign with Jonah in the belly of the sea monster:

> For just as Jonah was three days and three nights in the belly of the sea monster, so for three days and three nights the Son of Man will be in the heart of the earth. (Matt. 12:40)

Just as God was victorious over the sea monster and delivered Jonah, so also God will be victorious over sheol and deliver Jesus. The sign of Jonah in Q reflects the combat myth, a sign that became very popular in early Christian art.

More significant was the struggle with the sea itself.[13] The ocean was the source of chaos from which God created order (Gen. 1:1–2). Like God's conflict with the sea monster, it may well be that ordering of chaos came from the combat myth found in Near Eastern cultures. The term *tehom* does not refer to a dragon or monster, but poetically to the deep. References in the Hebrew Scriptures give the reader the impression that the combat myth lies under these poetic expressions (Ezek. 28:2). The word *yam* can simply mean "sea waters," but sometimes it parallels Rahab or otherwise appears as a personification in conflict with God:

By his power he stilled the Sea [*yam*]; by his understanding he
struck down Rahab. By his wind the heavens were made fair;
his hand pierced the fleeing serpent. (Job 26:12–13)

In the Jesus tradition the conflict with the waters plays a more
important role. Because in the Gospel of Mark the baptism of Jesus
occurs during the radical mission of John the Baptist, it would
appear that Jesus was baptized in some type of apocalyptic purification rite. Because the Jesus of the Jesus tradition hardly needed
purification, such an implication is missing. It was Ignatius of Antioch who first argued that the baptism of Jesus was to cleanse
the water (he was born and was baptized, that by his suffering he
might purify the water; IEph. 18:2). There is no reason to suppose
that Ignatius does not properly reflect the earliest tradition.[14] Just
as the Torah began with the conquering of the water, so the Jesus
tradition started with the Son of God and the Spirit conquering the
Jordan.

Once the presence of the myth is established, other instances in
the Jesus tradition become obvious. On the way to the region of
the Gerasene, Jesus was in a boat with the disciples. When a great
storm arose, Jesus controlled the waters (Mark 4:35–41). After
the feeding of the 5,000 Jesus conquered the water by walking on
the Sea of Galilee (6:47–52). These elements of the Jesus tradition
leave open the possibility that evil derives from an Ur-chaos that
once was overcome and still needs to be overpowered.[15]

Demonic Power

While the combat myth derives from ancient sources, the appearance of demonic power strikes a new note in the Jewish tradition.
There are some few signs of a demonic power in Jewish literature,
such as in *Tobit,* but it is a surprise to see what a significant role
demons and unclean spirits play in the Jesus tradition. The primary locus for demons comes in the healing stories.[16] From the
very beginning of Mark, Jesus speaks in synagogues and drives out
demons (Mark 1:34, 39). The first healing narrative occurs in a
Capernaum synagogue where he exorcises an unclean spirit (1:21–

28). The most amazing encounter with unclean spirits comes in the region of the Gerasenes when Jesus casts out multiple unclean spirits into a herd of swine. Following the Gerasene demoniac incident, Jesus gave the disciples power to cast out unclean spirits (6:7), and they cast out many demons (6:13). In the somewhat lamentable encounter with the Syrophoenician woman, Jesus eventually cast out, from a distance, the demon from the woman's sick daughter (7:26–30). The terms *unclean spirit* and *demon* are interchangeable in this narrative. Finally, he cast the unclean spirit out of the boy who had serious convulsions (9:25).

The presence of demons in the Jesus tradition has left open the possibility of a dualistic ontology. However, in a monistic theology demons and unclean spirits are personal psyches that have gone astray or have become individualized and lack a community (persons from whom Jesus has exorcised demons are normally returned to their social context). As such they hardly represent an ontological dualism. However, collective or corporate evil presents more of a problem. Although Satan in Hebrew Scriptures referred to the prosecuting attorney in the council of Jahweh (Job 1), by the time of the New Testament period the term *Satan* referenced the corporate head of the demonic world (see Luke 10:18). Mark uses the term *Satan* in the later sense. After his baptism Jesus was cast into the wilderness to be tempted by Satan (devil, in the Synoptic parallels). This is not a personal temptation but a challenge to act on behalf of Israel rather than universal good (Mark 1:13). Likewise, when Peter refuses to redefine the Messiah as one who suffers for the many, Jesus perceives his denial as a battle with the delimiting vision of Satan (8:33). Because Jesus could cast out demons, he was accused of being the prince of demons, Satan himself (3:20–27). In a fascinating controversy story Jesus argues that the leader of the demons would hardly prevent them from doing their assigned task. While the Jesus tradition kept demons and Satan as forces opposing God, and therefore sources of evil, the tradition did not alter the ancient monism received from Judaism. Instead, the demonic was that which had ceased existing in the corporate divine.

Healing

The earliest Jesus tradition describes the actions of Jesus, in contrast to his words, as primarily those of a healer. The Gospel of Mark (and Synoptic parallels) contain the healing of Simon Peter's mother-in-law (1:29–31), the leper (1:40–45), the paralytic (2:1–12), the man with a crippled hand (3:1–6), the Gerasene demoniac (5:1–20), Jairus's daughter (5:21–24a, 35–43), the woman with a flow of blood (5:24b–34), the deaf-mute (7:31–37), the blind man (8:22–26), the boy with convulsions (9:14–29), and finally blind Bartimaeus (10:46–52). Without reference to specific persons or diseases, Jesus often is described as a healer and exorcist on his mission journeys (1:32–39; 3:10; 6:5, 54–56; Gospel of Thomas 14). With such an emphasis on itinerant healing, it is little wonder that Jesus has been called a peripatetic healer or a wandering charismatic. Certainly his healing ministry breaks with the Jewish cultural pattern, where illness was more often than not a matter of divine punishment and healing a result of forgiveness:

> See now that I, even I, am he; there is no god beside me. I kill and I make alive; I wound and I heal; and no one can deliver from my hand. (Deut. 32:39)

To be sure there are some prophetic healing narratives such as raising the son of the Shunammite woman (2 Kings 4:8–37) or curing the leprosy of the Syrian official, Namaan (2 Kings 5). But the Jesus tradition pattern of a healing ministry signals a cultural break with prophetic Judaism.

One might suppose the difference arises from the focus on the love commandment. In the earliest level of the Jesus tradition, compassion and healing might have overridden concerns for the Sabbath, clean/unclean, and hierarchical authority. The later Jesus tradition, as it has been received, does not stress that compassion. Some narratives stress conflict with demons; some culminate with a return of the afflicted to their community (the leper); some mention a role in the Jesus movement (deacon, preaching the word, teaching, or simply a member of the movement); some do stress the compassion (and power) of Jesus (Jairus's daughter); and at least one has a theological component (forgiveness). By the time the earliest Jesus tradition had formed (prior to 60 c.e.), the act of healing had become a strong component of the faith community.

Commensality

For the Jesus tradition, perhaps the most radical cultural alterations occurred in commensality. The Jesus tradition dropped the kashrut regulations, altered expectations regarding table fellowship, and shifted the menu for primary fellowship meals.

The tradition says that nothing entering a person can be unclean, but what comes out of the heart can be unclean:

> "Do you not see that whatever goes into a person from outside cannot defile, since it enters, not the heart but the stomach, and goes out into the sewer?" [Thus he declared all foods clean.] And he said, "It is what comes out of a person that defiles. For it is from within, from the human heart, that evil intentions come." (Mark 7:19–21)

Generally speaking, Jesus shifted the law from act to intent or attitude. In the Gospel of Thomas he says, "Rather the true circumcision in spirit has become profitable in every respect" (53:3). In Mark 7:14–23 clean and unclean are shifted from foods that one eats to attitudes one holds or expresses (see also Gospel of Thomas 14:5). Kashrut obligations no longer hold.

Q (QS 34; Luke 11:39–40; Matt. 23:25–26) strongly attacks the ritual cleansing of dishes (i.e., cups) for much the same reason. The outside of the cup may be clean but "inside you are full of greed and wickedness" (Luke 11:39). The Gospel of Thomas puts a different slant on ritual washing by noting only the aphorism that makes the inside and the outside equal: "Don't you understand that the one who made the inside is also the one who made the outside?" (Gospel of Thomas 89; Luke 11:40). In its earliest form the tradition must have meant the outside actually was not unclean.

Likewise Jesus criticized the necessity for ritually washing hands (Mark 7:1–8). The critique was the same as with clean and unclean. God's intention has been set aside for a human tradition:

You abandon the commandment of God and hold to human tradition (7:8).

At the earliest level of tradition there is no indication that Jesus ate with Gentiles. The lack of such a narrative has puzzled many readers. Surely the earliest community had faced the issue of multiracial table fellowship. The closest to such a narrative would be the story of the Syrophoenician woman (Mark 7:24–30), though no meal is involved and the intent of the story actually delimits the mission of Jesus. The later Matthew tradition kept the story of the Syrophoenician woman as well as the delimiting mission command:

> These twelve Jesus sent out with the following instructions: "Go nowhere among the Gentiles, and enter no town of the Samaritans, but go rather to the lost sheep of the house of Israel." (Matt. 10:5–6)

The more universalizing Luke, on the other hand, eliminated the story of the Syrophoenician woman as well as the delimiting mission order. Luke's editing may be our best indication that Jews and non-Jews were already eating together.

Jesus did eat with persons who were unacceptable to Jewish religious leaders:

> When the scribes of the Pharisees saw that he was eating with sinners and tax collectors, they said to his disciples, "Why does he eat with tax collectors and sinners?"
>
> When Jesus heard this, he said to them, "Those who are well have no need of a physician, but those who are sick; I have come to call not the righteous but sinners." (Mark 2:16–17)

However, cross-gender table fellowship did not fare much better than cross-racial. There are no narratives in the earliest material to indicate Jesus ate with women present at the table. At the house of Simon the Leper a woman came to the table where Jesus was reclining (to eat). She was not a participant in the meal and her presence was unwanted by the presumed male guests (Mark 14:3–9). While the first hearers would have assumed women were surely present at the feeding of the 5,000 (6:35–44), Mark explicitly counts only the men:

> Those who had eaten the loaves numbered five thousand men. (6:44)

In the parallel narrative (Mark 8:1–9) gender cannot be ascertained:

> Now there were about four thousand people. (8:9)

The later tradition in Luke keeps the Markan gender designation (Luke 9:12–17), but Matthew, who keeps the 5,000 men, states the obvious:

> And those who ate were about five thousand men, besides women and children. (Matt. 14:21)

Apart from this one note there is no signal that men and women ate together with Jesus present.

Given the critique of kashrut in the Jesus tradition, the nature of the menu would need to change. One Jewish meal is described — the Last Supper. Jewish meals and Jewish food play no further role in the earliest levels of the narrative. While it is not certain what was eaten at early Christian meals, based on the loaves and fishes narrative it is best to assume the primary menu consisted of bread, fish, and wine. Since bread and fish constituted a common menu in the Mediterranean area, its adoption as the menu for even religious meals made commensality possible for everyone.

Eating meals in common may be the primary way in which community is formed and continued.[17] In order for communities of faith to have been formed in such multicultural cities as Antioch, Ephesus, Corinth, and Rome, there must have been deep struggles over laws of kashrut, table fellowship, and functionally appropriate foods. It could not have been otherwise (1 Cor. 8:1–13, 10:6–30; Gal. 2:11–14; Rom. 14:13–23).

The Jesus tradition does not reflect such intense conflicts. Whatever battles earlier levels of the tradition might have expressed, by the last stages (ca. 65), the issue was solved: foods were no longer classified as clean or unclean; Jewish Christians and Gentile Christians ate at the same table and ate the same food; men and women ate side by side; the use of a specifically Jewish menu had completely disappeared. So Jesus narratives regarding commensality were no longer needed. A new culture was underway: people ate together without regard for race or gender; the food served was not culturally specific, but a common meal (fish and bread).

Family

The earliest tradition radically strengthened the family unit. Early Jewish tradition itself held the same sense of bonding between man and woman: the two shall become one flesh (Gen. 2:22–24). The sexual union of a man and woman creates a single intention and purpose between the two (one flesh). Divorce is not possible because such a covenant unity could not be dissolved. Nevertheless, in actual practice divorce was allowed. Deuteronomy 24:1–4 forbids remarriage with a wife who had meanwhile married another man. A man could divorce his wife because of "nakedness of a thing." The passage doesn't really allow divorce but does indicate divorce was possible for some unclear reason (the LXX reads "shameful thing," though it might also refer to exposure). Later Judaism gave more reasons for divorce.

In a sense the Jesus tradition on divorce is quite simple. It returned to the Genesis description of marriage:

> Some Pharisees came, and to test him they asked, "Is it lawful for a man to divorce his wife?"
>
> He answered them, "What did Moses command you?"
>
> They said, "Moses allowed a man to write a certificate of dismissal and to divorce her."
>
> But Jesus said to them, "Because of your hardness of heart he wrote this commandment for you. But from the beginning of creation, 'God made them male and female.' 'For this reason a man shall leave his father and mother and be joined to his wife, and the two shall become one flesh.' So they are no longer two, but one flesh. Therefore what God has joined together, let no one separate." (Mark 10:2–9)

The early Jesus tradition added two items to the Genesis tradition. The woman can divorce her husband, and in either case remarriage after divorce constitutes adultery:

He said to them, "Whoever divorces his wife and marries another commits adultery against her; and if she divorces her
husband and marries another, she commits adultery." (Mark
10:11–12)

While Q (QS 56) does not alter the radical ontology of the Markan
tradition, the two Q traditions do present quite different sayings.
In Luke 16:18:

Anyone who divorces his wife and marries another commits
adultery, and whoever marries a woman divorced from her
husband commits adultery.

A divorced man who remarries commits adultery, and an unmarried
man commits adultery if he marries a divorced woman. Matthew's
Q reads much like Mark except that Jesus defends Moses (the Genesis account) as conveying God's original intention, even though the
callous Jews insisted on regulations for divorce:

He said to them, "It was because you were so hard-hearted
that Moses allowed you to divorce your wives, but from the
beginning it was not so. And I say to you, whoever divorces
his wife, except for unchastity, and marries another commits
adultery." (Matt. 19:8–9)

The reader may be astounded to see that Matthew's Q then gives
a reason for divorce: some type of sexual misconduct. This cause
for divorce may or may not be a reading of the elusive something
objectionable of Deut. 24:1 (NRSV). The Jesus words in the Sermon
on the Mount offers the same exception:

It was also said, "Whoever divorces his wife, let him give her
a certificate of divorce." But I say to you that anyone who divorces his wife, except on the ground of unchastity, causes her
to commit adultery; and whoever marries a divorced woman
commits adultery. (Matt. 5:31–32)

In the case of the Sermon, the divorcing husband makes the wife
commit adultery. Nothing is said about her remarriage, so apparently simply breaking the covenantal bond, unless it is already

broken by a prior act, is an act of adultery in itself. Otherwise it would appear that the Matthean community altered the Q tradition for exactly the same reasons given in the Torah: marriage was a bond that could and perhaps must be dissolved.

Other members of the family are included in the covenant bond. Jesus strongly upheld the commandment to honor father and mother. He accused the Jews of using religious obligations as an excuse for not supporting parents (Mark 7:9–13).

Despite sayings about the absolute nature of the marriage covenant, and despite the disturbing addition of the exception, divorce was not the primary issue in the Jesus tradition. The first Christians met in homes (Mark 1:29, 33; 2:1–4, 15–6; 3:20; 6:10; 7:17; 9:33; 14:15) that offered space for a new family of faith which superseded the blood family. Jesus made this very clear. While he was at home his blood relatives came to restrain him because their friends and neighbors thought he had lost his mind (Mark 3:21). Following the narrative his mothers and brothers arrive. The crowd told Jesus of their arrival. The response of Jesus makes clear the formation of a faith covenant based on a covenant with God:

> And he replied, "Who are my mother and my brothers?" And looking at those who sat around him, he said, "Here are my mother and my brothers! Whoever does the will of God is my brother and sister and mother." (Mark 3:33–35)

The Synoptic parallels are approximately the same (Matt. 12:46–50; Luke 8:19–21), except Luke makes it clear that the real brothers and sisters are those hearing the Word preached in the house churches. The logion in the Gospel of Thomas keeps the same intent except it concludes with a spiritual interpretation rather than a congregational one: "They are the ones who will enter my Father's domain" (99:3).

At times it is difficult to tell whether a saying deals with the blood family or the faith family. Acceptance of the children at first looks like compassion for children, but a closer examination indicates that the children are being accepted into the faith community, that is, the believer must enter the kingdom as a little child:

People were bringing little children to him in order that he might touch them; and the disciples spoke sternly to them.

But when Jesus saw this, he was indignant and said to them, "Let the little children come to me; do not stop them; for it is to such as these that the kingdom of God belongs. Truly I tell you, whoever does not receive the kingdom of God as a little child will never enter it."

And he took them up in his arms, laid his hands on them, and blessed them. (Mark 10:13–16)

The argument over which was the greatest was solved when Jesus took a child and identified acceptance of himself and even God with acceptance of this least in human consideration (Mark 9:33–37).

Lest there be any doubt about priority of the faith family, the Jesus tradition keeps a saying that ranks as the most startling family statement in the Gospels. Peter claims they have left everything to follow Jesus. Jesus replies:

Truly I tell you, there is no one who has left house or brothers or sisters or mother or father or children or fields, for my sake and for the sake of the good news, who will not receive a hundredfold now in this age houses, brothers and sisters, mothers and children, and fields with persecutions and in the age to come eternal life. (Mark 10:29–30)

Surprising as this replacement of the blood family by the faith family may be, Q (QS 43) keeps a much harsher tradition (Luke 12:51–53; Matt. 10:34–36; Gospel of Thomas 16). Set in an apocalyptic context based on Micah 7:5–6, the text says he has come to bring conflict in any given house, so that its members will be pitted against each other:

they will be divided: father against son and son against father, mother against daughter and daughter against mother, mother-in-law against her daughter-in-law and daughter-in-law against mother-in-law. (Luke 12:53)

It is not simply that members of the family are pitted against each other but, according to Luke's Q (QS 52), the one who follows Jesus will have to hate the entire family, including wife:

> Whoever comes to me and does not hate father and mother, wife and children, brothers and sisters, yes, and even life itself, cannot be my disciple. (Luke 14:26)

Attempts to circumvent the meaning of the Greek word *miseo,* "hate," have not succeeded. It simply means "hate." To be sure Matthew's Q puts a different slant on the aphorism by saying the disciple must love Jesus more than father, mother, son, or daughter (Matt. 10:37). The Gospel of Thomas reads much like Luke, with hate as the verb (55). Logion 101, if the reconstruction is correct, repeats the "hate" saying, but in a reversal of Matthew's Q says the disciple must "love father and mother as I [Jesus] do." Given the tendency of the Gospel of Thomas, it is possible to assume that "love of father and mother" refers neither to blood parents nor faith parents, but to divine parents.

The nature of family in the early Jesus tradition undoubtedly created conflict when it encountered another culture. On the one hand, there is a nearly absolute insistence on the indissolubility of the blood family. On the other hand, there is a nearly absolute insistence that maturation and spiritual growth are impossible unless one supersedes blood family and forms equally strong bonds with the faith community. When inculturation occurs, both intimations are present but many receiving cultures find it difficult to express both at the same time.

The Oral Tradition

By the time Paul spoke in north Galatia there existed in the early Christian world a translated tradition of the Jesus words and narratives. While it is not certain how much of this tradition was circulating before the Jewish War, it can be assumed that major elements of what is called Q, the Gospel of Thomas, and Mark were already present.[18] This study has examined only those parts of the Jesus tradition that affected adapting cultures and found that the

Jesus tradition considered good the creation of the earth as well as humanity. The ultimate source was monotheistic rather than dualistic. The one God was the ultimate authority, often expressed by the term *reign of God,* although both secular and religious authorities played a legitimate, subordinate role. Evil or sin enters human life because people fail to care for each other, often seeking their own personhood rather than the good of the community. Even so evil forces are loose in the world. The Jesus tradition shows elements of the Near Eastern combat myth, and, in contrast to Judaism, recognizes a demonic world that impinged on corporate life. As for Jesus, he spoke in Aramaic and his traditions were collected in Aramaic and then translated orally into Greek. Paul used that Greek oral tradition as he preached to Mediterranean communities, including the Celts of Galatia. Jesus did not alter the Jewish calendar, nor did he break with a linear sense of time. However, he did not strictly follow Jewish mandates for temporal celebrations, such as the Sabbath. Likewise, Jesus did not follow clean and unclean distinctions, so that commensality was made considerably more flexible. Jesus was a healer, though it is not clear from the received Jesus tradition why he cured so many — was it caring, defeat of demonic powers, or formation of community? Jesus insisted on the absolute unity of the blood family, but simultaneously called on his disciples to create a new faith family.

These hints or intimations of how the Jesus tradition would impact another culture existed. Paul must have carried some of these into the Greco-Roman world.

Notes

1. John S. Kloppenborg Verbin, *Excavating Q: The History and Setting of the Sayings Gospel* (Edinburgh: T. & T. Clark, 2000), 59–60; he argues for a date of about 50–60, perhaps time enough for Paul to have known it (80–87).

2. Matthew Black, *An Aramaic Approach to the Gospels and Acts* (Oxford: Clarendon, 1967), 14; Kloppenborg Verbin, *Excavating Q,* 72–80.

3. Maurice Casey, *Aramaic Sources of Mark's Gospel* (Cambridge: Cambridge University Press, 1998), 253–60. Casey stresses particularly words like *barnasha,* translated as Son of man.

4. Joachim Jeremias, *The Prayers of Jesus* (Philadelphia: Fortress Press, 1975), 29–65, 108–12.

5. See W. D. Davies and L. Finkelstein, eds., *The Cambridge History of Judaism,* vol. 2 (Cambridge: Cambridge University Press, 1989), 82–83.

6. Earle Ellis, *The Making of the New Testament Documents* (Leiden: Brill, 1999), 20–27.

7. K. E. Bailey, "Informal Controlled Oral Tradition and the Synoptic Gospels," *Asia Journal of Theology* 5 (1991): 34–54. Harvey Whitehouse considers imagistic or experiential religiosity significantly more functional than written or doctrinal. See his *Arguments and Icons: Divergent Modes of Religiosity* (Oxford: Oxford University Press, 2000), 1–12.

8. Bruce J. Malina, *The Social Gospel of Jesus: The Kingdom of God in Mediterranean Perspective* (Minneapolis: Fortress Press, 2001), 142.

9. William Klassen, *Love of Enemies: The Way to Peace* (Philadelphia: Fortress Press, 1984), 72–109.

10. Robert W. Funk, *Honest to Jesus: Jesus for a New Millennium* (San Francisco: HarperSanFrancisco, 1996), 166–68; Burton L. Mack, *The Lost Gospel: The Book of Q and Christian Origins* (San Francisco: HarperSanFrancisco, 1993), 38.

11. C. H. Dodd, *The Parables of the Kingdom* (1935; London: Nisbet & Co., 1950), 44.

12. Bernard F. Batto, *Slaying the Dragon: Mythmaking in the Biblical Tradition* (Louisville, Ky.: Westminster/John Knox, 1992), 102–52.

13. Philippe Reymond, *L'eau, sa vie, et sa signification dans l'ancien testament* (Leiden: Brill, 1958), 181–98.

14. Graydon F. Snyder, "The Historical Jesus in the Letters of Ignatius of Antioch," *Biblical Research* 8 (1963): 3–5.

15. Gunther Bornkamm, "The Stilling of the Storm," in *Tradition and Interpretation in Matthew,* ed. G. Bornkamm, G. Barth, and H. J. Held, trans. R. Scott (London: SCM, 1963), 52–57. Patrick Madden notes those scholars who consider the Walking on Water a form of the Combat Myth. See his *Jesus' Walking on the Sea: An Investigation of the Origin of the Narrative Account,* Beihefte zur NTW 81 (New York: de Gruyter, 1997), 24–32.

16. Stevan L. Davies, *Jesus the Healer: Possession, Trance, and the Origins of Christianity* (New York: Continuum, 1995), 15.

17. John Dominic Crossan, *The Historical Jesus: The Life of a Mediterranean Peasant* (San Francisco: HarperSanFrancisco, 1991), 341–44.

18. Gerd Theissen and Annette Merz, *The Historical Jesus: A Comprehensive Guide,* trans. John Bowden (Minneapolis: Fortress Press, 1998), 25–29, 37–41; John P. Meier, *A Marginal Jew: Rethinking the Historical Jesus,* vol. 1 (New York: Doubleday, 1991), 41–48, 123–39.

Chapter 4

The Jesus Tradition
in Paul's Teaching

Paul had an oral Jesus tradition that he shared with the Celts in Galatia. This oral Jesus tradition entered the ongoing Celtic oral tradition and eventually traveled to Gaul and Galicia. While this is an interesting and useful proposal, it is fraught with difficulties and serious complexities. First of all, can Paul's oral Jesus tradition even be identified?[1] In order to find the answer, it is necessary to determine what was available for Paul in oral form prior to about 50 C.E. Such a determination is not at all easy. Paul likely had access to some form of Q, the Gospel of Thomas, and the Gospel of Mark, but none of these were yet in written form. One is tempted to include the source of the Gospel of John, the Sign Source, but correlations between that Source and the letters of Paul are nonexistent, or so minimal as to render further analysis useless.

A fairly loose system of correlation can help to find the appropriation of the oral tradition in the letters of Paul (see appendix).

Paul's use of the Jesus tradition was relatively evenhanded throughout his mission. So culling Jesus material from all the genuine letters of Paul (1 Thessalonians, 1 Corinthians, 2 Corinthians, Galatians, Philippians, Philemon, and Romans) will approximate what Paul normally would have passed on to the various listeners. If that is true there is no need to ask about the specific Jesus tradition initially given to the Galatians. It would have been the same as that taught elsewhere. Admittedly this assertion presents serious difficulties. In 1 Corinthians Paul answered specific questions from the congregations. In some of his answers he used the Jesus tradition, which might not have been evident had the Corinthians not asked specific questions. In Galatians Paul spoke specifically to a Celtic culture.

70

When so many of the letters are situation specific, is it possible to say that Paul always relayed the same Jesus tradition to all who listened?

The appendix examines the minimal Jesus tradition available to Paul. There is, of course, a difference between the transmission of a tradition, the use of the tradition, and its adaptation to a given situation. The use of the authoritative Jesus tradition to address a given cultural situation is the first move toward inculturation. I will now attempt to distinguish between the general Jesus tradition and specific uses.

Language

Although Paul was fluent in Aramaic, his primary language was Greek. Without trying to evaluate the quality of that Greek, it is only necessary to say that Paul expressed himself in the common language of the eastern section of the Mediterranean world (*koine*). While he did retain some Aramaic phrases such as *abba* (Rom. 8:15) or maranatha, "O Lord Come" (1 Cor. 16:22), and while Acts reports he addressed the Jerusalem crowd in Hebrew, that is, Aramaic (22:2), the fact is the Jesus tradition entered the Roman world through the common language. Aramaicisms found in the Jesus tradition, like the use of *w* or the emphatic use of the participle, do not appear in the Pauline letters. One word, the Aramaic greeting *shalom*, has been combined with the Greek greeting to create "grace to you and peace." Terms that have meaning only in Aramaic have tended to disappear. The title for Jesus, Son of man, has been eliminated. The critical theological term, the kingdom of God, seldom occurs (see Gal. 5:21).[2]

The Jesus tradition has certainly been altered in order to make it more accessible or more relevant to its context. The sayings and parables were kept in fairly simple *koine* but were edited as the occasion required.

Calendar

The Sabbath is never mentioned in the genuine letters of Paul. That fact is a puzzle and a surprise. Paul and Pauline converts most likely observed the seventh day as their day of worship. That is, the calendar had not yet changed. Any number of references to worship appear in the letters of Paul: the fellowship meal in 1 Cor. 10:14–17; proclamation in 1 Cor. 11:4–5; the Lord's supper (Cor. 11:17–22); the remembrance Eucharist (1 Cor. 11:23–26); reflections on a complete worship service (1 Cor. 14:1–40); reading a letter before the congregation (1 Thess. 5:27); and congregational decisionmaking (1 Cor. 5:4). In no instance does Paul indicate these events occurred on any day other than the Sabbath.

The calendar of the Jesus tradition as transmitted through the Apostle Paul was firmly lunar. No annual (solar) celebrations are mentioned, except for the single oblique reference to the Passover in 1 Cor. 5:7–8. There Paul refers to Christ as the paschal lamb and church discipline as the feast of unleavened bread:

> Clean out the old yeast so that you may be a new batch, as you really are unleavened. For our paschal lamb, Christ, has been sacrificed. Therefore, let us celebrate the festival, not with the old yeast, the yeast of malice and evil, but with the unleavened bread of sincerity and truth.

Two exceptions to the above consensus exist regarding the lunar week: 1 Cor. 16:2 and Gal. 4:8–11 (Col. 2:16 is omitted as secondary Pauline). At first glance it would appear that Paul refers to worship on Sunday in 1 Cor. 16:2:

> On the first day of every week, each of you is to put aside and save whatever extra you earn, so that collections need not be taken when I come.

A second glance indicates there is no reference to Sunday worship. The congregational member is asked to put aside funds for Paul's collection. The collection goes for the poor of Jerusalem (Rom. 15:25–27), not support for the local congregation. When Paul visits the congregation, the funds put aside will be pooled and sent to Jerusalem by appropriate representatives. The collection was not made as a part of the congregational meeting. Why then the request to put aside money? It could be simply a matter of economic priorities, or it could be a very slight indication that Sunday, though calculated in Jewish fashion, was becoming a special day.

The second text has been dealt with in a previous chapter.

> Now, however, that you have come to know God, or rather to be known by God, how can you turn back again to the weak and beggarly elemental spirits? How can you want to be enslaved to them again? You are observing special days, and months, and seasons, and years. (Gal. 4:9–10)

If one accepts the south Galatian hypothesis, then some of the congregation came from a Jewish heritage where they had celebrated special days, months, seasons, and years. The Sabbath is not mentioned and everything else is quite general. If the problem is that some have reverted to the Jewish calendar, then it seems Paul was advocating a non-Jewish calendar. That is patently not true. Paul, as well as the Jesus tradition, continued to use a Jewish calendar. In Gal. 4:9–10 Paul must have been writing to persons who were not Jews, such as the Celts of north Galatia.

If the letter is addressed to the Celts of north Galatia, then Paul is asking them not to revert to the Celtic calendar and not to worship the Celtic divinities. In that case what Paul has proposed as an alternative to the Celtic calendar is not certain. Since there was not yet a Christian calendar, he presumably urged on the Celts the alternative of a Jewish calendar.

Political Authorities

While the Jesus tradition tends to undermine the dominant culture, Paul tends to relativize it. In the crucial passage he urges the Corinthians to participate in the cultural activities (celebrations, buying and selling) without granting such activities ultimate value:

> I mean, brothers and sisters, the appointed time has grown short; from now on, let even those who have wives be as though they had none, and those who mourn as though they were not mourning, and those who rejoice as though they were not rejoicing, and those who buy as though they had no pos-

sessions, and those who deal with the world as though they had no dealings with it. For the present form of this world is passing away. (1 Cor. 7:29–31)

Whether one is a slave or master, Jew or Greek, male or female, does not really matter. All is relative to the Lordship of Christ. In the end-time all human authorities will be rendered unnecessary:

> But each in his own order: Christ the first fruits, then at his coming those who belong to Christ. Then comes the end, when he hands over the kingdom to God the Father, after he has destroyed every ruler and every authority and power. For he must reign until he has put all his enemies under his feet. (1 Cor. 15:23–25)

What was called the kingdom of God in the Jesus tradition is now the reign of Christ (see also Gal. 5:21). One function of this Lordship of Christ is to rule over the authorities until the end-time when the reign of God obliterates the need for human authorities. For human authorities Paul uses three Greek words meaning ruler, authority, and power, terms that refer to authority in terms of its divine origins. The original mythology comes from Gen. 6:1–4, where sons of God seduce daughters of men and give rise to the Nephilim who exercise authority in human affairs (*T. 12 Patr.*, Reuben 5). Paul uses the term *Son of God* for Christ in order to emphasize his authority over these "wayward" sons of God. Many non-Jewish readers would have understood this ultimate function in the Roman society as that of the *filius dei* (emperor).

Human authorities had a legitimate function for Paul, as they did in the Jesus tradition. Nevertheless human authorities can interfere with our relationship to God by seducing us with feigned divine power. In a triumphant passage Paul assures us such interference will not be final:

> For I am convinced that neither death, nor life, nor angels, nor rulers, nor things present, nor things to come, nor powers, nor height, nor depth, nor anything else in all creation, will be able to separate us from the love of God in Christ Jesus our Lord. (Rom. 8:38–39)

Nothing, even divine powers in the form of human authorities, can separate us from the love of God.

The early Christians were not anarchists. The state had a legitimate function as the power that held together the human community until the end-time. At the apex of his writing skill, in a letter addressed to those who lived in the shadow of the Roman forum, Paul makes it clear that human authorities are legitimized by divine power:

> Let every person be subject to the governing authorities; for there is no authority except from God, and those authorities that exist have been instituted by God. Therefore whoever resists authority resists what God has appointed, and those who resist will incur judgment. For rulers are not a terror to good conduct, but to bad. Do you wish to have no fear of the authority? Then do what is good, and you will receive its approval; for it is God's servant for your good. But if you do what is wrong, you should be afraid, for the authority does not bear the sword in vain! It is the servant of God to execute wrath on the wrongdoer. Therefore one must be subject, not only because of wrath but also because of conscience. For the same reason you also pay taxes, for the authorities are God's servants, busy with this very thing. Pay to all what is due them — taxes to whom taxes are due, revenue to whom revenue is due, respect to whom respect is due, honor to whom honor is due. (Rom. 13:1–7)

In this most-maligned and -misused text of the New Testament, the Jesus tradition works on the grand scale. Authorities have received their power from God because they keep peace in the human community. In order to keep peace the authorities need to be obeyed, respected, and given appropriate revenue. This passage must be seen in light of Paul's relativizing: it is appropriate to obey political authorities as long as one does not give them ultimate value. In the end-time, in the reign of Christ, they will be found unnecessary and will cease to be.

For the process of inculturation the role of political authority ranks high in critical importance. The invading faith had to face the political realities of the invaded culture. The invading faith had to form new organizational structures for itself. Eventually these new religious authorities had to form some coalition with traditional political authorities. There is a slight intimation in the letters of Paul that some discord about appropriate power arenas had already begun. Some members of the Corinthian congregation had a quarrel about a civil problem involving perhaps ownership, property boundaries, or something of that nature. Paul was dismayed that the two Christians used a civil court:

> When any of you has a grievance against another, do you dare to take it to court before the unrighteous, instead of taking it before the saints? Do you not know that the saints will judge the world? And if the world is to be judged by you, are you incompetent to try trivial cases? Do you not know that we are to judge angels — to say nothing of ordinary matters? If you have ordinary cases, then, do you appoint as judges those who have no standing in the church? I say this to your shame. Can it be that there is no one among you wise enough to decide between one believer and another, but a believer goes to court against a believer — and before unbelievers at that? In fact, to have lawsuits at all with one another is already a defeat for you. Why not rather be wronged? Why not rather be defrauded? But you yourselves wrong and defraud — and believers at that. (1 Cor. 6:1–8)

Paul insists that they should be able to reconcile this problem within the boundaries of the congregation. How could they let their case be decided by nonbelievers? Nonbelievers could use the courts to make just judgments, but the courts cannot reconcile two parties who have already formed a family bond. This is an indication that Paul would prefer a church council to adjudicate even civil problems among members. If so, the conflict between church and state has already begun.

Despite the potential nationalism of Romans 13, Paul includes in the exhortatory section of his letter the Jesus tradition about love of enemies. In Rom. 12:14–21, Paul nearly quotes the Jesus tradition in appealing for nonviolence instead of vengeance:

Bless those who persecute you; bless and do not curse them. Rejoice with those who rejoice, weep with those who weep. Live in harmony with one another; do not be haughty, but associate with the lowly; do not claim to be wiser than you are. Do not repay anyone evil for evil, but take thought for what is noble in the sight of all. If it is possible, so far as it depends on you, live peaceably with all. Beloved, never avenge yourselves, but leave room for the wrath of God; for it is written, "Vengeance is mine, I will repay, says the Lord." No, "if your enemies are hungry, feed them; if they are thirsty, give them something to drink; for by doing this you will heap burning coals on their heads." Do not be overcome by evil, but overcome evil with good. (Rom. 12:14–21)

Not unlike the summary of the law in the Jesus tradition, Paul speaks of love as fulfilling the law:

Owe no one anything, except to love one another; for the one who loves another has fulfilled the law. The commandments, "You shall not commit adultery; You shall not murder; You shall not steal; You shall not covet"; and any other commandment, are summed up in this word, "Love your neighbor as yourself." Love does no wrong to a neighbor; therefore, love is the fulfilling of the law. (Rom. 13:8–10)

While the law of love has profound personal implications, as a social teaching it makes exclusive nationalism impossible.

Religious Authority

In contrast to the Jesus tradition Paul simply never mentions the Jewish religious establishment: no Pharisees (Phil. 3:5 refers to aristocracy, not leadership), no high priests, no priests, no Sanhedrin, no Sadducees, no Levis, no elders. Furthermore, there are no references to non-Jewish religious leaders. What accounts for this startling absence? Has Paul dropped the conflicts found in the Jesus tradition? If so, why? Or have conflicts between Jesus and religious authorities been added or exaggerated as the Jesus movement spread throughout the Mediterranean area? That is, are the conflicts with the Jewish leaders actually reflections of competition with neighboring synagogues in hellenistic cities?[3] There seems to be no satisfactory answer.

Paul apparently was more concerned about the function of religious leadership in his own congregations. The body of Christ, rather than the building in Jerusalem, is now the temple of God:

> Or do you [*pl.*] not know that your [*pl.*] body [*sing.*] is a temple of the Holy Spirit within [among] you [*pl.*], which you [*pl.*] have from God, and that you [*pl.*] are not your [*pl.*] own? (1 Cor. 6:19)

The Spirit organizes the body of Christ and creates those offices necessary for its functioning. In his famous body metaphor Paul maintains that the Spirit energizes the various parts of the body so that the body can work as a useful system:

> All these are activated by one and the same Spirit, who allots to each one individually just as the Spirit chooses. For just as the body is one and has many members, and all the members of the body, though many, are one body, so it is with Christ. For in the one Spirit we were all baptized into one body — Jews or Greeks, slaves or free — and we were all made to drink of one Spirit. Indeed, the body does not consist of one member but of many. (1 Cor. 12:11–14)

He uses the body metaphor (see also Rom. 12:4) to explain how the Spirit creates and energizes the various leadership roles in the church. While Paul at first gives equal value to each part of the body and therefore by analogy to each function in the church (1 Cor. 12:4–10; Rom. 12:6–8), he does finally list a successive order in 1 Cor. 12:28:

> And God has appointed in the church first apostles, second prophets, third teachers; then deeds of power, then gifts of healing, forms of assistance, forms of leadership, various kinds of tongues.

From this passage historians frequently have deduced that religious authority for Paul resided first with apostles, then with prophets, and finally with teachers. Other forms of leadership were secondary to these first three. Church historian Adolf von Harnack suggested that the first three were universal offices and the rest were local (eventually elder, bishop, and deacon).[4] It is more likely the genuine Paul viewed all leadership functions as equivalent within the harmonious body. There was no head (authority) of the body until the secondary letters, Eph. 4:11–16 and Col. 2:16–19. Paul must have known the tradition about religious leadership found in Mark and Q, but he was far more interested in the development of the new faith community than in competition with local synagogues.

Paul's defense of his own apostleship against other apostles probably does not speak to the issue of religious authority:

> for I am not at all inferior to these super-apostles, even though I am nothing. (2 Cor. 12:11)

The super-apostles have no authority over Paul; they simply compete with him. Nor does Paul often use his authority as an apostle. In the controversy over the man living with his stepmother, Paul insists that his position should be considered when the community met, but he does not speak as an apostle with ultimate authority. There is no question he used pressure on behalf of Onesimus when he wrote to Philemon, but again he did not speak as an apostle. Finally, then, the authority of the Pauline church lies primarily in the consensus of the community even though the gifts of the members of the body may differ.

Healing

Paul was no stranger to personal illnesses. Better known, however, than his eye problem (see chapter 2) would be his so-called thorn in the flesh:

> even considering the exceptional character of the revelations. Therefore, to keep me from being too elated, a thorn was given

me in the flesh (a messenger of Satan) to torment me, to keep
me from being too elated. Three times I appealed to the Lord
about this, that it would leave me. (2 Cor. 12:7–8)

Though much has been written about the enigmatic thorn in the
flesh, no one has been able to create a consensus about the metaphor. It could be anything that annoyed Paul. Even though what
Paul had in mind will never really be known, two aspects of the
problem would have been evident to his listeners/readers. The
"thorn" was given to him by a messenger of Satan. Satan here
would not have been the ultimate tempter or the power of darkness.
One must grant that a messenger of Satan could be the individualized demon found often in the Jesus tradition. However, the
function of this "demon" was not to alienate Paul from his community. It was to make him less arrogant by placing him on a level
playing field with his converts. That is hardly an evil function. Second, Paul prayed to God for its removal. Would the use of the Jesus
tradition (Lord) be so simple: a messenger of Satan could cause an
illness and prayer to God can cure it? In any case, the Lord didn't
cure it.

Even though Paul could not cure himself either of the thorn in
the flesh or the obnoxious eye disease, apparently he had the power
to cure others. In his argument with the super-apostles, among
many other claims, Paul claims that he can do the same miracles
performed by other apostles:

The signs of a true apostle were performed among you
with utmost patience, signs and wonders and mighty works.
(2 Cor. 12:12)

One would assume that a work referred to a miraculous healing.
What else might it have been? Paul repeated the claim in Rom.
15:19 (by the power of signs and wonders, by the power of the
Spirit) and Gal. 3:5 (work miracles among you). Otherwise, there
are no references to actual healing events in the letters of Paul.

Whether Paul healed or not, the healing ministry was an essential
aspect of a Pauline congregation. In 1 Corinthians 12 Paul describes

the various ministries and how they work together for the common well-being:

> and there are varieties of activities, but it is the same God who activates all of them in everyone. To each is given the manifestation of the Spirit for the common good. To one is given through the Spirit the utterance of wisdom, and to another the utterance of knowledge according to the same Spirit, to another faith by the same Spirit, to another gifts of healing by the one Spirit, to another the working of miracles, to another prophecy, to another the discernment of spirits, to another various kinds of tongues, to another the interpretation of tongues. (1 Cor. 12:6–10)

After the gifts of persuasion, knowledge, and faith, Paul mentions first the charisma of healing (one has to notice that works of power do not seem to be the same as gifts of healing). In the parallel passage found in v. 28, the works of power follow apostles, prophets, and teachers. Following miracles or works of power are the gifts of healing:

> And God has appointed in the church first apostles, second prophets, third teachers; then deeds of power, then gifts of healing, forms of assistance, forms of leadership, various kinds of tongues. (1 Cor. 12:18)

The gift of healing occurred within the congregation, with no apparent indication that healing was a ministry to outsiders. That line is a very fine one, perhaps too fine. In the Jesus tradition healing created the community itself and led converts into specific community roles. In Paul's adaptation of the Jesus tradition, the healing ministry is a community gift, not a community developer. Though it may indeed build up the congregation and eradicate boundaries, as with the Jesus tradition, healing in the Pauline community is a gift of the Spirit in its own right.

Sickness was more alienation from one's community (illness) than a problem that could be defined biomedically (disease). In terms of social anthropology, separation from community could

cover a number of problems that might not be considered biomed-
ical in nature. For example, lameness, deafness, and blindness are
certainly limiting, but not diseases in the scientific sense. Because
they do indeed limit corporate participation, in the social anthropological pattern they are illnesses, not medical problems. According
to the Jesus tradition, Jesus dealt with illnesses that caused alienation. In the letters of Paul there is one instance that demonstrates
the same perception:

> Whoever, therefore, eats the bread or drinks the cup of the
> Lord in an unworthy manner will be answerable for the body
> and blood of the Lord. Examine yourselves, and only then
> eat of the bread and drink of the cup. For all who eat and
> drink without discerning the body, eat and drink judgment
> against themselves. For this reason many of you are weak
> and ill, and some have died. But if we judged ourselves, we
> would not be judged. But when we are judged by the Lord,
> we are disciplined so that we may not be condemned along
> with the world.
>
> So then, my brothers and sisters, when you come together
> to eat, wait for one another. If you are hungry, eat at home, so
> that when you come together, it will not be for your condem-
> nation. About the other things I will give instructions when I
> come. (1 Cor. 11:27–34)

Paul had chastised the Corinthian house church for not sharing
equally in the supper of the Lord. Some ate their own preferred
food without sharing. Presumably others came without proper food
or lacked sufficient amounts for their families. Those who did not
share were guilty of profaning the corporate body. When they came
to the apex of the Lord's Supper, the *anamnesis,* they had already
failed to discern the meaning of the body of Christ. So when they
broke the bread with those with whom they had already failed to
share, they also profaned the crucified body of Christ. They were
ipso facto alienated. By definition they were sick and even dying.
Paul asks them to share in the Agape as befitting members of the body
of Christ. He does not say considerate and compassionate sharing
would solve the illnesses, but presumably that is what he meant.

Cosmological Good and Evil

Like Judaism in general and the Jesus tradition specifically, Paul's monotheism disallows an ontological power of evil. His theological worldview requires that evil be understood as an aberration of ultimate good.

The Combat Myth

Elements of the Near Eastern combat myth can be seen in the Hebrew Scriptures, elements that passed on into the Jesus tradition. The literal fragments of the myth may not be so apparent in the preaching of Paul, but its theological importance cannot be overestimated. Paul adheres to the apocalyptic branch of Judaism. Or, better perhaps, his conversion represents a radical shift from proleptic rabbinic Judaism to apocalypticism (2 Cor. 12:1–4; Phil. 3:4–11). Simply put, Paul's apocalyptic faith was that the promises of God for history would be realized, though only through the demise of the present historical process. For some Jewish apocalypticists that end could be the destruction of Jerusalem; for others it could be the fall of the Roman Empire. For Paul it was the crucifixion of Jesus.

Evil in the combat myth was disorder, not a force opposed to the divinity. In the Hebrew Scriptures the Spirit of God overcame the chaos of the *tohu* and *bohu,* the "trackless waste and emptiness." The Spirit brought order to the visible world. Adam, who participated in the formation of that order, eventually fell back into disorder. The Spirit continued to fight for order in the chaos (seas, oceans, sea monsters), but eventually, when the Jews were exiled from Jerusalem, the chaos became predominant. Resultant apocalyptic theology promised victory over the chaos and the beginning of a new creation.

Bringing order to the chaos occurs in the Jesus tradition in such stories as the baptism, the sign of Jonah, the stilling of the storm, and drowning of the Gerasene pigs/demons. In Paul the myth appears most prominently in Romans 6:

Do you not know that all of us who have been baptized into
Christ Jesus were baptized into his death? Therefore we have
been buried with him by baptism into death, so that, just as
Christ was raised from the dead by the glory of the Father,
so we too might walk in newness of life. For if we have been
united with him in a death like his, we will certainly be united
with him in a resurrection like his. We know that our old
self was crucified with him so that the body of sin might be
destroyed, and we might no longer be enslaved to sin. For
whoever has died is freed from sin. But if we have died with
Christ, we believe that we will also live with him. We know
that Christ, being raised from the dead, will never die again;
death no longer has dominion over him. The death he died, he
died to sin, once for all; but the life he lives, he lives to God.
So you also must consider yourselves dead to sin and alive to
God in Christ Jesus. (Rom. 6:3–11)

As Jesus Christ died, was buried, and raised, so we too die when we
are baptized in the water and are raised with Christ. On the cross
and by his death Jesus attacked that chaos signified by death. Death
was overcome and a new creation sprang forth. Jesus was the new
Adam who, in contrast to the first Adam, would not return to the
Ur-chaos. Those who are baptized into the water (chaos) participate
in that attack on the chaos and share in the new order.

Perhaps Paul's theology of baptism is the only remaining fragment of the combat myth, but it doesn't seem likely. Paul's
apocalyptic use of the death and resurrection of Jesus seems quite
parallel to the combat myth. By his resurrection from the dead
Christ has made all things subject to God. The disorder of the state
and all other institutions will have been destroyed (1 Cor. 15:28).
Disorder or chaos can be seen in institutional abuse, the violation
of rights, and unjust treatment:

Who will separate us from the love of Christ? Will hardship,
or distress, or persecution, or famine, or nakedness, or peril,
or sword? (Rom. 8:35)

The power of the disorder lies so deep in our culture that almost all powers might have worked against us had they not been overcome by the love of God in the resurrection of Christ:

> For I am convinced that neither death, nor life, nor angels, nor rulers, nor things present, nor things to come, nor powers, nor height, nor depth, nor anything else in all creation, will be able to separate us from the love of God in Christ Jesus our Lord. (Rom. 8:38–39)

Satan

A major element of evil in the Jesus tradition was the activity of the demonic, particularly demon possession. Demons and unclean spirits were sometimes the cause of illnesses and separation from the community. On a corporate level the demons were responsible to a power called Satan. This tradition passed on through Paul to a limited extent. Since there are no healing narratives in the letters of Paul, it is impossible to know if Paul spoke to his listeners about the bodily dangers of the demonic. He did consider failure to discern community a source of illness. In that sense Paul continued the Jesus tradition that evil derives from discord or disorder and alienation. Though he didn't use the word *demon*, Paul considered his own illness, the so-called thorn in the flesh, to be caused by a minion of Satan, an angel or messenger of Satan. A similar affliction must have prevented Paul from visiting the Thessalonians:

> For we wanted to come to you — certainly I, Paul, wanted to again and again — but Satan blocked our way. (1 Thess. 2:18)

Otherwise Satan is the source or power of disorder. In the Corinthian church a rather feisty Paul accused a man living with his stepmother of creating moral dishonesty. He advised the Corinthian community to hand the man over to discord rather than create pseudo-harmony by pretending the problem didn't exist:

> you are to hand this man over to Satan for the destruction of the flesh, so that his spirit may be saved in the day of the Lord. (1 Cor. 5:5)

Later Paul apparently relented of this questionable antagonism toward his detractor and advised the Corinthians to forgive the shunned leader, even to be reconciled to Paul himself. He reasoned that discord in the faith community might lead them all into the hands of Satan:

> Anyone whom you forgive, I also forgive. What I have forgiven, if I have forgiven anything, has been for your sake in the presence of Christ. And we do this so that we may not be outwitted by Satan; for we are not ignorant of his designs. (2 Cor. 2:10–11)

Other references to Satan in Paul show the same sense of community discord. In the so-called angry letter when speaking of the dissident super-apostles, Paul says Satan can even disguise himself as an angel. Perhaps more surprising is the reference to marriage. Some Corinthians try to understand sex by incorrectly exegeting only half of Paul's "better than" saying: Better not to touch a woman at all than...."[5] Paul responds that it is permissible to withdraw from sexual relations a short time for a matter of prayer. But a longer period could result in a separation, an individualistic asceticism (Satan) that brings discord to the marriage bond

> Do not deprive one another except perhaps by agreement for a set time, to devote yourselves to prayer, and then come together again, so that Satan may not tempt you because of your lack of self-control. This I say by way of concession, not of command. (1 Cor. 7:5–6)

Good comes from the God of peace; evil comes from Satan. In a straightforward statement of faith Paul wishes to add to the theological wisdom of the Roman congregations:

> For while your obedience is known to all, so that I rejoice over you, I want you to be wise in what is good and guileless in what is evil. The God of peace will shortly crush Satan under your feet. The grace of our Lord Jesus Christ be with you. (Rom. 16:19–20)

The problem of good and evil in Paul could not be stated more clearly: the God of peace will eventually put Satan under his feet. Satan is a strong power of discord but not a dualistic entity.

Family

Like the Jesus tradition, Paul maintains the inviolability of the family unit. He quotes the Jesus tradition regarding divorce:

> To the married I give this command — not I but the Lord — that the wife should not separate from her husband (but if she does separate, let her remain unmarried or else be reconciled to her husband), and that the husband should not divorce his wife. (1 Cor. 7:10–11)

The social context addressed here by Paul must have been quite complex. Though Paul affirms the inviolability of marriage, he faces situations in which adherence to the new faith community will have split the family unit. Following the words of the Lord he urges the husband or wife not to be divorced. If separation does become necessary, even then divorce ought not be an option. In Paul's version of the Jesus tradition the admonition against divorce holds for both wife and husband. As found in the Jesus tradition, Paul also upholds the power of the marriage bond. He argues against an ascetic marriage because the sexuality of the husband creates the identity of the wife and the sexuality of the wife creates the identity of the husband:

> For the wife does not have authority over her own body [sexual identity], but the husband does; likewise the husband does not have authority over his own body [sexual identity], but the wife does. (1 Cor. 7:4)

Because of the power of sexual bonding Paul, not the Lord (!), believes the wife or the husband can even affect the faith of the nonbelieving partner, and, of course, their children:

> For the unbelieving husband is made holy through his wife, and the unbelieving wife is made holy through her husband.

Otherwise, your children would be unclean, but as it is, they are holy. (1 Cor. 7:14)

Wife, for all you know, you might save your husband. Husband, for all you know, you might save your wife. (1 Cor. 7:16)

At the same time, like the Jesus tradition, Paul recognizes that the blood family ought not take precedence over the new faith family:

But if the unbelieving partner separates, let it be so; in such a case the brother or sister is not bound. It is to peace that God has called you. (1 Cor. 7:15)

Paul consistently speaks of new adherents as brother and sister and (Rom. 16:1, 14:10), or more often the inclusive (Rom. 1:13).

The centuries-old consensus that Paul was celibate and advocated celibacy has no foundation whatsoever in the letters of Paul. The primary passage quoted for celibacy, 1 Cor. 7:1–16, addresses married people, not singles. Singles are addressed for the first time in 7:25. Strangely enough, the argument for celibacy depends on Paul's wish that the married of Corinth would remain single as was he. Many readers have taken *agamos* to mean single, though obviously that cannot be. In v. 11 Paul wrote that if someone becomes separated let him remain single. Since those addressed had been married, the term must mean demarried in the sense of no longer married. The use of the term in v. 8 must mean widower:

I say to the widowers and to the widows, it is better to remain demarried as I am. (1 Cor. 7:8)

So Paul must have been married and somehow lost his wife. If she had ever accompanied Paul on his missionary journeys is not clear. He did complain to the Corinthians about privileges extended to wives of other apostles that were not extended to him and his natural wife who was also a sister in the faith community (9:5).

Directly quoting the Jesus tradition, Paul held the monogamous marriage bond inviolable. But also like the Jesus tradition he placed the family of the faith community above loyalty to the natural family. Like the Jesus tradition, he understood husband and wife might be separated by new religious loyalties. Like the Jesus tradition, he urged separated persons not to remarry. Unlike the Jesus tradition, he recognized the possibility of remarriage for those who had lost their husband or wife. Like the Jesus image portrayed in the Jesus tradition, Paul noted the value of being unmarried in the face of the end-time vision.

Food and Meals

With regard to meals Paul deals with five issues: food offered to idols; communal sharing; fasting; appropriate menu; and table fellowship. In 1 Cor. 8:1 Paul attempts to answer the question posed by some Corinthians (concerning food offered to idols). The answer occurs in 8:1–13 and again in 10:14–11:1. Paul concludes that one should never offend a brother or sister by what one eats. For that matter, it is dangerous to eat with people who do believe that food offered to idols is efficacious, since eating together creates community. Since the Jesus tradition was formed in hellenistic communities, it seems very strange that the Jesus tradition does not address the issue of food offered to idols.

When dealing with irregularities in the Agape meal (1 Cor. 11:17–34), Paul insists the Corinthians wait for each other (11:33) and share equally what has been proffered.[6] Again, though a crucial aspect of early Christian life together, there is no direct teaching in the Jesus tradition on equality at the table. However, in the Feeding of the 5,000 the five loaves were so shared that everyone had enough and there were baskets left over. When these baskets appear in later pictures of the Christian meal, they probably represent sharing with each other and those in need. Sharing together is critical for the Pauline Agape and for the Jesus Feeding, but Paul makes no reference to the Feeding of the 5,000.

Paul writes about fasting in Romans 14. Some in the community abstain from food on a certain day while others do not abstain at all.

Those who observe the day, observe it in honor of the Lord. Also those who eat, eat in honor of the Lord, since they give thanks to God; while those who abstain, abstain in honor of the Lord and give thanks to God. (Rom. 14:6)

The difference has caused conflict. Paul asks them to honor each other's convictions and not cause anyone to stumble. In Matt. 6:16–18 Jesus had asked his disciples not to fast in public, which shows that in the Matthean church fasting was indeed a problem. But in the early Jesus tradition there is no teaching on fasting that could have impacted Paul at the time he wrote the letter to the Romans.

The Pauline Christians must have eaten meat; otherwise there is no sense in the idol meat question. Paul urged the Corinthians not to eat meat if it would cause a brother or sister to stumble (1 Cor. 8:13). Eventually, though, some Christians became vegetarians. Paul did not discourage this conviction, but he did urge the Romans not to make an issue of it:

Welcome those who are weak in faith, but not for the purpose of quarreling over opinions. Some believe in eating anything, while the weak eat only vegetables. Those who eat must not despise those who abstain, and those who abstain must not pass judgment on those who eat; for God has welcomed them. (Rom. 14:1–3)

Despite considerable research and thought by scholars, the weak in the letters of Paul cannot be identified.[7] They obviously are not as flexible, or free, as the strong members. The strong need to be careful not to offend the more rigorous weak members. Are the weak members avoiding the kashrut question? Are they avoiding the question of meat offered to idols? From all the evidence, it is known that the Agape consisted of bread, fish, and wine. Did the vegetarians also shun the fish of the Agape meal? Again, however, there is practically no Jesus tradition on this issue. The Feeding of the 5,000 would make no sense if there were vegetarians in the earliest congregations. Paul must have been dealing with an anomaly in Romans 14.

That leaves table fellowship. Paul relativizes cultural norms and customs. He gives no apology whatsoever for his willingness, in the light of cultural expectations and regulations, to modify his behavior for the sake of the Gospel:

> For though I am free with respect to all, I have made myself a slave to all, so that I might win more of them. To the Jews I became as a Jew, in order to win Jews. To those under the law I became as one under the law (though I myself am not under the law) so that I might win those under the law. To those outside the law I became as one outside the law (though I am not free from God's law but am under Christ's law) so that I might win those outside the law. To the weak I became weak, so that I might win the weak. I have become all things to all people, that I might by all means save some. (1 Cor. 9:19–22)

A major key to Paul's gentile mission was his willingness to modify those Jewish regulations that prevented table fellowship. At first he scoffed at the problems of eating meat offered to idols because idols didn't exist and therefore the ontology of the gods was irrelevant. Then he realized that what really counted was the quality of the table fellowship. That is the issue addressed in the problematic 2:11–14 of the Letter to the Galatians:

> But when Cephas came to Antioch, I opposed him to his face, because he stood self-condemned; for until certain people came from James, he used to eat with the Gentiles. But after they came, he drew back and kept himself separate for fear of the circumcision faction. And the other Jews joined him in this hypocrisy, so that even Barnabas was led astray by their hypocrisy. But when I saw that they were not acting consistently with the truth of the gospel, I said to Cephas before them all, "If you, though a Jew, live like a Gentile and not like a Jew, how can you compel the Gentiles to live like Jews?" (Gal. 2:11–14)

The narrative is fairly straightforward. Paul and the Jewish Christians of Antioch shared meals together with the Gentile Christians, probably the Agape and the Eucharist. Either the kashrut rules had been compromised or, possibly, the meal (bread, fish, and wine)

actually contained no unclean foods. The Apostle Peter had previously participated in these meals. But when Jewish Christians came
up to Antioch from Jerusalem, being unaccustomed to eating with
Gentiles, they were unable to participate in the Agape. At that point
Peter himself withdrew to the tables of the Jerusalem visitors (protecting the weak or avoiding conflict). Paul does not say some ate
kosher food and others did not. He only says they did not eat at
the same tables.

If the issue is that of clean and unclean food, the impact of the
Jesus tradition at work is visible in the Pauline material. The Jesus
tradition sharply criticized kashrut regulations and argued, meta-
phorically, that it is what comes out of the mouth (words, attitudes)
that make us clean or unclean (Mark 7:14–23; cf. Rom. 14:14).

The issue in Gal. 2:11–14 does not appear to be simply clean
and unclean food. The Jewish types retired to their own tables. Of
course, there could have been two different menus — one kosher
and one not. But it seems more likely the issue involved sitting at
the same table. The problem of eating at the same table or eating
in the same room was well known.

Non-Jewish writers generally assumed that Jews could not eat
with non-Jews.[8] Tacitus notes:

> They sit apart at meals and they sleep apart, and although they
> are a race most given to lust, they abstain from intercourse
> with foreign women; among themselves nothing is unlawful.
> (*Hist.* 5.5.2)

Jewish sources are not quite as clear. The author of Daniel portrays
Daniel as not wishing to eat the food of King Nebuchadnezzar:

> But Daniel resolved that he would not defile himself with the
> royal rations of food and wine; so he asked the palace master
> to allow him not to defile himself. (Dan. 1:8)

It is not certain whether Daniel and the young Jewish men ate alone,
nor is it absolutely clear whether Daniel refers to the defilement of
unclean food or the disgrace of eating with idolaters. Other Jewish
sources are not more precise. When Judith ate with Holofernes she

ate her own food. Her rationale was indeed avoidance of disgrace rather than defilement.

> Then he commanded them to bring her in where his silver dinnerware was kept, and ordered them to set a table for her with some of his own delicacies, and with some of his own wine to drink.
> But Judith said, "I cannot partake of them, or it will be an offense; but I will have enough with the things I brought with me." (Jdt. 12:1–2)

The Jesus tradition shattered the Jewish exclusivism. Jewish leaders complained that Jesus ate with tax collectors and sinners (Luke 5:30; Matt. 9:10–13). In the parable of the banquet the outcasts are invited to the meal after the upstanding citizens of the town refuse to accept the invitation (Luke 14:21; Matt. 22:10; Thomas 64:11). The Jesus tradition does not include, however, any action or teaching that impinges on the problem of eating with non-Jews.

It is possible, then, that the Antioch episode did involve idolatry rather than kashrut. The representatives from Jerusalem must have known about meals eaten together. They must have known Peter already had crossed the line. And, perhaps, the food offered was not subject to kosher regulations. But outside Palestine wine was normally offered to a god before it was served. For a Jew, to drink such wine would be idolatry (*m. Abod. Zar* 5:5). Perhaps the disciples from Jerusalem withdrew because they could not determine how the wine had been prepared before it was served. In such a case the problem in Galatians is nearly identical with that of 1 Corinthians 8 and 10. The koinonia of the Agape was disturbed by differing views on idolatry. Even if this be true, nevertheless, as in the case of 1 Corinthians and Romans, there is no Jesus tradition on food offered to idols. It was a conflict arising out of Paul's mission to the Gentiles and not an issue for those holding to the early Jesus tradition.

Differences between the theology of Paul and the Gospels are well known and have been thoroughly examined. That theology called Pauline did not pass into the isles. For the most part the Jesus tradition he taught in oral communication did reach the At-

lantic Celts. The Jesus tradition was not radically altered by the
Pauline transmission. Like Jesus, Paul taught as Jew. To be sure,
his language lacked the Semitic flavor of the Jesus tradition, but
his thought world still derived from his Jewish heritage. He kept
the Jewish calendar, though, like Jesus, he did not strictly honor
Jewish celebrative days. Like the Jesus tradition he insisted on the
ultimacy of God's sovereignty. Like Jesus Paul understood the legitimacy of political authority, but also like Jesus he understood
that love of enemy would undermine any imperial authority not
true to God's sovereignty. Unlike Jesus he did not criticize the religious authorities, but instead developed a fictive kinship that was
itself the authority (the body of Christ). Unlike Jesus, on occasion
he made the family of Jesus an embryonic political authority. Like
Jesus his monotheistic faith disallowed any ontological dualism.
Evil entered when as individualists we failed to love our neighbor,
that is, thwart the family of God. As in the Jesus tradition, there
are also in Paul hints of a Near Eastern combat myth and the role
of Satan, both of which are powers that could disrupt the human
covenants. Unlike Jesus, Paul did not stress healing, though he held
it in high regard as a gift of the faith community. Like Jesus Paul insisted on commensality as the focus for community formation. Like
Jesus Paul insisted on the sanctity of the family and the importance
of covenantal sexuality. Despite Jesus' apparent celibacy, and only
a few references to Paul's marriage, there is no hint of sexual asceticism. However, both understood the critical importance of the
missioner for God being unhampered by family obligations.

The Jesus tradition passed on to the Celts by Paul was not identical to Q, the Gospel of Thomas, or Mark. But it was close enough
for us to speak of Paul as the legitimate carrier of the Jesus tradition
to those who lived beyond the Greco-Roman world.

The Jesus Tradition, Paul's Lifestyle, and the Galatians

It would be simplistic to suppose the impact of the Jesus tradition
was limited to the oral tradition of Q, the Gospel of Thomas, and
the Gospel of Mark. Paul himself must have made a deep impres-

sion on the Celts of north Galatia. Is it possible that any of Paul's personal behavior might have reinforced the Jesus tradition in such a way that it passed into the Celtic belief system? An examination of the Letter to the Galatians would indicate Paul enjoyed hospitality among the Galatians, had meals in common with Celts (non-Jews), both men and women. Paul showed indignation at wavering Celtic disciples and animosity toward Celtic leaders who argued for a co-operation with the dominant Celtic culture. Precedents for these behaviors can be found in the Jesus tradition. In QS 51, the story of the great supper, Jesus approves inviting as dinner guests those who otherwise would have been shunned. Yet, there is no indica-tion in the letters of Paul that this parable affected his picture of a common meal.

The early Jesus tradition shows antagonism from Jesus toward those who heard his words but did not do them (QS 14). If Paul knew the Jesus tradition of loving an enemy (QS 9), he did not demonstrate that quality toward those who, in his opinion, misled the Galatians.

The Celts apparently assimilated quite easily. The variety of Celtic tribes, customs, and language indicate this open stance. There is very little information about Irish hospitality and mealtimes. Cer-tainly Christian students from all over the continent were accepted to study in the Irish monasteries. Eating together was not the way in which community was formed. The early Irish Christians were very stubborn. Resisting encroachment from the Romans was a mark of their faith. For example, they refused to change their calendar until the seventh century and then only with great reluctance. Did Jesus' words and Paul's practice alter the assimilative nature of the Celts? Or was the stubbornness a product of constant Roman pressure on the Celts to flee westward?

Two more lifestyle issues are even more critical. The Irish monks and leaders were ascetics. Did that come through the Jesus tradi-tion? Some argue the Jesus tradition was indeed ascetic from the beginning. The words of Jesus in QS 8 praising the poor would have been a call for a type of monastic movement.[9] It cannot be denied that the Jesus tradition eschewed the value of wealth. Q1 has the parable of the barns (QS 38) or the advice to sell your possessions

(QS 40). While Paul must have had access to these sayings, there is no trace of them in his letters. There is no evidence that Paul was deliberately destitute and so the conclusion can be made that, even though there is a strong tendency in the early Jesus tradition to shun wealth, insistence on poverty did not pass into the early Irish tradition from Paul's interaction with the Celts of Galatia.

Celibacy would be a more difficult matter. The early Jesus tradition contains very little about sexuality. Jesus does warn about placing too much emphasis on the primary family (QS 52). At the same time, the permanence of the marriage bond was nearly absolute. In contrast to material asceticism, Paul did deal with sexuality. It can be assumed that his wife was with him on the first trip to Galatia. At least he wrote a few years later how upset he was that his wife was not given the same rights as other apostolic wives (1 Cor. 9:5). He encouraged strong sexual bonding and advised the incipient encratics of Corinth to cease and desist (1 Cor. 7:5). Paul cannot have exhibited a lifestyle in Galatia that would have encouraged sexual asceticism. Asceticism must not have passed from the Jesus tradition through Paul to early Irish Christianity. The origin of asceticism in Irish Christianity is very difficult to explain.

More difficult yet is peregrination. Many have assumed that the early Jesus tradition, especially Q, derived from and called for itinerancy.[10] For sociologists of the New Testament it has been traditional to speak of Jesus as a wandering radical, an itinerant missioner, even a Cynic philosopher.[11] Itinerancy in Q can hardly be denied. The call to mission (QS 20) is more than enough evidence. Followers of Jesus cannot take care of family matters like burying the dead or bidding farewell to family. They might not even have a place to sleep (QS 19). Food, drink, and clothing for the journey will be a gift of God (QS 39). However one might interpret these passages, the itinerant call can hardly be erased. Paul appeared before the Galatians as a missioner. Did he use the Q texts to support his mission? No. Could the Celts of Galatia have taken his trips as itinerancy? Yes. There were two types of missioners in the earliest church: itinerant charismatics and authorized community organizers. Paul was the supreme example of an itinerant charismatic.[12] Paul was the lead missioner of the early church.

His authority came from a divine call rather than from Jesus or the first apostles. In fact, Paul was not a member of any faith community. He defended his legitimacy by his function, not his tradition in the faith.

Yet, it is not that simple. Some claim that it would be easier to call for itinerancy when one is stationary. Others have made the same argument. It would be difficult for a group of itinerants to put together documents for use by the community. Furthermore, Q reflects community needs and advice like that found in Galilee during the first half of the first century.[13]

The Celts of Galatia were not nomadic. They must have traded with the Celts to the west, but they had fixed homes in Galatia. Did Paul's life as an itinerant carry with it a Jesus admonition to wander? When Irish Christianity broke forth in the fifth century it was highly itinerant. Had it not been for peregrination, Irish Christianity would not have spread to Iona and Scotland. Had it not been for peregrination, the Irish monks would not have carried their learning to the continent. Surely Paul was known among the Celts as a peregrinator and almost surely the tradition of the mission to Spain carried with it that perception of itinerancy.

Notes

1. See Victor Furnish, *Jesus According to Paul* (Cambridge: Cambridge University Press, 1993), 40–65, and Frans Neirynck, "Paul and the Sayings of Jesus," in *L'Apôtre Paul: personnalité, style et conception du ministère,* ed. Albert Vanhoye (Leuven: Leuven University Press, 1986), 265–321.

2. George Johnston, "Kingdom of God Sayings in Paul's Letters," in *From Jesus to Paul: Studies in Honour of Francis Wright Beare,* ed. Peter Richardson and John C. Hurd (Waterloo, Ontario: Wilfrid Laurier University Press, 1984), 143–56.

3. G. F. Snyder, "The Ironic Dialogues in John," in *Putting Body and Soul Together,* ed. V. Wiles, A. Brown, and G. F. Snyder (Valley Forge, Pa.: Trinity Press, 1997), 23.

4. Adolf von Harnack, *The Mission and Expansion of Christianity,* trans. James Moffatt (New York: G. P. Putnam, 1904), 398–461.

5. G. F. Snyder, "The *Tobspruch* in the New Testament," *New Testament Studies* 23 (1976–77): 117–20.

6. Gerd Theissen, *The Social Setting of Pauline Christianity* (Philadelphia: Fortress Press, 1982), 145–74.

7. Ibid., 21–143.

8. See examples in Esler, *Galatians*, 95.

9. J. C. O'Neill, "New Testament Monasteries," in *Common Life in the Early Church: Essays Honoring Graydon F. Snyder*, ed. Julian V. Hills (Harrisburg, Pa.: Trinity Press International, 1998), 118–32.

10. Gerd Theissen, "The Wandering Radicals: Light Shed by the Sociology of Literature on the Early Transmission of Jesus' Sayings," in *Social Reality and the Early Christians: Theology, Ethics, and the World of the New Testament*, trans M. Kohl (1973; Minneapolis: Fortress Press, 1992), 33–59.

11. As only one example see Crossan, *The Historical Jesus*, 72–88, 345–48.

12. Theissen, *Social Setting of Pauline Christianity*, 27–67.

13. William E. Arnal, *Jesus and the Village Scribes: Galilean Conflicts and the Setting of Q* (Minneapolis: Fortress Press, 2001), 202–3.

Chapter 5

Paul and Spain

No one doubts the presence of extensive trade routes between Iberia and Eire. In addition to the normal archaeological indications of trade, in recent days studies have even shown that the Irish are closer to the DNA structure of the Spanish than any other ethnic group.[1] In antiquity northern Spain and Ireland were very close. Because of the direct sea route, trading was more common than from Gaul to Ireland. Consequently, there was a stronger interchange of ideas and customs. A close relationship between Britain and Ireland would have been expected, but that has not been the case. As for Christianity, the Irish version differs sharply from that of Romano-Britannia. One could explain this sharp difference in several ways. First, as explained by W. H. C. Frend, the differences have been exaggerated.[2] Second, it is possible that the western island seriously altered the Christianity that crossed the sea from Britain. Or, finally, could it be that the Irish Celts absorbed a Jesus tradition that had already entered the Celtic cultural stream through some route other than through Britain? The first two options are highly improbable. Very likely, early Christianity came to Eire from the Celtiberians in north Spain or — even more likely — from Galicia in northwest Spain (the Hispanic equivalent of Galatia or Celts). That part of the puzzle seems simple, since the trade routes would have already been in place.

What would be considerably more difficult to explain is how the Jesus tradition ever arrived in Galicia. It is too romantic to suggest Paul sought a ride with his Galatian friends in one of their famous carts. Though, indeed, the final destination of some Galatian trading missions could well have been Galicia.[3] But, alas, there is no apparent place for such a trip in the chronology of Paul's life.

Nevertheless, it has always been assumed that Paul went to Spain. He spoke of the trip in Rom. 15:24:

> But now, with no further place for me in these regions, I desire, as I have for many years, to come to you when I go to Spain. For I do hope to see you on my journey and to be sent on by you, once I have enjoyed your company for a little while. (Rom. 15:23–24)

And again in 15:28:

> So, when I have completed this, and have delivered to them what has been collected, I will set out by way of you to Spain.

Paul may have implied a visit to Spain when he said his ambition was to proclaim the Good News in a place where Christ had never been named (Rom. 15:20).

The earliest corroboration of Paul's trip to Spain comes from Clement, who wrote in his letter to the Corinthian churches that Paul taught righteousness to all the world, East and West, when he had reached the limits of the West, and gave his testimony to the rulers (1 Clem. 5:7). Clement does not say explicitly that Paul went to Spain, but then on the continent only Spain would qualify as the "limits" of the West. Later authors did speak more directly about Spain. The Muratorian canon (about 200 C.E.) defends the early date for Acts by noting that Luke did not record the passion of Peter or "the journey of Paul, who from the city (of Rome) proceeded to Spain" (lines 38–39).

Similarly the *Acts of Peter* (180–190 C.E.) leaves no doubt about Spain. Before shifting to Peter the Acts begins with a narrative about the decision of Paul to leave Rome and sail for Spain (1:1–2 [*Actus Vercellenses*]). On the other hand, tradition has firmly established that Paul was executed in Rome during the time of Nero (*Acts of Peter* 1:1 [*Actus Vercellenses*]; *Acts of Paul* 11; Eusebius, *Hist. Eccl.* 3.1; 2.25.5). If Paul had traveled to Spain he would have returned to Rome by about 63 C.E. After announcing in Romans (55–57 C.E.) his intention to go to Spain, he still had before him the trip to Jerusalem and the imprisonment in Caesarea. That leaves practically no time for a trip to Spain.

There is yet another concern. Because the Pastoral Epistles differ so widely from the authentic epistles, it has been assumed that they were written from prison at a time other than when the Prison Epistles were written. The trip to Spain allows the occasion for a second imprisonment in Rome when the older, less fiery, more pastoral Paul could have written these two sets of directions to his cohorts, Timothy and Titus. Since modern scholarship has rejected the Pauline authorship of the Pastoral Epistles, there is no reason for a second imprisonment in Rome. Nor is there any need for a trip to Spain.

Four discreet possibilities exist. Paul traveled to Spain from Rome and wrote the Pastoral Epistles upon his return. Or Paul traveled to Spain but did not write the Pastoral Epistles upon his return to Rome. Or Paul never traveled to Spain and wrote the Pastoral Epistles before his martyrdom under Nero. Or Paul neither traveled to Spain nor wrote the Pastoral Epistles. Given the chronological crunch, the last choice seems most likely. How then should the tradition that Paul journeyed to Spain be treated?

The Great Commission to the apostles was to carry the gospel to the ends of the earth:

> But you will receive power when the Holy Spirit has come upon you; and you will be my witnesses in Jerusalem, in all Judea and Samaria, and to the ends of the earth. (Acts 1:8)

The Commission was not to accost the power centers of the Roman Empire, but rather to cover the known world.[4] Depending on how one translates *ethne*,[5] as nation or Gentiles, the Matthean Great Commission may refer to all nations or all non-Jewish peoples:

> Go therefore and make disciples of all nations. (Matt. 28:19)

It does not refer to power centers like Rome. The Book of Acts then confuses the issue. While the Great Commission refers to spatial or geographical expanses, the author of Acts has the story end in Rome. As a consequence most people read Acts as if it were a *Heilsgeschichte* that started in the divine center of the world, Jerusalem, and ended in the political center of the world, Rome. Perhaps that may have been the intent of the author. But Rome was not the spatial limits of the known world. Spain was.

It was understood that eventually each apostle would become responsible for some section of the world. How this happened is certainly a mystery. Eusebius said it was done by drawing lots (*Hist. Eccl.* 3.1): Thomas went to Parthia, Andrew to Scythia, John to Asia (Ephesus), Peter to central Asia, and Paul from Jerusalem to Illyria.

The same narrative occurs at the beginning of the *Acts of Thomas* where Thomas refuses the call to India, but does eventually capitulate:

> At that time we apostles were all in Jerusalem, Simon called Peter and Andrew his brother, James the son of Zebedee and John his brother, Philip and Bartholomew, Thomas and Matthew the publican, James (the son) of Alphaeus and Simon the Cananaean, and Judas (the brother) of James; and we divided the regions of the world, that each one of us might go to the region which fell to his lot, and to the nation to which the Lord sent him.

The sending of the apostles to all the nations is well attested in the early church material. In the *Kerygma* Petrou the Lord says,

> I have chosen you twelve because I judged you worthy to be my disciples (whom the Lord wished). And I sent them, of whom I was persuaded that they would be true apostles, into the world to proclaim to men in all the world the joyous message. (Clem. Al., *Strom.* 6.5.43; parenthesis added by Clement)

It is nearly impossible to distill from the mass of information a clear picture of apostolic assignments. But essentially there is this list:

Peter	Rome
Andrew	Scythia
Thomas	India
Mark	Egypt
Philip	Hieropolis
John	Ephesus

This discussion deals with apostolic mission, not known apostolic travels. There is no historical evidence that Mark ever traveled to Alexandria. The John of Ephesus would have been John the Presbyter, not John the Apostle. Despite the ancient tradition, still alive today, that Thomas founded the church in India, there is no factual data behind the assertion. The keystone for apostolic mission would be, of course, the presence of Peter in Rome. Despite the presence of a burial under St. Peter's, there is still a lingering doubt that Peter ever made it to the capital city.[6] The importance of Peter in Rome would be the "rock" double entendre in Matthew 16 and the tradition that Peter was the first to the see the resurrected Lord (1 Cor. 15:1–5).

Paul was to go to Spain. Even though he said he was headed for Spain, there is far less factual evidence of Paul in Spain than of Peter in Rome. On the other hand, there are no written words of Peter about his mission to Rome, but, as Paul told the Celts in Galatia, going to *all* the Gentiles was his apostolic mission (1:16; 2:9; 3:8, 14).

If this is correct, then it creates something of a quandary about the actual intrusion of the Jesus tradition into Celtic Spain. There are three considerations:

1. Since the Celts maintained trade routes throughout northern Europe, there is every reason to suppose the impact of Paul and the Jesus tradition in Galatia also reached Galicia. However, there is no specific connection between Galatia and Galicia. If the Jesus tradition reached Galicia, then it also must have also reached the Celts in Gaul or Helvitus or Germania. One must suppose this would have been true. The tradition of Paul going to Spain was eschatological. Paul was going to the end of the world and that end was Spain, not Gaul.

2. In terms of communication between continental and insular Celts of Ireland the link is Spain, the trade route. Very little went from Gaul through Britannia, or the Romano-Britons, to Ireland. Spain was, in fact, the point of departure. So even if the Jesus tradition reached most of the Celts of Europe by means of Galatia, the only contact that matters for our

thesis is the route through Spain. The pre-Patrick Jesus tradition arrived by way of Galicia. The jump to Ireland was an
unanticipated next step in the history of the Jesus movement.

3. There is more to Paul's trip to Spain than meets the eye. The
    presence of Paul, his gospel, and the Jesus tradition could have
    been carried to Spain by Paul's associates rather than Paul
    himself. Most obvious would be the possibility that Paul's
    cohort Phoebe might have expedited the mission to Spain.
    After telling the Romans about his plans for Spain, Paul then
    mentions Phoebe's journey from Corinth to Rome:

> I commend to you our sister Phoebe, a minister of the
> church at Cenchrea, so that you may welcome her in the
> Lord as is fitting for the saints, and help her in whatever
> she may require from you, for she has been a benefactor
> of many and of myself as well. (Rom. 16:1–2)

> Phoebe was a minister (deacon is an inappropriate translation)
> in the church at Cenchrea and a benefactor for many. Though
> much debated it is assumed she was, in the normal sense of
> the word, a wealthy financial benefactor. What, then, would
> she have need of from the Roman Christians? Certainly one
> obvious possibility was to set up the Spanish mission for, with,
> or in the place of the apostle Paul.[7]

The assumption that Paul himself went to Spain has existed until
our time. For example, in 1892 Frederick Meyrick wrote:

> There is no reason for doubting that S. Paul fulfilled his
> expressed purpose of visiting Spain. We know that he was
> strongly averse to giving up the plans that he had formed for
> his missionary journeys.
> After his first imprisonment at Rome, he had time and
> opportunity for carrying out his cherished purpose.[8]

The rejection of the Pastoral Epistles as authentic letters of Paul
made the visit to Spain by Paul both unnecessary and highly problematic. Chronologies by Robert Jewett and Gerd Lüdemann show
the near impossibility of such a journey.[9] The Spain tradition must

imply the impact of Paul on the Galatians, and subsequently the Galicians.

Notes

1. For a helpful discussion see W. H. C. Frend, "Romano-British Christianity and the West: Comparison and Contrast," in *The Early Church in Western Britain and Ireland,* ed. Susan M. Pearce, BAR British Series 102 (Oxford: British Archaeological Reports, 1982), 5–11. He concludes that Irish Christianity could not have been the heir of Christianity in Romano-Britain or Gaul (11).

2. John Thomas McNeill, *The Celtic Churches: A History A.D. 200 to 1200* (Chicago: University of Chicago Press, 1974), 10.

3. See R. D. Aus, "Paul's Travel Plans to Spain and the 'Full Number of the Gentiles' of Rom XI 25," *NovT* 21 (1979): 244–46. For a view that limits the mission to the land of Israel, see Daniel Schwartz, "The End of the GH (Acts 1:8): Beginning or End of the Christian Vision?" *JBL* 105 (1986): 669–76.

4. James LaGrand, *The Earliest Christian Mission to "All Nations" in the Light of Matthew's Gospel* (Grand Rapids, Mich.: Eerdmans, 1999), 37–42.

5. For details see Edgar Hennecke, *New Testament Apocrypha,* trans. R. McL. Wilson et al., vol. 2 (Philadelphia: Westminster Press, 1965), 43–50.

6. On the importance of the myth of apostolic presence see G. F. Snyder, "Survey and 'New' Thesis on the Bones of Peter," *The Biblical Archaeologist Reader,* vol. 3, ed. Edward F. Campbell Jr. and David Noel Freedman (Garden City, N.Y.: Doubleday, 1970), 405–24. E. Dinkler, "Die Petrus-Rom-Frage," *Theologische Rundschau* 25 (1959), 189–230, 289–335; 27 (1961), 33–64.

7. Robert Jewett, *A Chronology of Paul's Life* (Philadelphia: Fortress Press, 1979), 45; Karl Donfried, "Chronology," *ABD* 1:1021.

8. Frederick Meyrick, *The Church in Spain* (London: Wells Gardner, Darton & Co. 1892), 18.

9. Jewett, *Chronology of Paul's Life,* 45; Lüdemann, *Paul, Apostle to the Gentiles* (Philadelphia: Fortress Press, 1984), 45.

Chapter 6

The Celts in Spain

It seems strange that the most problematic bridge between Galatia and Eire could at the same time be the most certain. On the certain side:

1. The Iberian Celts formed, with Brittany, Cornwall, and Ireland, a far western trading unit that were called the Atlantic Celts.[1]

2. The northwestern corner of the Iberian peninsula, Galicia, was inhabited by Celts from the early part of the first millennium B.C.E.[2] Villares speaks of a strongly castro-oriented Celtic population: "This castro population appears to be the result of different contributing groups, those referred to as original ethnic Galicians, and those who entered Galicia during the first centuries of the final millennium before Christ."[3]

3. The early Celts spoke a form of Celtic that matches the goidelic of Eire.[4]

4. The early Celts, sometimes called the castro Celts, built hillforts like those found in Ireland: "For the Spanish peninsula, in their use of hill sites with fortifications, the castros represent approximately, in their general conception, the oppida of celtic Gaul."[5]

5. The hills of Galicia contained considerable metal deposits that gave rise to the same type of metalwork for which the Irish Celts were famed. Otherwise, it is the "richness of minerals that very early caught the attention of early inhabitants for the far regions of the Spanish peninsula."[6]

6. Galician metal pieces not only were traded in eastern Europe, but also to the western isles.

106

7. The interchange between Iberia and Ireland was not only economic, but demographic.

On the other hand, there are disturbing questions that cannot be easily answered:

1. Archaeological evidence in Ireland does not support any substantial trading between 600 B.C.E. and 200 B.C.E.[7]
2. While the original language of Galicia was goidelic, it shifted to brythonic about the fourth century B.C.E.[8]
3. The relationship between the Celts of Galicia, the more interior Celtiberians, and the more eastern La Tène culture cannot be clarified by archaeological evidence.
4. Metal trade from the eastern Mediterranean is more obvious in southern Iberia (Cadiz) than Galicia and the north.
5. There is no evidence for Christianity in Spain before 200 C.E.
6. There is no evidence that the Jesus tradition entered Ireland from Iberia.

Excellent studies regarding the Celts in Spain have been written and there is nothing new to add. A short summary will suffice to see that Spain could have been the port from which the Jesus tradition moved into Ireland.

In the first millennium much of Spain was influenced by trade with the eastern Mediterranean. Among the earliest traders were the Phoenicians who used Gadir as a port and eventually established colonies up the east coast (eighth to sixth centuries). According to archaeological evidence (vases, metalwork, weapons) there was extensive Spanish interaction with Greeks and north Africans. Historically speaking, because of the connection with North Africa, central/southern inhabitants of Spain were caught up in the Punic wars. Eventually this resulted in Spain being annexed by the Romans. Although there are Celtic names and remains throughout central and eastern Spain, the primary Celtic population resided in the northcentral region, the Ebro Valley, and are called Celtiberians. How the Celtiberians came to exist in Spain has been much debated. A preferred thesis would be that proto-Celts were already living in the peninsula, as there were proto-Celts in Ireland. In north-central Iberia these proto-Celtics assimilated the Celtic culture as it crossed over from Gaul. Assimilation was more of a characteristic of the Celts than conquest or even mass migration. The combination of these proto-Celts with the Gaul type created a Celtic culture peculiar to Spain.[9]

While this may be true of the Celtiberians, it was not true of those proto-Celts living in that northwestern part of the peninsula called Galicia. Their culture was not influenced by the eastern influx. Rather than assimilating, the Galicians remained aloof from the changes in central Spain. They had more in common with the cultures found in Brittany, Cornwall, and Ireland. In short, the Atlantic Celts formed a culture apparently only lightly touched by the Mediterranean cultures and La Tène. That this Atlantic culture differs from the more eastern groups can easily be seen in language, artifacts, buildings, and lifestyle. To what extent it is really Celtic would be harder to determine.

As a geographical area Galicia is certainly a rugged, mountainous terrain.[10] Strabo, writing in 18 C.E., said, "Northern Iberia, in addition to its ruggedness, not only is extremely cold, but lies next to the ocean; consequently it is an exceedingly wretched place to live in."[11] The area was heavily forested, due in part to nearly ten months of daily rain. Given the heavy rainfall, many rivers were formed that flowed into the Atlantic (particularly the Duero, the Lima, the Minho, and the Ulla). While the shore was rocky and often stormy, over time the inlets or rias developed into natural harbors from which to ply the Atlantic trade.

Like other Celtic groups Galicians used feasting as the basis for communal formation: "the dinner is passed around, and amid their cups they dance to flute and trumpet, dancing in chorus (Strabo, *Geography* 3.3.7). Not only did the feasts tie together the local community but they also celebrated the seasons of the year. And like many cultures there was feasting for the dead who were spiritually still a part of the community.[12] Though the first Galician Christians would also have included the dead in their celebrations, obviously they had a much more difficult time with seasonal fertility rites, the ritualization of natural phenomena, and the Celtic calendar.[13]

From the middle of the first millennium B.C.E. the Celts of Galicia developed characteristically Celtic hilltops called castros (the oppida of Roman designation). In terms of archaeology, the Castro culture can be identified by its hilltop settlements, pottery types, and stone sculpture.[14] Though estimations vary, there were probably about 2,000 castros in Galicia.

Galicia should not be identified with the Gallic Celtiberians of the East, but with the Atlantic Celts of the West. Their language survived as Gaelic, Manx, Breton, Welsh, and Cornish. Archaeological remains of the Atlantic Celts show the general style of Celtic art, even some La Tène.[15]

The situation now becomes rather clear. There was a proto-Celtic culture in the western coast of both the continent and the islands. It is visible in megaliths, circular burial chambers oriented toward the sun, nature-oriented art, and hillforts. Around 600 B.C.E. the far western cultures formed a trading community now called the Atlantic community. At the same time, the Celtic culture associated with La Tène moved west through Gaul, Italia, and Iberia. For the most part the La Tène–type culture assimilated the prior central tribes, so that a variety of Celtic types resulted in northcentral Europe. The Gallic type interacted with the eastern part of the isles to form what later would go by the name Great Britain. In Iberia the northcentral proto-Celtic culture became Celtiberian. Eventually, in the first century B.C.E., the Romans conquered Gaul and Iberia. Despite the romanization, elements of the Celtic culture continued.[16] All the while the Atlantic community maintained a kind of Celtic culture that was in existence prior to the formation of Celtic Gaul and Celtic Iberia and relatively free of orientalizing. How that happened is still open to debate. Presumably the first wave of what are called Celts, speaking goidelic, arrived in Galicia and Brittany prior to the arrival of the La Tène culture. While the more interior Celts of Gaul and Iberia interacted with the new La Tène types, the earlier, coastal proto-Celtic culture was transferred to Ireland, Wales, Cornwall, and Scotland from Galicia and to the eastern isle (Britain) from Brittany.[17] The later invasion of Britain by the Romans greatly altered the Celtic culture there. However, the Romans only marginally affected Ireland, Wales, and Scotland. Even though the Romans eventually conquered Galicia and Brittany in the first century B.C.E., Galicia never readily submitted to romanization.[18]

The furthermost western Celtic communities strongly resisted romanization. In fact even romanized "Britain" also failed to influence its neighbors to the west and north. After the east section of Romano-Britain was conquered by the Anglo-Saxons (410 C.E.) and Britain proper was formed, the possibility of romanizing the Celts of Ireland, Wales, and Scotland disappeared. By this analysis it cannot be said that the insular north (Scotland) and insular west (Ireland) maintained the purest Celtic culture, but that they were the least affected by Roman culture. The intent of this study was to examine an ancient culture relatively free of Roman influence — a culture that also became Christian. Early Irish Christianity serves well as such an example.

At this point it all seems rather obvious. The route to Ireland was through Galicia. Tradition nearly unanimously agrees that Paul went to Spain. Sometime before Galicia was romanized, the Jesus tradition carried by Paul or Paul's cohorts was passed on to Ireland through the normal trade routes.[19] The Jesus tradition was readily accepted in Ireland because the Celtic culture of Galicia was very similar to that of the western isle. Would that it were so simple. There are still nearly insurmountable data problems:

- Apart from tradition there is no indication that Paul ever went to Spain.

- The idea that Paul's people went to Spain cannot be verified.

- There is no tradition or evidence for the Jesus tradition in Spain before 200 C.E.

- There is no reason to localize Christianity in Spain to the remote section called Galicia.

- There is little Irish tradition identifying Spain as the origin of its first Christian faith.

Despite this lack of evidence, another kind of logic comes into play:

- The Jesus tradition did arrive in Ireland before Pelagius and Patrick.

- The Jesus tradition did not come from romanized Gaul or Iberia.

- The Jesus tradition entered Ireland without resistance.

- The Jesus tradition must have come from a people with whom its Celtic culture was empathic.

Improbable as the above thesis may appear, the alternatives are quite implausible.

- A non-Roman Jesus tradition traveled from Palestine through North Africa to Cadiz and on to Ireland through the Atlantic trade route.

Or:

- A Celtic mercenary witnessed the Jesus events in Jerusalem and carried the untouched "Good News" to Ireland through Italy, Gaul, and the Atlantic Celtic community (Brittany or Galicia).

The logic is simply stated: if not... then how? It did happen. Probably no demonstrable proposal will ever gain consensus. So this study will go with Paul and the Galatians. An early Jesus tradition was received in Ireland before that tradition had been romanized. Until then, Ireland itself had strongly resisted Roman culture or any other culture influenced by Rome. As a result, a nonromanized Jesus tradition entered a culture that itself had not been romanized. Now it is time to describe what happened to Jesus in Ireland.

Notes

1. Cunliffe, *Ancient Celts,* 145–47. Cunliffe speaks of these areas as the Atlantic Façade. See the critique by James, *The Atlantic Celts,* 10.

2. P. Bosch-Gimpera, "Two Celtic Waves in Spain," *Proceedings of the British Academy* (1940): 30.

3. Ramón Villares, *História da Galiza* (Lisbon: Livros Horizonte, 1991), 25.

4. Peter Berresford Ellis, *The Celtic Empire: The First Millennium of Celtic History c. 1000 B.C.–51 A.D.* (London: Constable, 1990), 12, 44.

5. Alain Tranoy, *La Galice romaine* (Paris: de Boccard, 1981), 75. The houses in the castros of Galicia were normally round. See Collis, "The First Towns," 168. For descriptions of an excavated castro, Ullastret, see Paul MacKendrick,

The Iberian Stones Speak: Archaeology in Spain and Portugal (New York: Funk and Wagnalls, 1969), 61–72, and for a picture of an excavated hilltop in Galicia, Briteiros, see 87.

6. Tranoy, La Galice romaine, 96. Also Villares, História da Galiza, 29, and Strabo, Geography 3.2.9.

7. James, World of the Celts, 154.

8. Bosch-Gimpera, "Two Celtic Waves in Spain," 92–115.

9. Francisco Marco Simón speaks of the assimilation as "akkumulativen Keltizität." See his Die Religion im keltischen Hispanien (Budapest: Archaeolingua Alapítváry, 1998), 10. He adapted the term from C. F. H. Hawkes, "Cumulative Celticity in Pre-Roman Britain," Études Celtiques 13, no. 2 (1973): 607–28 (Hawkes uses the term la celticité cumulative on 608).

10. Tranoy, La Galice romaine, 24.

11. Strabo, Geography 3.1.2.

12. Julio Caro Baroja, Los pueblos del norte de la península Ibérica (Madrid: Burgos, 1943), 51–53, 73. See Joyce E. Salisbury, Iberian Popular Religion, 600 B.C. to 700 A.D.: Celts, Romans, and Visigoths (New York: E. Mellen Press, 1985), 280–81.

13. Simón, Die Religion im keltischen Hispanien, 21–22.

14. Cunliffe, Ancient Celts, 135; Villares, História da Galiza, 26–28.

15. David Rankin, "The Celts Through Classical Eyes," in The Celtic World, ed. Green, 22–23. Besides linguistic and archaeological evidence regarding the Atlantic Celts there are few literary references. A sixth-century B.C.E. reference, in the Masilliot Periplus as found in the Ora Maritma of Rufus Festus Avienus, describes Britain as insula Albionum. There is mention of gens Hiernorum or the race of the Irish. A further reference to islands called the Oestrymnides probably refers to Cornwall. Pytheas, in recounting a voyage of about 320 B.C.E., refers to the British as Pritanii. Historians assume the shift in consonants indicate that in Britain the early Celtic, goidelic, was replaced by the brythonic between the sixth and third centuries. About the third century B.C.E. Britain would have become more associated with Gaul, while Ireland remained with the Atlantic Celts.

16. For example, Jerome noted the Galatians spoke the same language as the inhabitants of Treveri. (Comm. Gal. 2, 3).

17. Considered, but not quite accepted by Peter Harbison, Pre-Christian Ireland: From the First Settlers to the Early Celts (London: Thames and Hudson, 1988), 170.

18. There are too few Roman artifacts to assume a Roman takeover; see MacKendrick, The Iberian Stones Speak, 94.

19. Herm, The Celts, 261.

Chapter 7

The Insular Celts

The definition of the appellation *Celt* and even determining their geographical location have become a conundrum of the highest order. Archaeological data from Hallstatt would place the origins of Iron Age Celts at about 600 B.C.E. What are more specifically called Celts, the La Tène culture, would have appeared about 400 B.C.E. But the so-called proto-Celts of the insular world and the Atlantic community evidence a type of Celtic lifestyle by the beginning of the first millennium B.C.E., or even earlier. Indications for an early common community come from language, megaliths, hilltops, symbols, and archaeological data. Scholars are correct in saying this makes any definition of the term *Celtic* very difficult.[1]

Prior to about 600 B.C.E. the isles had a fairly common culture. While this fact puts in doubt what should be a clear picture of Celtic migration from the continent, and is highly important for the long-range history of Celtic culture, it doesn't affect this study. The only concern here about insular Celtics is that the romanized Celts were limited to southcentral Britain and that the Jesus tradition entered Ireland and Scotland (including the Pict territory) by some means other than through previously romanized Celts of Britain. The proto-Celticism of the Atlantic community was a general Bronze Age (even Stone Age) culture of middle/northern Europe that finally took specific Iron Age form at Hallstatt, later La Tène. In that case, a general proto-Celtic culture would have existed in the British Isles well before the Hallstatt finds.

Evidence of the Celts in Britain

By 300 B.C.E. the area now called Great Britain was peopled by a variety of Celtic tribes, a fact evident by the discovery of swords

113

made with smelted iron or steel. These instruments were traded to various tribes and even to Romans on the continent. The Celtic tribes also traded constantly with the Gallic Celts. As for the Romans, their desire to invade Britain first came in 55 B.C.E., a few years after Caesar's takeover of Gaul.[2] It is difficult to decide why Caesar wanted to gain control in Britain — perhaps to plunder, to establish a trading partner, or to strengthen his own political image. Although Caesar did make military forays into southern Britain, the full-fledged Roman invasion of Britain under Claudius did not happen for nearly another century (43 C.E.). Because of this invasion some Celtic tribes were conquered and some were forced father west and north. Romanized Gallic tribes also followed Roman troops into Britain and set up trading relationships with those Celts who did not flee. For almost four hundred years Britain was under Roman control and influence. The Anglo-Saxon invasion (410) then drove out the Romans (436) and created the culture called British and the language called English.[3]

Evidence of the Celts in Ireland

Generally what is said here of Ireland holds for the entire insular world until the impact of the Romans and the presence of romanized Gauls on the southern section of the main island. At the same time, there were considerable differences among the insular people, probably due to geography and trading partners. While the Iron Age Celts in Ireland are the focus of this study, a quick overview of prior archaeological periods would set the stage.

The Neolithic Age

In prehistoric times the islands must have been a long peninsula, connected to the continent at the promontory called Brittany.[4] The western island probably connected to the eastern island at its northernmost tip. While all of this is speculation, its importance should not be underestimated. Since they lived on a peninsula, it is easy to assume that what was later the islands shared a common language and culture with the non-Mediterranean people of the continent.

Such an assumption would help clarify the proto-Celtic issue: similarities in language, in architecture, and in artifacts. Having a common language does not necessitate a common culture. A proto-Celtic language could have been the language of the prehistoric people of the peninsula. When it became an island, something like goidelic developed in Ireland as well as other parts of the Atlantic community. The evidence for communication between Spain and Ireland is quite certain. Meanwhile, brythonic developed in Gaul and then Britain, where intercommunication is quite apparent. In other words it is not necessary to consider invasions or even massive migrations in order to account for the language. In fact, there is no evidence of such invasions or migrations. So the issue of commonality overrides almost everything under discussion here. Did the Celts invade or immigrate to Ireland about the time of Hallstatt? There is no evidence. Did the Celts of the La Tène type invade or immigrate to Ireland? There is no such evidence. Much of what is now called Celtic was there before La Tène.

Archaeologists in general think in terms of invasion or migration. That is, the presence of artifacts that signify a cultural shift can best be explained by the movement of people from the outside dominant culture moving into the weaker, recipient culture. The scholarly need for a shift in population makes the Irish question extremely difficult. There is no easy explanation for the presence of a goidelic-type language and a Celtic-type culture that shows so little influence from the continental La Tène type. There are two alternative explanations, however. Inculturation occurred; that is, values from another culture were brought in by traders, visitors, families, or whatever. These attitudes and values eventually would have appeared useful to the recipient culture and been accepted. Normally people accept cultural change because of some lack in their basic cultural paradigms.[5] Another set of paradigms would better serve the basic purposes of the recipient people (a paradigm shift). No revolution would be necessary. That could explain the presence of the Atlantic-type Celts without any sign of an invasion or immigration.

Another possibility that historians and archaeologists tend or wish to overlook concerns human behavior. The collective human psyche will evolve in set ways regardless of outside influence. Given the same historical origin, similarity of basic cultural presuppositions, and comparable geographical settings, various people, without contacting other groups, will develop similar if not identical mores, architecture, tools, art, and religious faith.

A prehistoric culture existed in Ireland that does not stand in serious conflict with what is called Celtic. Around 7,000 B.C.E. people lived in caves, hunted with flint knives, and left behind piles of shells and bones called middens (e.g., at Cushendun in County Antrim). Sometime about 4,000 B.C.E. the inhabitants of Ireland began to build a type of stone edifice that would identify them with the Neolithic period. At the same time the basis for living shifted to agriculture: cattle, sheep, pigs as livestock, and wheat and barley as crops.[6] By the fifth millennium any possibility of a walking connection with Scotland or Britain would have long since disappeared. The animals and the farmers had to have come by boat. Where did they come from? Obviously no great distance. Scotland to County Antrim? Is there any indication such a transition occurred? Not really.

Neolithic monuments are counted among the greatest legacies of Ireland. These megalithic structures sometimes may have served as burial places for important leaders, or sometimes may have served as assembly points for worship. It is possible they served both purposes.

Court Tombs. The most numerous Neolithic monument in Ireland are the court tombs, of which there are over three hundred. A court tomb consisted of orthostats set next to each other to form a burial gallery. At the entrance, usually facing the rising sun, a forecourt was built, normally in a semicircular form.[7] While the court tomb has been identified as a burial place, actually there are few signs of burials, even though many have ceremonial burials pits or signs of eating. The tomb might well have been a temple and the actual burials were elsewhere. A considerable number of court tombs had been expanded with subsidiary galleries. The most striking feature is a large stone artistically placed on top of the gateway stones. Portal tombs, as they are called, like the court tombs, appear almost exclusively in northern Ireland (north of Galway).[8] They are found about the same time (3200 B.C.E.) in Brittany and Iberia.

Passage Tombs. These Neolithic structures also number about three hundred. Unlike the royal tombs they tend to occur in clusters as if that area served as a necropolis. The most famous cluster, which includes Knowth and Newgrange, occurs in the Boyne Valley, though there are at least eight other such necropoli. As is well known, the passage tomb consists of a circular stone edifice with a passage, facing the sun of the winter solstice and ending in a central tomb. Unquestionably Newgrange, and even Knowth, rank among the greatest stone monuments ever built. Constructed about 2500 B.C.E. they match Stonehenge and the pyramids in antiquity, skill of construction, and remarkable size.[9] For unknown centuries they have been visited and admired by thousands.

Neolithic art is of very special interest in the passage tombs. The huge decorated stone at the front of Newgrange has been designed with spirals that tail out into an adjacent spirals (plate 1). Not only spirals but also lozenges and chevrons appear on the back of Newgrange and in Knowth. Only rarely does the design seem to suggest a human face. This art appears well over a millennium before the earliest possible formal celticization of Ireland. Yet one would be hard put not to see in these Neolithic designs and art forms a continuity with even the Christian art such as found in the Book of Kells.

Granted Newgrange and Knowth are unique, similar passage tombs can be found in the Atlantic community. Comparable grave-goods and art can be found in Brittany and Iberia. But the Irish material would appear to be earlier, not later, than that of the Atlantic community. What is the source of the unique artistic conception and the high-level skill required to build these magnificent monuments?

The Early Bronze Age

The period 2000–1200 B.C.E. in Ireland is marked by the use of bronze or copper. Just as the Neolithic Age was marked by the advent of cattle and farmers, the Bronze Age was marked by the apparent advent of the so-called Beaker people. Their beakers were pitchers and cauldrons molded from copper. The appearance of the Beaker people marked the advent of the Bronze Age on the continent. There the beakers tended to be used in tombs, so also in Ireland they are found in the numerous wedge tombs (about 400 total) and stone circles. Sometimes they are also found in settlement remains. The advent of the Early Bronze Age also brought the use of metal to form axe heads, swords, and spearheads.

Like the megalithic monuments, the less-spectacular stone circles found in Ireland are also found in Brittany. It has been long assumed that Stonehenge itself is a product of Ireland, but Brittany may also be the origin of Stonehenge and Irish stone circles. Or, perhaps, influence or immigrations were not necessary. For example the 4,000–year-old stone monument near Salem, New Hampshire (called the American Stonehenge), can hardly be the result of proto-Celts who traveled to America. During the Stone Age many peoples around the world built massive stone monuments.

The Late Bronze Age

Megalithic monuments waned by 1200–700 B.C.E. Irish artisans turned their attention to metalwork. Gold became the favored metal for smiths, who turned out large numbers of torcs, earrings, bracelets, dress fasteners, and gorgets. These objects were not only well designed, but their decorative style and artistic skill is almost unmatched in the ancient world. And again, even before celticization, one can see ornamentation that foreshadows Celtic/Christian art. In any case, the Late Bronze Age ended with the advent of the Hallstatt influence.

The Iron Age

From 700 to 100 B.C.E. the celticization process became evident. Iron weapons such as swords and spearheads appear in Navan or Armagh, the later headquarters for Saint Patrick. While these may have arrived through Hallstatt influence, they generally are not identical with continental metalwork. Apparently native Irish smiths were adapting what they saw.

Some La Tène art work also appears. One of the most obvious comes in stone art such as that on the Turoe stone in County

Galway. The design is a curvilinear type with "trumpet ends" and stylized animal heads. No one knows the purpose of stones like the Turoe stone, but it is generally agreed that the La Tène design matches better with Celtic objects in Britain than with those of the Atlantic Celts.

In a sense the proto-Celtic history does not affect this thesis because it is focused on romanization versus nonromanization. But that is not quite true. How did Christianity develop?

- Where and with whom was the outside connecting link to Ireland made? Scotland to County Antrim? Wales to the central harbors or Iberia to the southwest?

- Were the changes from prehistoric to agricultural to Celtic to Christian primarily exogenous alterations created by invasions or mass movements? Or were the changes due primarily to endogenous alterations and natural developments?[10] Were they simply triggered, perhaps, by the visits of families or the incursion of traders from the Atlantic community?

- Did the first Irish Christians come from Romano-Britain and practice a Roman-style Christianity? Or did they come from Iberia before romanization there had occurred?

There must have been mutual exchange between Ireland, on the one hand, and Scotland or Wales on the other. Neither had a dominant influence. Christianity entered Ireland peacefully without the threat of dreaded romanization.[11] There are archaeological indications of a relationship between Romano-Britain and Ireland, but the Roman influence on these particular British relationships was minimal, or the Roman influence was filtered out by the Irish. Thus, between the Iron Age and early Christianity the Celts experienced a peaceful inculturation from a source that differed from Roman Christianity.[12]

Notes

1. James, *The Atlantic Celts*, 15–25; see also the language chart on p. 40.
2. Caesar, *Gallic War* 2.4, 4.20–30; John King, *Kingdoms of the Celts: A History and a Guide* (London: Blandford, 1998), 86–87.

3. Ibid., 100.

4. Davies, *The Isles*, 7–8.

5. Howard Clark Kee, "From the Jesus Movement Toward Institutional Church," in *Conversion to Christianity: Historical and Anthropological Perspectives on a Great Transformation,* ed. Robert W. Hefner (Berkeley: University of California Press, 1993), 47–63. Gager also assumes conversion occurs when the basic paradigm no longer operates satisfactorily. John Gager, *Kingdom and Community: The Social World of Early Christianity* (Englewood Cliffs, N.J.: Prentice-Hall, 1975).

6. Flanagan, *Ancient Ireland*, 31–34; Harbison, *Pre-Christian Ireland*, 47–52.

7. Flanagan, *Ancient Ireland*, 47.

8. Harbison, *Pre-Christian Ireland*, 52–56.

9. Ibid., 56–85.

10. Harold Mytum, *The Origins of Early Christian Ireland* (London: Routledge, 1992), 15.

11. Barry Raftery, "Ireland: A World Without the Romans," in *The Celtic World,* ed. Green, 651.

12. Vincent Hurley confirms our thesis that Ireland was the first country outside the Roman Empire to be Christianized. See his "The Early Church in the South-West of Ireland: Settlement and Organisation," in *The Early Church in Western Britain and Ireland,* ed. Pearce, 297.

Plate 1. Newgrange Entrance Stone

Plate 2.
Aberlemno Cross Slab,
Aberlemno Churchyard
(Pict)

Plate 3.
Pict Slab (*front*),
Scotland

Plate 4. Interlacing on the Ruthwell Cross, Scotland

Plate 5. Jesus Healing, Vatican Museum

Plate 6. Daniel and Seven Lions, Moone Cross

Plate 7. Adam and Eve, Cain and Abel,
Monasterboice, South Cross, East Side

Plate 8. Reask Stone,
Dingle Peninsula

Plate 9.
High Cross, Monasterboice,
South Cross, East Side

Plate 10. Adam and Eve Cycle, Vatican Museum

Plate 11. Moses Striking the Rock, Monasterboice,
South Cross, East Side

Plate 12. Multiplication of Loaves and Fishes;
Moses Striking the Rock, Vatican Museum

Plate 13. Mary and Manger Scene, Vatican Museum

Plate 14. Arrest of Jesus, Monasterboice,
South Cross, West Side

Plate 15. Crucifixion, Monasterboice, West Cross, West Side (head)

Plate 16. Resurrection, Monasterboice, South Cross, West Side (head)

Chapter 8

Early Christians in Ireland

The proof of early Christianity in Ireland is indeed limited. Even the few pieces of evidence are not undisputed. According to Prosper of Aquitaine, in 431 Pope Celestine sent a certain Palladius to Ireland as a minister to "those of the Irish who believed in Christ." If this account is accepted, there were Christians already worshipping in Ireland that early. Some minor traditions indicate a Christian presence in south Ireland (the Corcu Loegde in Cork, and the Dési in Waterford). Patrick himself said many Christians had been taken captive along with him.[1]

The debate over whether Palladius and Patrick were the same person is an irresolvable problem because it cannot be proved one way or the other.[2] For the sake of providing a history, suppose Patrick was born in England, in a home of some wealth. During an Irish raid he was seized and taken to Ireland.[3] He was raised there, probably in the north, as a slave, until he escaped in a merchant ship headed for Gaul. Eventually he returned to his family, but was called by God to continue on to Ireland as a missioner. He may have arrived in Ireland in 431 (supposedly one year later than Palladius).[4] Patrick may indeed have made some considerable impact on Ireland. In sharp contrast to the struggles and persecutions in the Roman world, the Christian intrusion into Ireland produced little resistance and very likely no more than one or so martyrs. At the same time it is highly likely the rapid conversion to the Jesus movement in the Roman world occurred because of the high number of slaves, freed people, and widows in urban populations. This might well have been the case in Ireland at the time of Patrick. It could be that his primary converts were tradespeople and slaves, some of whom might have been taken from England, or did commerce with the continent, and so were already acquainted with Christianity.[5]

Characteristics of the First Irish Christians

Despite Patrick's prominence, his form of Christianity did not take hold in Ireland. If his goal was to install a Roman structure, he failed. There were no dioceses with bishops and no parishes with priests. About a hundred years after Patrick, a quite different form of Christianity emerged. Just as the earlier Celts were organized around hillforts, so the Christians were organized around monasteries. The feastings of the kings had shifted to ascetic menus and lusty Celtic leaders had become monks. The rejection of Patrick's Roman program led to the development of a monastic life where beliefs and practices differed from those of Roman Christianity.

Immanence of the Other World

The geographical and familial closeness of the king or leader in sparsely populated Ireland probably led to the perception of God as an immanent king rather than a distant or otherworldly ruler. In the Jesus tradition as well as in Irish Christianity the relationship to God shifted from high transcendence in Judaism to terms of familial closeness like *Father* and *Abba*.

Individualistic Spirituality

The monastic movement reflected an individualism that matched the sparseness of Irish population. In terms of piety the "we" of early Christian prayers shifted to "I."[6] While the Jesus tradition did occasionally stress individual responsibility for faith (Mark 1:35–36, 7:24), spirituality was almost always a matter of corporate involvement.

Spirituality Expressed by Pilgrimages

Following the Celtic pattern of migrating, and the insular need for ocean voyage, the early Irish Christians expressed their faith either by travel, or by purposeful sharing of their Celtic faith (peregrination).[7] In the Jesus tradition, both Jesus and the disciples were itinerants. They had homes, but they expressed and expanded their new faith by traveling.

The Goodness of Creation and Humanity

Patrick and/or Palladius may have been sent to Ireland to thwart the spread of Pelagianism. Whether this is true or not, Irish Christianity embraced a theology that threatened the orthodoxy of Rome. Pelagius's belief in the goodness of people who had a free will and who could determine their own destiny was so widespread it took a massive intellectual and political battle by Augustine of Hippo to curtail this so-called heresy. The Roman counterattack on Pelagius failed in Ireland. In both the Jesus tradition and Irish Christianity people are born good. Sin enters in the failure to love the neighbor.

Christian Life Centered in Monasteries

Irish Christianity after Patrick revolves around the primary saints and the monasteries that were founded up through the ninth century. Regardless of the number of Christians before Patrick and regardless of the number he may have converted, the emergent Irish Christianity was elitist in the sense that the monasteries were locations of power and scholarship. The monks, in that sense, assimilated the functions of the Druids, bards, and brehons, while their monasteries replaced the Celtic tradition of hillforts.

Chronological Stages

For purposes of chronological organization, four eras in early Irish Christianity can be defined:

Monastic Movement and Pilgrimages (ca. 400–520)

It may be that Patrick established bishoprics, as for example in the places associated with his name, like Armagh. But the romanizing program did not last. It is possible that he converted masses of the Celtic populace, but monasticism became the primary expression of Irish Christianity. It is not certain how monasticism was injected into the post-Patrick period. As a Christian way of life it was already popular in the fourth century. Athanasius's *Life of Anthony* was first circulated in 361. The impact of that work on Irish Celtic Christians cannot be determined, but Anthony does appear on their stone crosses. In contrast he does not appear on any extant Roman or Gallic art works.

About the same time Saint Martin of Tours began establishing monastic communities on the continent. No known direct contact can be established to pre-Patrick Ireland, but his name is mentioned in legendary lives of saints like Patrick and Ninian. A more likely influence would have been Ninian himself, who presumably founded a monastery at Whithorn, just opposite the northeastern tip of Ireland. Ninian died about 432, so again these are pre-Patrick influences that might have triggered a monastic Christian momentum — a movement Patrick and Palladius were sent to stop.[8]

By the time of people like Saint Brendan, the monastic movement had taken over. Ireland was ruled by abbots, not bishops or kings. About 500, Saint Boite founded Monasterboice in County Louth. Somewhat later Ciaran founded Clonmacnois in County Offaly. Around 520, Finnian must have established Clonard in County Meath. These foundings are not as impressive as they might appear. An early monastic community must have consisted of a few wooden huts set in something like a hillfort. There would have been a larger hut for the abbot and extra huts for food accommodations and storage. These huts must have been constructed like the beehive huts found especially in County Kerry and the later stone huts of Skellig Michael.

In addition to establishing many monastic communities, the monks traveled. There is no reason to ask about the origin of Irish wanderlust. For the insular Celts there was practically no choice. Even Caesar was so impressed by Celtic sailing boats that he copied (and feared) them. Some suggest the Irish Celts sailed as far as America.[9] A reconstruction of some boats would indicate a length of forty feet, perhaps fourteen oars, and a crew of eighteen. While specifics on the traveling monks are lacking, twelve seems to have been the acceptable number per boat.

It is not so easy to say why the monks traveled. Did they simply engage in an ancient insular tradition? Certainly the Christian voyages paralleled the incredible adventures found in more secular literature such as the *Voyage of Bran,* or *Immram Brain.*[10] "Rowing about" [*Immram*] indicates the adventuresome nature of the trips. In the well-known Irish tale, "Immram Curaig Maíle Dúin" (about the eighth century C.E.), the voyagers hoisted the sail and, without a rudder, allowed the wind to take them wherever God wished.

Were the monks engaged in a favorite, almost mandatory, urge to make a pilgrimage? Indeed, the Irish monks became pilgrimage addicts, though to be frank, the first voyagers didn't really go anywhere. The earliest extant account of an Irish Christian voyage, *Navigatio Sancti Brendani,* comes from Saint Brendan, founder of the Clonfert monastery. It describes a fantastic adventure filled with miracles, demonic and divine encounters, transmogrifications, and all the elements of a fictive Celtic voyage.[11]

Later, when the voyages really did become pilgrimages, their possible function as a penance or exile must be given serious consideration. For example, the voyage of Columba that ended in the founding of Iona may well have occurred as a punishment for interfering in family politics.[12] Whatever the reason, such journeys did serve to expand the Celtic faith in Christ (*pro Christo peregrinari*).

The first Celtic Christians were not bumbling monks who believed in impossible miracles and wandered in boats around the island. For some reason (possibly Celtic tradition) such remarkable stories seemed important to the faithful, even though they surely do not actually reflect what happened. By the time of monastic expansion under the leadership of Saint Columba, Irish monasteries were already becoming centers of art and scholarship. About 558, Comgall, an Irish Pict, founded the great Bangor monastery that became an important training center for scholars. In addition to learning, the copying of manuscripts had already started. The first extant example of a copied manuscript comes from 600 C.E., the *Codex Ussherianus Primus,* a pre-Jerome version of the gospels. The presence of this manuscript indicates copying was already occurring in the sixth century. The *Cathach of Saint Columba,* possibly copied by the saint himself about the beginning of the seventh century, shows the beginning of decorative initial letters. It wasn't until the middle of the seventh century that examples of what was to be the genius of Irish calligraphy appeared: artistic initials and the gradually diminishing size of each successive letter, the "diminuendo effect."[13]

This first period is well known for many other saints and monasteries. One of the most famous was Saint Coemgen, or Kevin, who after monastic training sought solitude in the beautiful valley of Glendalough in County Wicklow. Like other saints of this period many stories are told of his miraculous relationship to nature, especially birds and beasts. But far more important was his founding of a most influential monastery. Kevin probably died about 615 at an old age.

There were also women saints. Saint Ita, who died about 570, ran a school in Kileedy. But better known is Saint Brigit who was born about 450, just after the death of Patrick. This mother of Ireland, known to us by several legendary lives, like *The Life of Brigit*, worked primarily in benevolent causes.[14] She replaces, of course, the Celtic goddess Brigid, a connection made apparent with the location of her nunnery at Kildare, the prior location of a Celtic oak tree sanctuary.

Insular Expansion (ca. 563–600)

While Patrick may be celebrated as the patron saint of the Irish, that honor truly belongs to Saint Columba. He was born of royal family on December 5, 521. While, as a descendent of Niall, he might have become the king of Tara, he chose instead the monastic life. Studying under Finnian of Clonard he became associated with other Finnian disciples who were largely responsible for the rapid development of the monastic movement in Ireland. Columba himself was responsible for the founding of Derry, Durrow, and Kells. Columba was not only impressive and brilliant, but apparently somewhat irritable in his earlier years. According to a later *Vita*, at age 42 he came into conflict with Finnian of Moville over a manuscript Columba may have inappropriately copied. Finnian protested to the king Diarmait that "copyright" customs had been violated. The king ruled in favor of Finnian with the words, "As the calf follows the cow, so the copy follows the original." At that point Columba departed on his peregrination.[15] He and twelve companions set sail and on May 12, 563, landed on the island of Hy, later called Iona. Though Iona was either Pict or Scot, it became the point of departure for Irish Christianity to the rest of the islands and eventually to the continent itself.[16]

Columba's accomplishments are numerous. He formed friendships and agreements with rulers in the insular world, resulting in the formation of monasteries and, so to speak, the Christianizing of peoples outside Ireland. This was particularly true of northern Britain, such as the Picts and Scots. Columba was willing, even eager, to utilize the Celtic heritage of Ireland. The intense scholarly interest of the monks almost surely went back to the intellectual training of the Druids. In 575, at a national convention of Christians in Ireland, Columba helped defeat a proposal to suppress the Celtic bards. Just as the Celtic Druids shifted over to Christian scholarship, so the Celtic bards engendered the Irish love of and skill for composing music and poetry (even to this day). Adomnán's *Life of Columba* states that the great saint died on June 9, 597.[17]

At the behest of King Oswald of Northumbria, already a notable Christian, the Iona monks sent Saint Aidan to the king's domain. Aidan choose the semi-island Lindisfarne as his headquarters. He was joined there by many Picts and Scots in what was essentially an Irish/Celtic enterprise. Meanwhile, from the south (Canterbury), there was another attempt to Christianize Anglo-Saxon Britain. Augustine and forty Benedictine monks represented, of course, Roman Christianity. Clashes with the northern Irish groups were inevitable. The primary issues were organization (monk versus bishop), calendar (the date of Easter), and the mark of a monk (type of tonsure). The struggle between the Celtic types and the Roman types continued until early in the eighth century. Even then, whether the Irish actually conformed to the Romans is dubious.

Certain Irish characteristics were too deep to be dislodged. Chief among them was Irish calligraphy and manuscript illumination. The *Cathach* copied by Saint Columba has already been mentioned. Despite the destruction of manuscripts by invaders such as the Vikings, key works exist — like the *Book of Durrow* from Ireland — where the anticlassical style has been established (late seventh century). Even more clear would be the Hiberno-Saxon style as seen in the marvelous *Book of Lindisfarne*.[18]

At times, to the dismay of those who wanted to study only scriptures, the Irish monks also copied classical literature. Early in the development of the monastic movement such authors as Virgil, Horace, and Juvenal were known. Eventually the use and copying of classical literature became a key element in the revitalization of continental culture.

While finally the Celtic Christians bowed to the practices of the Roman church, the British and the Irish did not share the same attitude toward political authorities. The struggle in Northumbria ended with a British Christianity that considered the king the ultimate authority. The Irish left Lindisfarne, sometimes friendly to political authorities, but finally obedient to the abbot.

Continental Expansion (597–800)

Sometime about 590, another Columba, named Columban (born about 540 somewhere in Leinster), changed the course of history as radically as did Columba. Following the sack of Rome by Alaric in 410, the Western empire disintegrated. It was into this world, prior to the formation of the Holy Roman Empire, that the Irish *peregrini* poured into the Western continent. About 590, Columban asked for and received permission to make a peregrination to the continent. He and twelve others set off for an unknown destination. Irish pilgrimages at this time were religious journeys in their own right. It was not necessary to arrive at a holy place; the journey itself was holy. This point cannot be overly emphasized. The Irish had a *consuetudo peregrinandi* (custom of making pilgrimages).[19] In the ninth century three Irish monks said they were wishing, for the love of God, to be in foreign lands, they cared not where.

Columban and his crew came to Frankish Gaul and found it in dangerous disarray. Eventually Columban made friends with a king in Burgundy where he was allowed to start a monastery. After many misadventures and conflicts, the pilgrimage of Columban resulted in monasteries such as Luxeuil, Saint Gall, Bobbio, and Lure, to mention a few. The result can hardly be overestimated. Columban brought "back" into the continent the scholarship and manuscripts that had been lost after the demise of the Roman Empire. Without the Irish resources our Western civilization would have been considerably impoverished, if not defunct.[20]

On the other hand, while not necessarily heretical, the Irish monks were neither subordinate to temporal power nor polite to papal/Roman authority. The Columban discipline was strict, even severe. He did not hesitate to chide Pope Boniface for allowing laxity among his leaders. And, he argued, the Irish were the true disciples of Peter and Paul. Despite the great contribution of the Irish monks and a generally favorable reception by royalty and political leaders, they were hardly universally accepted.[21] The Roman ecclesiastical leaders complained about the uncouth lifestyle of the monks, the competitive preference of the people for the Irish monks, and the general insolence of the Irish saints in regard to Roman papal authority.

The Retreat to Ireland (800–1000)

As the pilgrims were gradually replaced by scholars, the contribution of Irish Christians increased. Not only did many young European scholars travel to Irish centers of learning like Iona, but Irish scholars created centers of learning on the Continent where monasteries may have been established. At first the Irish scholars were well received. Charlemagne created an Irish-style circle of scholarship in his Aachen court. It was said of Charlemagne that *amabat peregrinos* [he loved the pilgrim]. Irish scholars brought back to the Continent illuminated manuscripts of the Gospels, and the influence of the Hiberno-Saxon style can be seen in continental manuscripts like the Trier Gospels or the Stockholm Gospels. They also brought a Christian scholarship that differed from the Roman. To name a few, Sedulius Scottus of Liège, following the poetic heritage of the Irish bards, wrote unique theological poetry in Latin. The Irish scholar John Scottus Eriugena (about 810–77) was asked to write a refutation of the super Augustinian Gottschalk.[22] In his *On Divine Predestination,* he denied the predestination of evil people, and at the same time he almost denied the real existence of evil. He translated from the Greek the work called *Pseudo-Dionysius,* a work basically Neoplatonic with a mystical bent.[23] Like Pelagius he stressed the goodness of creation (*On the Division of Nature,* ca. 867).

The Irish peregrination did not last. The continental Benedictine monastic style won the day. Papal authorities squelched the invasion of the Irish. The manuscripts were eventually destroyed or transported to safe libraries. The Irish returned home where, instead of peregrinations, they produced incomparable works of art: stone crosses and even more elaborate illuminated manuscripts. The Irish Christians traveled, but they did not conquer. They inspired, but did not use persuasion. They were disciplined but not administrators. They produced more poetry and stories than scholastic theology.[24] In the end Rome did win the West, but it could not and did not destroy the early Christianity of Ireland.

Notes

1. Máire de Paor and Liam de Paor, *Early Christian Ireland* (London: Thames and Hudson, 1958), 29; Brendan Lehane, *Early Celtic Christianity* (London: Constable, 1994); Mark Redknap, "Early Christianity and Its Monuments," in *The Celtic World,* ed. Green, 738.

2. McNeill, *The Celtic Churches,* 30–31, 50–67. The debate began in 1942 with the analysis of T. F. O'Rahilly, *The Two Patricks* (1942; Dublin: DIAS, 1957). Also E. A. Thompson, *Who Was St. Patrick?* (New York: St. Martin's Press, 1985).

3. Thomas Charles-Edwards, *Christianity in Roman Britain* (London: Batsford, 1981), 307; R. P. C. Hanson, *The Life and Writings of the Historical Patrick* (New York: Seabury Press, 1983), 19.

4. Seán Mac Airt and Gearóid Mac Niocaill, eds., *The Annals of Ulster (to A.D. 1131),* part 1 (Dublin: Institute for Advanced Studies, 1983), 39.

5. Rodney Stark, *The Rise of Christianity* (San Francisco: HarperSanFrancisco, 1997), 161; Ludwig Bieler, *The Works of St. Patrick* (London: Longmans, Green & Co., 1953), 9. D. Dumville, "Some British Aspects of the Earliest Irish Christianity," in *Ireland and Europe,* ed. Ní Chatháin and M. Richter (Stuttgart: Klett-Cotta, 1984), 16–24.

6. Diarmuid O'Laoghaire, "Irish Spirituality," in *Ireland and Europe,* ed. Chatháin and Richter, 73–82.

7. Peter Harbison, *Pilgrimage in Ireland: The Monuments and the People* (Syracuse, N.Y.: Syracuse University Press, 1991), 29–32.

8. John B. Bury, *The Life of St. Patrick and His Place in History* (1905; Mineola, N.Y.: Dover Publications, 1998), 38, 313; John A. Duke, *The Columban Church* (Oxford: Oxford University Press, 1932), 24–26; *Lives of the Saints*, trans. and with an introduction by J. F. Webb (Baltimore: Penguin, 1965).

9. For example, the origin of the mysterious 4,000–year-old Stonehenge near Salem, New Hampshire.

10. Séamus Mac Mathúna, *Immram Brain: Bran's Journey to the Land of the Women* (Tübingen: M. Niemeyer, 1985).

11. Oliver Davies, ed. and trans., *Celtic Spirituality* (Mahwah, N.J.: Paulist Press, 1999), 155–90.

12. McNeill, *The Celtic Churches,* 89; Duke, *The Columban Church,* 61–63.

13. Carl Nordenfalk, *Celtic and Anglo-Saxon Painting: Book Illumination in the British Isles, 600–800* (1977; New York: George Braziller, 1995), 11–13.

14. Davies, ed. and trans., *Celtic Spirituality* 122–39 (Cogitosus version), 140–54 (Irish version).

15. See Duke, *The Columban Church,* 61–63, and Francis J. Byrne, "The Ireland of St. Columba," *Historical Studies* 5 (1965): 37.

16. Already Iona was the burial ground for the kings of Dalraida (Pictish northern Ireland).

17. See Adomnán of Iona, *Life of St. Columba,* trans. Richard Sharpe (London: Penguin, 1995).

18. Nordenfalk, *Celtic and Anglo-Saxon Painting,* 17.

19. Jonas, *Life of St. Columban,* ed. Dana Carleton Munro (Felinfach: Llanerch, 1993); Walahfrid Strabo, *The Life of St. Gall,* ed. Maud Joynt (London: SPCK, 1927), sec. 2, 64–65.

20. The assertion of Cahill, *How the Irish Saved Civilization.*

21. William Shaw Kerr, *The Independence of the Celtic Church in Ireland* (London: SPCK, 1931), 44–48; Liam de Paor, "The Aggrandisement of Armagh," *Historical Studies* 8 (1971): 98.

22. Heinrich Zimmer, *Pelagius in Irland* (Berlin: Weidmann, 1901), 4–5.

23. Paul Rorem, *Pseudo-Dionysius: A Commentary on the Texts and an Introduction to Their Influence* (New York: Oxford University Press, 1993), 30.

24. Early Irish Christians expressed their faith and their history more in poetry than in propositional truths. So Byrne, "Ireland of St. Columba," 38.

Chapter 9

Early Christian Art and Architecture

Ornamentation

Celtic Christian art pieces were ornately decorated. Perhaps no other culture, except perhaps Islam, has so extensively utilized ornamentation as the basis for its art. In Irish Christian book illumination four basic types of ornamentation are used: spiral, interlacing, animal fantasy figures, and human fantasy figures. Often within a page the ornamentation was contained in fillets and circles called *bosses*. Bosses likely originated in Celtic military art and have many parallels in Irish stone crosses.

The spiral was the basic ornamentation, found early in the western island. Excellent fourth-millennium examples have come from the Boyne Valley, especially Newgrange (plate 1). Already in Newgrange the spirals connected in such a way that the tail of one created the head of the next.[1]

Early in Irish Christian book illumination the spiral gave rise to interlacing — a style that intertwined four strands in a complex curvilinear fashion, though rectilinear could also occur.[2] Spirals and interlacing appeared in fillets or ribbons, circles or bosses, and rectangles. The artists then added zoological representations to the ends of the spirals or interfacing. While snakes and dragons were most common, eventually birds and other animals were added. The effect was mystifying and even exhilarating. Eventually human bodies were added, often with feet at one end of the spiral and the head at the other.[3]

Illuminated manuscripts may be the most available media for observing Celtic Christian ornamentation, but it is not the only one.

The Bronze Age Celts had developed metalwork to a high artistic level. The ornamentation found on post-Patrick metal shows the same style as found on the manuscripts and in earlier Celtic art. Stone crosses show the same ornamentation as on the metalwork. The Pictish cross, the Aberlemno cross (plate 2), shows spirals ending in animals to the left and right of the cross, interlacing on each cross piece, and bosses at each juncture. One of the most marvelous stone pieces from medieval Europe, the Ruthwell cross, shows Irish interlacing raised to the highest level (plate 4).

Irish ornamentation stands in sharp contrast to early Roman-style Christian art. For the Romans, fresco art (catacomb art) was done quickly with a minimum of detail. Ornamentation would have consumed more time than was available. On sarcophagi, where ornamentation would have been quite possible, the pictures run together without any decorative ribbons or margins. Pictorial representations overlap each other and extend right to the edge of the sarcophagus.

By the middle of the fourth century, some Roman Christians provided dividers for the pictures. There were columns (see, for example, plate 5), like the sarcophagus of Junio Bassus or Lateran no. 171 (Vatican Museum). Trees were used on others, like the Miracles sarcophagus in Arles or Lateran no. 164 (Vatican Museum). On the elaborate sarcophagus of Junio Bassus, the artist used pediments to connect the columns at the upper level and architraves to connect the columns on the lower level. On and above the pediments are architectural designs and above the architraves are animals. Nevertheless, ornamentation in early Roman Christian art is found so seldom, it must be concluded that ornamentation was not critically important.

In contrast to the Irish manuscripts of the New Testament, the great codices of the Continent, such as Sinaiticus and Vaticanus, have no illumination. Since these uncials are splendid copies done by very skilled calligraphers, it must be assumed that there simply was no history of or interest in manuscript ornamentation. In fact, Jerome warned against illumination because it might interfere with the exact copying of the text (*Ep.* 22:32, 107:12).

Symbols signified a crucial aspect of the Roman Christian faith, especially in a contextual sense. For example, the fish or the anchor would signify faith existence in an alien culture. Later these symbols were used in pictures derived in part from biblical material. Like the symbols, the pictures were designed to encourage the viewer to face certain social difficulties. For example, the Orante symbol would be found in situations like Daniel and the Lions' Den, where it signified the delivering power of God.

The Irish Christians received less social encouragement from symbols and pictures. Ornamentation was a religious experience in its own right. The one who designed and executed the spiral or interlacing experienced God in a poetic or musical way. The person who saw the intricate designs followed the lines to a spiritual experience analogous to what the artist intended.

Animals

Celtic animal forms were nearly always of a fantasy nature. They often complete a spiral or interlacing pattern. This is true both on stones and in illuminated manuscripts. Animals can also appear as ornamentation in spaces that might otherwise not have been sufficient for pictures or other ornamentation. These decorative animals are not symbolic but reflect the world of the artists. Nearly every kind of household and farm animal (cats, dogs, cows, mice, deer, ducks, geese, and so on) can be found.[4] In addition to everyday animals used as decorations, there are independent animals that may be characterized as fantastic, grotesque, or totally imaginary. There is no acceptable consensus about the source for these latter animals. For the most part they had to come from the creative imagination of the artist. Many of the animals drawn did not exist at all or did not exist in Irish territory, so one has to assume they took form in the mind of the artist without any immediate model. However, even if the animals were known in Irish territory, the artist may not have made them recognizable (e.g., the fantasy animals decorating a stone at the Miegle Museum).

In the Celtic world the boundary between human and animal was not firm.[5] In Celtic literature transmogrification was frequent, and in pre-Christian art human-type gods and goddesses usually had some animal characteristics. Like the spiral and the interlacing, the fantasy animals must have expressed a religious perception that allowed entrance into the divine world. Because of the high quality of Celtic art, it can be assumed that most artists could have produced a clear representation of a model animal rather than a fantasy. Some examples of animal representations seem more clumsy than even fantasy required (e.g., animals on stones at the Miegle Museum). These expressed more psychic sensations like fear or violence.

Humans were seldom portrayed as they really would have appeared. The same is true of most animals. The portrayals were signifiers. There were not intended to make the observer reflect on the animal itself. There was a quality in the animal itself or in the artistic representation of the animal that gave the observer a message. So the lions attacking Daniel represent a ferocity that the hero could withstand (plate 6). The crude bears in Miegle strike fear in the observer. It is not the intention of the artisan to portray accurately the animal in question. After all the observer may never have seen such an animal. There is a striking contradiction to this observation, which at the same time serves as its confirmation. Of the 347 pictures found on 111 Irish crosses (see below), twenty-nine involve horses. The horses are clearly and precisely portrayed.[6] These horses indicate that stone sculptors could indeed portray figures as they appeared and the Celts knew horses very well. It is not reasonable to think that only horses could be portrayed naturally while almost everything else had to appear as fantasy. Yet how can some conclusion like that be avoided? Are these scenes of warriors and huntsmen not pictures of real life in Celtic Ireland, while nearly every other animal found on the crosses and slabs reflects a symbolic or psychic world?

Lion

Other than horses the most common animal in Irish Christian art was the lion, a beast it may be assumed was never seen by most Irish. It occurs in the picture of Daniel in the Lions' Den (12 out of 347 pictures) and David and the Lion (9 out of 347 pictures). Daniel in the Lions' Den was also a frequent picture in early Roman

Christian art, although with quite a different iconography. There are no examples of David and the Lion in Roman Christian art.

The Irish lions are not symbolic of state persecutions, as with the Roman Christians, but, like the bears, are fierce animals in conflict with the two biblical heroes who resist psychic fear.

Sheep

There are no horses in early Roman Christian art to compare to the hunting and warrior scenes of Irish Christian art. On the other hand, there are no sheep in early Irish art (a notable exception would be Christ in Glory). Generally sheep are accessories for the figure of the Good Shepherd, but unbelievable though it may seem, in Irish art Good Shepherds with sheep are nearly nonexistent. The Shepherd with Sheep and the praying Orante are the two most popular human symbols in early Roman Christianity and yet they do not exist in Ireland.[7]

Many observers would like to associate the sheep of early art with the Bible, in the Jesus stories or parables about shepherds caring for sheep. That is not likely the case. Very seldom do early Christian symbols actually illustrate the Bible. The Orante and the Shepherd, as symbols, first arose as the Jesus tradition entered the Roman culture (by at least 180 C.E.). When, after the emperor Constantine (313 C.E.), the Good Shepherd was identified with Jesus, then sheep could be used to signify the disciples, as seen in the New Testament.

Given the ubiquitous nature of sheep and shepherds in Roman Christian art, it is incredible to discover only one shepherd with sheep in Irish Christian art, at Armagh (a shepherd with wolves occurs on the Market Cross in Kells). Sheep, shepherds, and orantes are found frequently on fourth- and fifth-century Gallic sarcophagi (e.g., Arles). The Jesus tradition must have crossed over to Ireland before these symbols became popular on the Continent. Their absence is a significant indication of nonromanization.

At the same time, there is another possibility to consider. The Celts of Ireland did have sheep, so they were aware of their propensity to gather around the leader (shepherd). If the idea of endogenous development of language and symbols is credible, then the early Irish Christians could have used sheep even though they were unaware of Roman symbolism. They did not. In early Irish Christianity symbols of Christian collectivity are nearly missing. Such communal signs as the Agape meal, as well as the gathered sheep, are rare. With some whimsy, perhaps, it might be said the early Irish symbolized their sense of the Christian life with individualized hunting scenes (peregrination), while the Roman Christians symbolized their life together with a shepherd among his devoted sheep.

Fish

Fish are very important in early Roman Christian art. If the Multiplication of the Loaves and Fishes are counted together with the early Christian meals, there are about fifty pictures that contain the fish as a food. Along with the boat and the anchor, the fish is an aquatic symbol of Christian existence in an alienating environment, as well as a symbol of the Christian meal.[8] One early church father even took the Greek name of fish, *ixthus,* as an acrostic that meant Jesus Christ Son of God Savior. In Irish art there are six pictures I have classified as Loaves and Fishes (6 out of 347), but five are pictures of the Multiplication where the fish are nearly insignificant. The only clear use of fish is found on the Moone Abbey cross, where there are two fish and five circles. Two things can be assumed: (1) as with the sheep, a collective symbol such as the Agape meal of bread and fish was not that critical in Irish Christian life; (2) the fish as a symbol of life in an alien environment was totally unnecessary, since the Celtic culture of Ireland had not been inimical to the emerging Jesus tradition.

The same is true of the sea monster. The sea monster, a constant threat found in Greek and Jewish literature and art, occurs frequently in early Roman Christian art. Jonah is shown cast from the boat and swallowed by the sea monster. In both of these pictures. Jonah is depicted as an Orante, a victorious person. Along with the meal, the Jonah story occurs more often than any other biblical portrayal. It was a popular symbol of deliverance from the grasp of an alien social environment and a hostile Roman state. In Irish art there are two instances (2 out of 347) of Jonah cast from the boat, and there is only one instance of a supposed sea monster. Of course, there was no need to signify an environment hostile to Christianity.

Birds

Regarding birds, the raven is found in the picture of Paul and Anthony (12 out of 347). Stories of the first monastics featured birds feeding the monks.[9] In pre-Christian Celtic iconography the raven was the transmogrification of a warrior goddesses, but also could signify the presence of otherworldly divine beings. Presumably this signification was transferred to Paul and Anthony.[10] On the other hand, the only bird found in early Roman Christian art is the dove. It occurs frequently as a separate symbol that can best be identified as Peace. It also appears as the divine presence at the baptism of Jesus or even the saving presence with the Three Young Men in the Fiery Furnace.

Serpents

Most important for any study of early Irish art is the serpent in the pictures of Adam and Eve (27 out of 347), since the picture of Adam and Eve is the most frequent piece of sculptured art. In some a serpent is curled around a tree, while in others it is not present at all (plate 7). The serpent has many meanings: rebirth (because of the peeling of the skin); fertility (because of the phallic symbolism); temptation (because of its subtle appearance and mobility). To be sure the serpent in the Genesis 3 story was subtle and seductive, but there is no particular reason to suppose that is true for the serpent in early Roman Christian art. The picture of Adam and Eve stood alongside pictures of threat and deliverance such as Noah in the Ark, the Sacrifice of Isaac, Daniel in the Lions' Den, the Three Young Men in the Fiery Furnace, and Susanna and the Elders. The serpent in the Adam and Eve pictures may indeed be a threat, but what is the threat and from what are the couple delivered? That problem will be discussed later.

In Irish art Adam and Eve often stand in succession with the Sacrifice of Isaac (17 out of 347) and perhaps Cain and Abel or Daniel in the Lions' Den (plates 7 and 6). Although it is possible, it would take considerable esoteric theological sophistication to see in the figure of Isaac the kind of sacrifice needed to overcome the sin of Adam and Eve. More reasonable would be the argument that God's first creatures faced times of testing and conflict like Cain and Abel, Abraham and Isaac. As will be discussed later, the crossless crucifixes at the top of the stone cross may well imply withstanding the same testing of faith. In this case, the Irish Adam and Eve, and the serpent, when present, do not refer to an Augustinian-type fall, but to a birth/fertility event that could result, after birth, in many tests of faith. These life-long tests, or conflicts, were not unlike the annual rebirth of the serpent as it naturally lost its skin. As the early Roman Christian serpent had nonbiblical precedents, so did the fertility serpent in Irish Christian art. For example, the snake can be found as a fertility symbol attached to the Celtic goddess Sirona. Throughout Celtic imagery the serpent references fertility or healing. The ram-horned serpent, not found in Irish Celtic art, certainly symbolizes fertility, regeneration, and healing. The Irish Christian serpent (plate 3), also often seen in illuminated manuscripts, kept that same meaning of birth (phallic) and rebirth (shedding of skin).[11]

Geometric Symbols

Irish Christian art adapted the Celtic ornamentation, especially the spiral and interlacing. At least two other graphic symbols need to be noted.

Swastika

Though not frequent, the interlacing pattern can shift to a swastika. The swastika was associated with the Celtic sky/sun god and the notion of fertility. It moved in a circle not unlike the spoked wheel that also symbolized the sun. The circle of the Irish cross derived from the Celtic spoked wheel and the swastika shares the same origin. It does occur occasionally in the context of the circular cross.

The Celtic Circle

As a Celtic symbol the swastika was closely associated with the spoked wheel.[12] The spoked wheel was used in jewelry, metalwork, clothing, and military equipment. Like the sky chariot of Roman art, it has no extended meaning other than the movement of the sun. The movement of the wheel might reference regeneration, but normally that is a function of the sun. In Celtic art the spokes could be horizontal or diagonal. Of the fifty-two so-called crucifixions in Irish Christian sculptured art, all spokes are diagonal. If Jesus does appear with horizontally outstretched arms, they will be sculpted along the lines of the horizontal spokes of the wheel. If the hands of Jesus are actually attached to the spokes as in a crucifix, it is indeed difficult for the modern observer to discern.

The circle is the primary geometric figure in Celtic and Irish symbolism. Builtforms were almost always circular. Starting with Newgrange and the Boyne Valley tombs on to hillforts, public buildings, homes, crannogs, to beehives and monasteries, the circle is assumed. Squares and rectangles are seldom seen, though early places for church meetings might be rectangular (e.g., St. Kevin's or the Gallerus oratory). Basically speaking, these geometric forms are very informative. The Celtic circular builtforms stress the potential unity of human and divine. In the Celtic architecture that unity almost surely involved the rotation of the sun, though the domes or circles of any culture signify the upward yearning for the heavenly. Squares, such as the first locations of Roman Christian house churches, stress the relational nature of the human community. Longitudinal builtforms, on the other hand, stress the movement of the community toward life goals and the divine presence. So stated, the circle deeply reflects the spirituality of Irish Christianity, just as the longitudinal basilica reflects the Roman Christian expectation of the eschatological consummation of the divine presence among us.

Besides the swastika, spoked wheel, and circular builtforms, there are other circles, some of which appear puzzling to those immersed in early Christian Roman art. In Roman early church portrayals of the meal, whether eucharistic or the Agape, there were always loaves of bread present. There were also baskets of bread in portrayals of the Multiplication of the Loaves and Fishes. In early Roman Christian art these breads were depicted by circles. Sometimes the circles existed independently, as in the narthex of S. Maria in Trastevere, Rome, but normally they occurred with the meal. Agape meals with the circular bread are the most frequent portrayal in early Roman Christian art.[13] But there are no such meals in Irish Christian art. How could the most important element of the Jesus tradition, the Agape meal, not appear in the art? The answer can most likely be found in the frequent pictures of the Temptation of Anthony or the Raven Feeding Paul and Anthony. The epitome of Irish monastic life was to fast and depend on divine intervention for food. The epitome of Roman Christian life was the formation of community through eating the bread, fish, and wine offered by the followers of Jesus.

There is, of course, the possibility that even those circles with the fish are not bread. Bread was not a staple in a land where dairy products and fruits seemed more abundant. In manuscript art circles are to be found everywhere. Should they be thought of as eucharistic bread? Presumably not.[14] Actually there are remarkably few descriptions of the Eucharist in early Irish Christian literature or art.[15] Among a people who drank beer and mead, what function would the wine have had? Again, in contrast to the Roman Christian art, there is no cup of wine in the 347 pictures that are catalogued. In addition to the nature of the eucharistic food, eucharistic theology needs to be considered. In a Christianity that stresses the goodness of creation (Adam and Eve, Pelagius), is there need for a sacrificial meal (flesh [bread] and blood [wine])? Once again the romanization of the New Testament may have escaped the Irish. What better way to celebrate the goodness of creation than with bread and mead?

There are thousands of circles in the illuminated manuscripts. There are circles on the stone crosses and slabs. The circles on the crosses are bosses, that is, raised circles (embossed). Such bosses derived from the raised circles found on Celtic shields. Since they served no military function, they probably signified the power of the sun. These bosses entered two-dimensional Irish art as circles, often connected, of course, with spirals and interlacing. But they entered three-dimensional art (crosses and slabs) as raised circles. The early Irish Christians saw the ubiquitous circle at the top of their crosses. Those circles signified the rotating sun (spoked wheel) as seen in the Celtic circular shields with their raised bosses. The circles were used by the Celts to call upon that divine protection offered by the sun god(dess). In the center of these solar circles can sometimes be found David and his harp (e.g., Casteldermot, South Cross and North Cross; Durrow Abbey; Ullard), that is, music for the solar dance, or more often, of course, Jesus with arms outstretched over the horizontal spokes.

This is a serious crossroads. In Roman Christian life the early Christians (including their artists) attacked and even assimilated the sun god. In Mausoleum M under the Vatican they showed Jesus in Apollo's chariot crossing the sky. An even more blatant attack can be seen on the doors of S. Sabina where Elijah mounts the chariot of the sun. Christian artists depicted the wise men who bowed before Jesus as magi dressed in Mithraic costumes. The Roman solar calendar was assimilated by Christians to suit their festivals.

But in Ireland it was not so. Worship of the sun and the new Jesus tradition coalesced. Druids and Celtic bards moved into church positions. Symbols of Celtic sun worship (spirals and interlacing) became the basic ornamentation for cross and manuscript illumination. So it makes sense that the Celtic cross had a circle at the top. Jesus was not hung on that cross. Jesus was adored on that cross. Much like the crucifixion in the Gospel of John, Jesus the incarnate was lifted to the highest point so that all the world could see the *doxa* (glory) of God. There is no suffering Jesus on the cross.[16] Rather Jesus has overcome the conflicts. With him we can, too. The doxa and the sun are identical.

Pictish Circles

A word should be said about Pictish circles (plate 3). A *Z* with two circles and a *V* with two crescents (never otherwise) are among the most frequent symbols found on Christian Pictish stones. As far as circles are concerned, an object that looks like a mirror also can occur. There are no known, extant non-Christian antecedents for these symbols. For reasons that can no longer be fathomed, early Pict Christians attached the sun symbol to a *Z* and the moon symbol to the *V*. It could be that the two symbols are calendric: the sun rises and sets and remains the same from day to day. The moon waxes and wanes from day to day and is not the same every night. These symbols could then reference solar and lunar calendars. Since Northumbria was the center of the calendric argument over the paschal celebration, it would be reasonable to suppose the people of the northern isle might still have struggled with the issue of a constant sun and a changing moon.

Human Forms

The Roman artist approximated an accurate, though often idealistic, portrayal of the human body. The shape and stance of the form was altered, of course, to symbolize desired characteristics. Statesmen were tall and formal. Athletes were muscular and eager. Gods, goddesses, and mythological figures carried the mark of their authority: Neptune with a trident; Cupid with a bow and arrow. To what extent art actually reproduced personal traits is unknown. The first Christians continued that classical sense of bodiness. Due to the time limitations for painting fresco art and after 1,800 years of deterioration, catacomb art may seem rough-hewn. While early Christian sculpted art might appear somewhat crude in comparison to classical sculpture, the observation still holds true: the human form approximated reality. And, as in classical art, the heroes of the faith could be identified by set iconographic characteristics (even over a fairly broad geographical area). For example. Jesus is young with curly hair. Paul is older, short and bald.

The situation in Irish Christian art is startling different. By their metalwork and illuminated manuscripts it is clear that Irish artists were highly skilled. And some sculpture artists could approximate exciting reality such as prancing or running horses. However, they almost never sculpted the human body in a realistic way. It has even been suggested the Irish artisans loved to create horses but merely copied the Roman Christian scenes.[17] That seems highly unlikely, but there is indeed a striking difference between the horses and the hunting scenes, on the one hand, and the people on the other.

Irish Christian people cannot go unnoticed. Strictly speaking they tend to have a triangular (a chevron) or circular head, no neck, and a square body with feet pointed in opposite directions (*contraposto*). Of course, there is no such human body. This unrealistic presentation cannot be explained as artistic ineptitude or carelessness. In fact, some of the humans drawn in carefully illuminated manuscripts follow the same style. The body form is an attempt to reproduce Celtic characteristics. The same characteristics can be seen on the plaque found at Aghaboe, Leix, or the three *genii cucullati* (hooded spirits) from Hadrian's Wall, a carving from Margidunum or a carving from Thorpe.[18] Celtic and Celtic Christian human figures were quite simple because accoutrements took away from the essence of the person. Furthermore, the head was the most important part of the body. The artists emphasized that tradition by setting large heads, without necks, on nondescript squares. Variations could be made with the head in order to establish identity; for example, the heads might have the characteristic Celtic moustache or coiffure.

There were only two human symbols in early Christian Roman art: the Good Shepherd and the Orante. The Good Shepherd, taken from Hittite art and frequently used in the Roman world, was invariably portrayed realistically. He was tall, carried a sheep or ram on his shoulder, was dressed in shepherd's clothing, and might have a shepherd's staff. There was absolutely no question about his identity.

The female Orante was somewhat different. Though she was realistically portrayed as a woman with raised hands, she existed only as a human symbol. She appeared on Roman coins with the rubric PIETAS. In Christian art she often appeared in funerary inscriptions with the rubric PAX. Otherwise the Orante was the major figure in pictorial representations that centered on deliverance: Noah and the Ark, Daniel in the Lions' Den, the Three Young Men, the Jonah cycle, and Susanna and the Elders. Rarely she appeared as Isaac.[19]

The Irish artist allowed the context to carry the meaning without identifying the human body involved. The Roman artists set an identity for the body and used that identity to create contexts.

Early Irish Christian Sculptured Art

In order to compare early Irish Christian art with early Roman Christian art, it will be necessary to index and describe both. I have produced in *Ante Pacem* an index of early Roman Christian art before Constantine.[20] While there are excellent books on post-Constantinian art, an actual index does not exist. As for the Irish art, I have taken the list of 115 crosses and slabs and count 347 biblical scenes (see table 9.1 on the following page). The number of times a particular scene occurs will be indicated. I found this method very imprecise. I have not personally seen many of the scenes listed and, unfortunately, other historians and photographers often differ as to the identity of what they have seen. This issue is exacerbated by the fact that human figures are simple and often indistinguishable from one another. And sometimes, as in early Roman Christian art, I suspect the theological bias of the viewer determined the identity of what was seen. There is not much that can be done about the imprecision. Nevertheless, this list does approximate Irish Christian art sufficiently enough to make a comparison with the Roman Christian list found in *Ante Pacem*.[21]

While this count takes into consideration all the known crosses in Ireland, the artistic examples mentioned in this text are taken primarily from crosses at Kells, Clonmacnois, Monasterboice, and Moone Abbey.[22]

The Origin of Circular Crosses

The circle was the central form in Celtic art, ornamentation, and architecture. The distinguishing mark of an Irish cross is, of course, the circle at the top. The circle derives from Celtic representations of the sun, such as the spoked wheel. But how did the circle become such a unique, essential element of the Irish cross? It can only be assumed that the cross resulted from an encounter between the worship of the

Table 9.1. Index of Art on Irish Crosses

ART	NUMBER OF APPEARANCES
Adam and Eve	27
Arrest of Jesus	5
Baptism of Jesus	8
Betrayal of Jesus	5
Cain and Abel	6
Celtic Images	14
Crucifixion	52
Christ in Glory	2
Daniel in the Lions' Den	12
David and Goliath	3
David with Harp	7
David and the Lion	9
David and Saul	1
Denial of Peter	1
Evangelists	3
Fantasy Animals	19
Feeding of 5,000	3
Flight into Egypt	2
Hand of God	2
Historic Irish Figures and Events	19
Hunting [Horsemen]	21
Jacob and Angel	8
Jonah and Sea Monster	2
Journey to Emmaus	2
Judgment of Solomon	2
Loaves and Fishes	6
Last Judgment	6
Massacre of the Innocents	4
Mocking of Jesus	1
Moses Striking Rock	3
Moses with Arms Held Up [Aaron and Hur]	4
Nativity	2
Noah's Ark	4
Paul and Anthony [Raven]	12
Pilate Washing Hands	4
Presentation at the Temple	1
Return of Prodigal	1
Sacrifice of Isaac	17
Shepherds	2
Soldiers Guarding Tomb	4
Temptation of Jesus	1
Temptation of Saint Anthony	8
Three Young Men in the Fiery Furnace	7
Twelve Apostles	4
Warriors	8
Wedding at Cana	2
Wise Men	12

sun and the Christian kerygma. In contrast to Roman Christianity, where the sun worship was assimilated by Christianity, in the Irish world an amalgamation was formed. The sun circle and the so-called crucifix became one symbol. There are very few crucifixion scenes without the circle (the Athlone plaque or the Durham Gospel Fragment II, fol. 38v).[23] There are many crosses without crucifixions, both internal circles (e.g., the Reask stone, plate 8) and external circles (e.g., Ahenny, south cross). In other words, while the crucifixion almost never stood alone as a symbol of Irish Christianity, the crossless circle rather often could be found on Christian slabs or crosses. A Christian cross could exist without Jesus, but not without the sun.

Because the slab without the crucifixion and without the external circle would seem to be the type from which evolution of the high crosses began, some suspect the original came from Whithorn in Scotland. Some slabs there do appear to be early because of the less elaborate carving. On the other hand, slabs like the Reask stone might be equivalent (plate 8). In any case it would seem there was an evolution from slabs with internal circles and no crucifix, to slabs with an internal circle and crucifix, to crosses with an external circle and no crucifix, to, finally, high crosses with circle and crucifix (plate 9).

Comparative Chronology

In early Roman Christianity symbols and some artistic material began to appear about 180 C.E. Many historians would place the Capella greca in the catacomb of Priscilla (Rome) at about that time. Other catacombs may or may not contain earlier inscriptions and symbols. Some inscriptions in Phrygia would surely precede this date, but there is no accompanying art. So, in my opinion, it took about 150 years for a Christian culture to develop artifacts that could be distinguished by later historians as Christian.[24] Surely there must be a considerable gap between the time a new faith enters a culture and the time it has the consciousness and artistry to display its own signifiers. This is particularly true when the new faith brings no developed art or symbols.

This must have been the case in Ireland as well. If the new faith entered the Celtic world of Ireland about 300 C.E. then the new Christian cultural symbols might be expected to appear around 450 C.E. Because of the language, some would date the "Latinus Stone" at Whithorn at 450 C.E. According to our chronological analogy, this would be about the same amount of time it took for Roman Christian art to appear. Other stone or slabs come from the sixth century, but the *terminus ab quo* of Irish crosses as they are known probably ought not vary much from the beginning of the seventh century

Early Christian Architecture

Celtic architecture was from the beginning circular. Since form and function match in Ireland, it would be difficult to argue that circular buildings, spoked wheels, poetry, dance, and music are not bound to each other. As in Christian art there is a symbolic interplay between Jesus with outstretched arms, the sun wheel, and David with the harp. This is the very soul of early Irish Christianity.

Self-denying monks lived in beehives and circular huts. Eventually there were buildings other than circular huts, such as Skellig Michael. The chapel at Gallerus from the sixth century has the same interlocking or corbeled stone work as the huts, but actually is more rectangular in shape. The inside is quite plain, with no archaeological indication of a hierarchical worship. Eventually even more elaborate rectangular buildings, such as Saint Kevin's chapel, were constructed.[25]

Of the early churches that remain, several have remarkable entrances that point to early Celtic traditions. Some Romanesque-type entrances have heads set in systematic order. The style is reminiscent of the use of heads in oppida and hillforts, especially in southern Gaul. These heads referenced saints, however, rather than conquered victims. Heads were crucial to Celtic self-identity and cultic practices. The Celtic custom has not been terminated but altered. The life of the saint is now the goal.

There are not many round and domed builtforms in early Roman Christianity. What there is tends to be associated with the heroons (monumental burials) of the Greco-Roman world. Because the daemons of the dead could wander only a few feet from the burial site, a circle made the best use of the space. While not all heroons were circular buildings, nevertheless this functional truth affected the form of the gravesite. At the time of Constantine, *coemeteria subteglata* were first formed with a circular apse around the honored dead and then elongated by the addition of a nave. The buildings were used for celebrations with the martyrs and family dead. The circle contributed to the formation of the apse in later churches and cathedrals.

Likewise the first Christians were buried with Christ in baptism, so eventually a builtform that emulated the heroon and the apse of the *coemeteria subteglata* was quite in order. However, there are no separate baptistries until after Constantine (the baptistry at Dura-Europos was designed within an existing house church). Likewise there are no extant early Christian Irish baptisteries.

The first meeting places for Mediterranean Christians were houses. The places for meeting tended to be square rooms with flat roofs. In wealthier homes the meeting might have occurred in the open peristyle with the triclinium serving as the locus for the Agape. In either case the architecture reflected the nature of the church — a family — where brothers and sisters met to worship the Parent. The Son, Jesus, was present in their midst. The leaders were fellow family members.

It wasn't until after Constantine that church buildings became rectangular halls with, perhaps, a nave, side aisles, and a clerestory. The theology had changed. The church was an organization and when it met it faced the divine presence in the front or apse. Post-Constantinian Christians were led in acknowledgment and appropriation of this divine presence by persons selected or appointed for worship leadership (i.e., priests). The Roman Christian church had become a rectangle.

Notes

1. On the many variations see Laing and Laing, *Celtic Britain and Ireland,* 204–9; and J. Romilly Allen, *Celtic Art in Pagan and Christian Times* (London: Whiting & Co., 1887; London: Bracken Books, 1993), 162–92.

2. Nordenfalk, *Celtic and Anglo-Saxon Painting,* 14–17.

3. For a mass of intricate examples see Allen, *Celtic Art,* 257–95. For aesthetic analyses and examples see Gwenda Adcock, "Theory of Interlace and Interlace Types in Anglican Sculpture," in *Anglo-Saxon and Viking Age Sculpture and Its Context,* ed. James Lang, BAR British Series 49 (Oxford: British Archaeological Reports, 1978), 36–45.

4. Drawings of nonsymbolic animals can be seen in de Paor and de Paor, *Early Christian Ireland,* 89. Miranda J. Green, *Animals in Celtic Life and Myth* (London: Routledge, 1992).

5. On the relationship between human and natural see Green, *Animals in Celtic Life and Myth,* 1–4.

6. The reality of horses and hunting scenes is particularly typical of Pictish stones. Stewart Cruden, *The Early Christian and Pictish Monument of Scotland* (Edinburgh: Her Majesty's Stationery Office, 1964), 9, and Green, *Animals in Celtic Life and Myth,* 7–21.

7. A remarkable exception could be Jonah as an Orante on the slab at Gallen Priory.

8. Snyder, *Inculturation of the Jesus Tradition,* 94–95.

9. For ravens and for eagles, see Bede, *Life of Cuthbert,* in *Lives of the Saints,* trans. Webb, 12, 20.

10. Rarely there is a bird annexed to the crucifix circle, such as on the west side of the Clonmacnois cross below the circle. No certain interpretation has been offered.

11. Françoise Henry, *Irish Art in the Early Christian Period (to 800 A.D.)* (Ithaca, N.Y.: Cornell University Press, 1965), 165, 215.

12. Green, *Wheel as a Cult-Symbol,* 155–59.

13. The Jonah story, when counted as separate sections, would be nearly as frequent.

14. In the famous Monogram Page of the Book of Kells (Fol. 34R) the calligrapher drew two mice eating in a circle while two cats and more mice looked on. In this whimsical cartoon do we have an artistic reference to the eucharistic bread?

15. *Life of St. Columba,* I.44, II.1.13. See Adomnán of Iona, *Life of St. Columba,* trans. Richard Sharpe (London: Penguin, 1995), 306.

16. It must be noted that Jesus suffering on the cross was also quite late in Roman Christianity.

17. Joseph Anderson, *Scotland in Early Christian Times* (Edinburgh: D. Douglas, 1881), 122–25; Cruden, *Early Christian and Pictish Monuments,* 9.

18. Henry, *Irish Art in the Early Christian Period,* plate 47; King, *Kingdoms of the Celts,* 46; Laing and Laing, *Celtic Britain and Ireland,* 60–61.

19. For example, in the Sacrament Chapels in the Callixtus catacomb.

20. Graydon F. Snyder, *Ante Pacem: Archaeological Evidence of Church Life Before Constantine* (Macon, Ga.: Mercer University Press, 1985), 42–43.

21. The data were extracted from Eric H. L. Sexton, *Irish Figure Sculptures of the Early Christian Period* (Portland, Me.: Southworth-Anthoensen Press, 1946). Additional information was found in Arthur Kingsley Porter, *The Crosses and Culture of Ireland* (New Haven: Yale University Press, 1931), and Peter Harbison, *Guide to the National and Historic Monuments of Ireland* (Dublin: Gill

and Macmillan, 1992), and his *Irish High Crosses: With the Figure Sculptures Explained* (Syracuse: Syracuse University Press, 1994). For identification of the scenes Harbison was invaluable.

22. For the Kells crosses, see Helen M. Roe, *The High Crosses of Kells* (Meath: Meath Archaeological and Historical Society, 1966). Many would consider the Scottish high cross of Ruthwell the most important extant sculpture from Anglo-Saxon Britain. The cross is not included in the Irish data, though it has many Celtic-type characteristics. The additional figures would be Mary and Martha, Jesus Healing the Blind, Christ and Mary Magdalene, the Annunciation, John the Baptist, Christ on the Beasts, Paul and Anthony Breaking Bread, and the Flight into Egypt. See Brendan Cassidy, ed., *The Ruthwell Cross* (Princeton, N.J.: Princeton University Press, 1992), and Albert S. Cook, *The Date of the Ruthwell and Bewcastle Crosses* (New Haven: Yale University Press, 1912).

23. Laing and Laing, *Celtic Britain and Ireland*, 150; Nordenfalk, *Celtic and Anglo-Saxon Painting* 57.

24. Stark thinks the later date is a matter of demographics (too few Christians at first). See Stark, *Rise of Christianity*, 8–9. Finney agrees that Christian art was at first indistinguishable from non-Christian. It was the acquisition of property that produced enough wealth to seek specifically Christian symbols and art. See Paul Corby Finney, *The Invisible God: The Earliest Christians on Art* (Oxford: Oxford University Press, 1994), 110.

25. On early architecture see Hughes and Hamlin, *Modern Traveller to the Early Irish Church*, 54–79.

Chapter 10

The Hebrew Scriptures in Sculptured Art

Visual images offer a means of learning at least equal to that of the printed word. Visual images often reflect more accurately the cultural traditions than does the printed word. In early Roman Christian art the biblical images found in the catacombs reflect more the Jesus tradition (as seen in chapter 4) than the kerygma of Paul. So now it is time to approach Irish Christian sculptured art. What tradition does it reflect and what message did the artists intend to convey? How does the Irish use of biblical images compare to that of the Roman Christians? Or, put another way, what is the biblical theology of Irish sculptured art and how does it contrast to the biblical theology of early Roman Christian art?

This congruent biblical theology will be based on a sequential analysis of the Irish art, from Adam and Eve to the glorification of Jesus. There are very serious problems: the art comes from different places and different times; consequently, a biblical sequence does not really exist. Occasionally there is a movement up from Adam and Eve to Cain and Abel and to the Sacrifice of Isaac. Occasionally there is a movement up from Betrayal and Arrest of Jesus to the "Crucifixion circle." Other than these two, the sequence seems random. There is no Irish cross that portrays the biblical narrative as outlined here.

Although in Roman Christian art most of the biblical narrative can be found in the *Capella greca* (catacomb of Priscilla, Rome), there is no apparent order there either. As with Irish art the sequential biblical narrative does not exist. Is there an order no longer discernible?[1] Did each seemingly random scene carry with it more of the narrative than is now apparent?[2] The presence of several copies of any given biblical scene implies that it lies in the corporate consciousness of eighth- and ninth-century Irish Christianity. So the biblical narrative also lies there. It is logical, then, to assume the same for Roman Christianity.

These scenes are called biblical. They are not biblical illustrations. In Roman Christianity there is no illustrative art until well after Constantine (Maria Maggiore in Rome or S. Apollinare Nuovo in Ravenna). Neither should the biblical scenes on the Irish crosses be understood as illustrative. Symbolic visual images must be understood as polyvalent. The art of Irish Christianity and Roman Christianity carry at least three dimensions: (1) the biblical reference itself; (2) the historical context in Ireland or Rome that made the biblical scene important; and (3) the faith journey described by the biblical scene. Needless to say, to interpret simultaneously a scene all three ways will not be simple but it will be necessary.

Creation

The primary symbolic force of most cultures has been the sun. Such symbols take many forms: sky chariots, circles, wheels, rays, light. The Celts were no exception, and the wheel, the circle, and the spiral were their primary sun symbols. Symbols of the sun reflected not only the source of life, but also new life. As the sun set and rose, so life sets and rises. So wheels and circles were used in funerary settings. Models of spoked wheels have been found in Celtic graves and in cultic places wheels were carved into rocks. One of the more important Celtic finds was the Trundholm chariot (1300 B.C.E.) in which the sun was carried on a horsedrawn cart. The sun itself was the creative divinity. The sun god can be more easily identified after contact with the Romans. The Celts were generous with their divinities. They readily accepted the gods of cultures with which they had a forced encounter. Consequently, many Roman gods and goddesses appear in Celtic guise. Jupiter, the Roman Zeus, was adapted as the sun god. Among other symbolic manifestations, Jupiter appeared on giant Jupiter columns found across the continental Celtic world (about 150). The columns are high (perhaps 45 feet) with a statue of Jupiter riding a horse. He often carried a spoked wheel as a shield, while his horse trampled some unidentifiable monster that was obviously related to otherworldly darkness. At times he carried thunderbolts.

The Irish crosses are high and do not have an image of Jupiter at the top. However, the crosses do direct the viewer's attention to the sky and are topped off by the sun symbol, a spoked wheel. Jesus often stands in the middle of the wheel in a pose that must be identified as Jesus on the cross. To be sure Jesus must be the new sun god, but not like any other Celtic adaptation. As the spoked wheel signified the setting and rising of the sun, the end and rebirth of life, so Jesus represented death to conflict and birth in spiritual maturity. The two symbols, the sun and Jesus, have become one.

There are also artistic references to Jesus and the sun god in early Roman art. The most obvious would be the mosaic in Mausoleum M under the Vatican. Jesus has mounted a biga and rides into the sky with rays from his head streaming into the golden sky. Pictures of Elijah mounting a chariot have the same implication (door of S. Sabina). Another obvious encounter with the sun god can be seen in some pictures of the three wise men who, dressed like Mithraic magi, pay homage to the baby Jesus (Vatican Museum, Pio Clementine). To be sure, in addition to Apollo, the early Roman Christians did assimilate Roman deities like Neptune and Orpheus, or Roman figures like Hercules and Endymion. But there is no equivalent for the Irish identification of Jesus with the sun.

Adam and Eve

As noted the most frequent scene in Irish sculptured art is Adam and Eve (27 out of 347). Furthermore, most of the Adam and Eve scenes occur at the base of the cross (19 out of 27; see plate 7). It would be difficult to deny that many of the cross artisans intended to see a progression from the creation symbol of Adam and Eve to the new creation symbol of Jesus in the solar spoked wheel. It would also be difficult to deny that viewers saw in the circle a second, spiritual creation that derived from the first, physical creation. One could wish for an inscription or a literary reference that would confirm this apparent faith progression. There is none.

It is not always appropriate to use theological writings to interpret religious art, but at this point it seems necessary. There is a distinctive Irish theology. While all aspects of that theology are certainly not unique to Ireland, the composite is distinctly Irish. The function of Adam and Eve in relationship to Jesus is so important in early Irish theology it requires attention at this point. The premiere Irish theologian Pelagius (ca. 350–418) was born and raised either in Ireland or in Wales. He was present in Rome at the end of the fourth century and the beginning of the fifth. Although Pelagianism was eventually condemned as a heresy, it did not at first seem unorthodox. Pelagius came from the Antioch school that read the New Testament in its apparent literary sense — that is, no allegorical reading. His view of creation, freedom, sin, faith, and grace did not differ much from other scholars of his time, Augustine included. Pelagius believed Adam and Eve were created good and free. There was no original sin inherent in their "fall," no fault that would be passed to all humans at their birth. Instead, in their freedom they chose to "sin" and then continued habitually to sin. Again in their freedom they chose to respond to Jesus and were graced to choose for life rather than the habit of sin. In his commentary on Rom. 5:12: "Therefore, just as through one person sin came into the world, and through sin death," Pelagius wrote that it was caused by "example or by pattern." And on Rom. 5:15 he argues that Christ not only freed us but also previous generations (that is, the opportunity for freedom had always been present).[3]

It would be foolhardy to suppose the Irish artisans who created the crosses, or even their clients, knew the theology of their earlier compatriot Pelagius. It would be equally foolhardy to assume that monumental public art failed to reflect the metaphysical basis of a culture. The very frequent pictures of Adam and Eve at the base of Irish crosses signify the creation of humans as physical beings (plate 7). Sometimes they are tending the animals. Other times they stand on each side of a tree and sometimes a serpent may be coiled around the tree. The serpent does not refer to original sin (as in Augustine or the traducianists, who believed that guilt was

inherited), but to human fertility. The cross, or circle, references
the spiritual rebirth that makes the full life possible. Intermediate
scenes illustrate life, the faith journey, between the physical birth
and the spiritual birth.

Pictures of Adam and Eve are not as frequent in early Roman
Christian art (4 out of 181; plate 10). They do tend to appear more
often in later sarcophagi. But even the few examples in existence
are puzzling. Their contextual placement seems totally arbitrary.
Unlike the Irish crosses, no progressive movement can be discerned.
Most interpreters tend toward the traditional. Some see a reference
to original sin. Others see a loss of Paradise.[4] Signifying original
sin would be highly unlikely, since the Augustinian debate would
have been early fifth century. It is highly unlikely early Christians
would have adopted Manichean or traducianist ideas into their art.
As for the Fall from Paradise, that may be, but there is no Jesus to
act as a faith or spiritual redeemer. Jesus on the cross first appears
at the beginning of the fifth century. The Adam and Eve portrayal
normally occurs close to deliverance stories such as Noah and the
Ark, Moses Striking the Rock, Daniel in the Lions' Den, the Three
Young Men in the Fiery Furnace, and Susanna and the Elders. If
Adam and Eve should fit in the deliverance context, then the scene
likely refers more to the Christian rebirth — that is, baptism — than
to the Fall.[5] More likely the Roman Adam and Eve does not differ
that much from the Irish. The story signals the beginning of each
life, a life that will be caught in social and political entrapments.
Deliverance from those entrapments comes when the person joins
with Jesus in the new community of faith.

Scenes of Conflict

Again, while it might be foolhardy to suggest a progression from
Adam and Eve at the base of the cross to Jesus at the head, several
scenes reflect such a movement. These are among the most frequent
scenes on Irish crosses, all from the Hebrew Scriptures: Cain and
Abel (6 of 347); Noah in the Ark (4); Sacrifice of Isaac (17); Jacob
and the Angel (8); Moses with Arms Held Up (4); Moses Striking
the Rock (3); Samson (2) David and Goliath (3); David and the

Lion (9); Daniel in the Lions' Den (2); Three Young Men in the Fiery Furnace (7); and Jonah (2).

The scenes from the Hebrew Scriptures found in early Roman Christian art almost invariably refer to divine deliverance in the face of external threat (often signified by the presence of the deliverance symbol, the Orante). Scenes from the New Testament tend to stress healing and extraordinary actions. While these New Testament scenes extend the deliverance motif into acts of compassion on the part of Jesus, they do not move on to the cross. The Roman Christian artistic series ends with the ministry of Jesus and the resultant fellowship/Agape meal of the early church. That is, the end result of the biblical history comes when the faith community eats together and in that meal lives out the redemptive act of Jesus (bread and wine).

In contrast, the Irish Christian use of the Hebrew Scriptures does not feature deliverance so much as victory over traditional history. Many of the stories are the same as the early Roman, but the lack of the Orante or any delivering figure demands quite a different interpretation. Given the movement from physical birth (Adam and Eve) to spiritual birth (Jesus in the sun circle), it can be assumed that the Irish scenes from the Hebrew Scriptures lead up to the head of the cross. These scenes are almost invariably conflict situations. The conflicts show primarily how the old Celtic world was integrated into the new Celtic Christian world. In order to better understand both the Irish and the Roman scenes, they must be compared in a presumed chronological/biblical order.

Cain and Abel

Cain and Abel as a picture usually occurs close to Adam and Eve, sometimes even as a double in the same panel (plate 7). Such proximity makes the subjects fairly easy to identify. The Cain and Abel scene consists of two men confronting each other, with Cain holding a machete-like sword as a weapon. The biblical narrative begins with Adam and Eve, then points to the conflicts that follow. The first conflict in the series involves siblings and their relationship to God. The scene is a painful one. On the faith level, sin enters when conflict occurs and is repeated. The Cain and Abel story signifies the beginning of that conflictive process.

On the historical level, the Celts sacrificed animals. Early Irish Christians, following the Jesus tradition, repudiated animal sacrifice (the Cleansing of the Temple). Being almost vegetarian, they offered only products of the field to the monastic community. To what extent that created a conflict with their sibling Druids cannot be easily determined. Surely murder was not involved, since there are so few known martyrs. Nevertheless, in early Irish Christian art life involved conflict and that conflict was first signified by the struggle between Cain, who as a Druid offered animal sacrifice, and Abel, who as an Irish Christian did not.

In contrast there are no Cain and Abel pictures in either early or post-Constantinian Christian Roman art. Certainly the first Roman Christians experienced conflict with other religious groups (the traditions of Acts 16 and 19),[6] some of whom did employ animal sacrifice. That conflict can be seen in such early Christian art as the subservience of the Mithraic magi before Jesus. While the Roman Christians rejected all sacrificial systems, they could hardly be considered Abel-like vegetarians. Though the early art shows fish as the primary meat, they apparently did not hesitate to eat other kinds of meat. The Cain-Abel conflict story was not appropriate for the Roman Christians.

Noah in the Ark

On the Irish crosses the Ark is not easily distinguished. At the Kells, for example, it would appear to be a type of Viking ship with a prow and seven shields on the side. Three or four persons are sailing in this supposed Ark. The figure of Noah is not very clear; a dove hovers over the boat. There are only four of these scenes and only two of Jonah. The Noah story offers an opportunity for the artisan to celebrate overcoming the conflict with the waters that separated the new Irish faith community from the Continent. Given the necessity and enjoyment of boat travel, one wonders why the biblical boating narratives appear so seldom. Since the artistic narrative from the

Hebrew scriptures stress conflict, one could assume the oft-traveled water did not present any life-threatening problems.

In early Roman Christian scenes Noah stands in a cubical box, an Orante though dressed in masculine clothing. The Noah figure has been saved from the threat of a flood. It cannot be assumed that the early Christians actually faced floods or experienced the frights of ocean travel. Nautical scenes in early Christian Roman art referred more to the alien culture in which the early Christian found themselves.[7]

They used symbols like the anchor, the fish, and the boat to encourage the faithful to trust in divine protection from the threats of Roman life. Not until the Trier Noah sarcophagus is there an Ark that actually looks like a boat. After Constantine the Noah scene loses its deliverance motif and will be found occasionally as a biblical illustration (Monreale, Sicily).

The Sacrifice of Isaac

The so-called Sacrifice of Isaac occurs more frequently on the Irish cross than any scene other than Adam and Eve. Furthermore, it occurs often enough just above Adam and Eve in the upward progression (eight times) to make one suspect it is a primary conflict scene. The iconography of the Sacrifice is fairly simple. On the Moone cross Isaac kneels with his head on a table and a sheep practically on his back. Abraham sits in front of Isaac with a bird on the back of the chair. The bird could very well be delivering instructions to Abraham. There is no wood for the sacrifice.

On the West Cross at Monasterboice, East Side, Isaac leans over an altar with some wood in his hands. Abraham, standing in this case, has a sword in his hand. There is no deliverance figure. The conflict has nothing to do with Isaac. The conflict lies in Abraham, who is learning not to offer human sacrifice. The Celts did offer human sacrifices, often for penal purposes but not always. When the Jesus tradition came to Celtic Ireland, human sacrifice was totally eliminated. This conflict scene signifies that cultural shift.

The Irish use of the Sacrifice of Isaac comes close to the actual Pentateuchal intent of the story. The Roman use does not even approximate the biblical narrative. In a few very early scenes Isaac appears as an Orante, so Isaac apparently has been delivered from a threatening religious persecution.

In the few pre-Constantinian examples of the Sacrifice, Isaac does not always appear as an Orante, but contextually the picture appears with the other deliverance scenes from the Hebrew Scriptures. Normally Abraham stands with a knife, Isaac carries wood toward an altar, a lamb is caught in a nearby thicket, and the hand of God appears above the whole scene. The two Jewish portrayals of that time are nearly identical with the Christian (Torah niche of the Dura-Europos synagogue, and Beth Saida in Israel). Sometime in this early period the Jewish interpretation of the Isaac narrative shifted. Perhaps to counter the sacrifice of the cross, attention centered on Isaac rather than Abraham. It has been argued that the Sacrifice of Isaac was the prototype for the Sacrifice of Jesus. In Rom. 8:32 Paul writes of the love of God:

> He who did not withhold his own Son, but gave him up for all of us, will he not with him also give us everything else?

The phrase "did not withhold your son" is also used of Abraham in relation to Isaac (Gen. 22:12). The notion that the Binding of Isaac was a sacrifice (known as the Aqedah) appeared in Judaism about the time the New Testament was formed. Even though Paul's comment in Rom. 8:32 could be understood that way, it was only later that identification of Isaac and Jesus became more certain (Irenaeus, *Haer.* 4.10.1). Jesus on the cross is very late in all Christian art. The Sacrifice of Isaac was used instead of the cross to portray the meaning of self-sacrifice (S. Vitale in Ravenna).

Jacob Wrestling with the Angel

There are several scenes in which a biblical hero does battle with extraordinary figures. While the contextual situation may not always be obvious, it is clear these scenes reference battles or conflicts on the way to the victory of Jesus in the head of the cross. Jacob Wrestling with the Angel may at first seem inconsequential in this progression. Unlike in Roman Christianity, angels do not often appear in Irish material, nor were angels a part of the Celtic heritage. In order to understand this scene it is necessary to return to the biblical meaning rather than Celtic iconography. Jacob wrestling with the angel occurred when Jacob entered the promised land. As the angel was the protector of the land of Palestine, so the angel in these Irish scenes is the protector of Celtic Ireland. Jacob signifies and commemorates the crossing of those carrying the Jesus tradition into the new promised land of the western isles. A conflict had been required.

Given this analogical interpretation of the Jacob story, it seems strange that there are no examples of Jacob Wrestling with the Angel in early Roman Christian art. The Jesus tradition did infiltrate Roman culture. Eventually Rome became the promised land. But once again analogy has its limits. There is no "delivering" motif in Jacob Wrestling with the Angel. The Irish Jacob made a compromise with the angel and entered the land. There is no reason for Jacob to appear in the early Roman Christian list of deliverance stories.

Moses with Arms Held Up

This is one of the most remarkable of the scenes from the Hebrew Scriptures. In Exod. 14:15–29, Moses stretches out his hand to open the Red Sea for the Israelites and then closes it for the Egyptians. In the Irish portrayal of this key redemptive event, Moses stands with his hand stretched at right angles (usually) to his body. The similarity to those scenes of Jesus in the solar circle can hardly be ignored. Jesus also stands with arms at right angles with no sign of a cross or wounds. In all of the Moses scenes two men help him hold up his arms. In the Jesus scenes two soldiers often stand by. The iconography is strikingly similar. Since there are no other scenes with outstretched arms, it can be assumed that the artisans took their iconography for Jesus and transferred it to the primary saving event in the history of Israel. But since Christian biblical art, either Roman or Irish, seldom actually illustrates a specific event, might it be better to say that the iconography of the outstretched arms represents the gift of entering a new promised land. In the Exodus narrative Moses was leaving Egypt and entering, eventually, the promised land. For the Irish it was the joining of the Jesus tradition with the Celtic sun tradition in this new land called Ireland.

There is no scene in early Roman Christian art equivalent to Moses with Arms Held Up. Although the Exodus was indeed a saving narrative, the early church did not place it among deliverance events. While the early church utilized stories involving deliverance from political persecution, apparently this story implied more the crossing into a new land than it did a saving flight from the pharaoh.

Moses Striking the Rock

According to Exodus, once in the desert the Israelites lacked water. Under duress Moses struck a rock. Water flowed out. This scene occurs three times (out of 347) in the Irish art (plate 11). It occurs five times in early Roman Christian art (plate 12). Moses Striking the Rock continued to be a popular scene in early Christian art after the fourth century. Obviously it serves as a saving event, or even a deliverance event. Striking the Rock can hardly be a realistic reference since there is no lack of water in either Italy or Ireland. In pre-Constantinian Roman art Moses Striking the Rock stands in the series of deliverance motifs.

In Irish art Moses Striking the Rock has quite another meaning. Underground water sources were in touch with the Otherworld and were cherished by the Celts as healing springs. As mentioned, such springs existed in Galatia. There were many other healing springs on the continent and in Britain. One thinks of such popular springs as Bath (Sulis Minerva) in Great Britain or Fontes Sequanae in Gaul. Not quite as well known were the Christian healing springs in Ireland, often connected with saints like Brigit or Patrick. Though originating dates would be difficult to ascertain, an Irish example would be Patrick's Pool on the island called the Purgatory of Patrick in Lough Derg.[8] Simply put, the picture of Moses Striking the Rock signifies the Christianization of the Celtic healing springs. The Celtic practices of human sacrifices (heads) at the wells would have been terminated to be replaced by remembrances of Irish saints. The result is not unlike the Jesus tradition that had Jesus cleansing the water of the sea monsters.

The David Cycle

Life-and-death struggles were popular with the Irish artisans. There are only two examples of Samson, one with him fighting a lion and one with him destroying the temple. The temple picture presents a remarkable composite of biblical narrative, personal conflict, and history. The long-haired Samson uses a staff to push over the temple, which consists of three arches that exhibit the heads of terminated enemies. Many such arches existed in Celtic temples and towns (e.g., Entremont). Samson is destroying the practice of headhunting.

A similar composite can be seen in David's fight with Goliath (3 out of 347). David plays a major role in early Irish art. His struggle with the lion occurs nine times. In addition to the struggle scenes he is pictured playing the harp seven times. All together the person of David occurs nineteen times. In sharp contrast, the figure of David almost never occurs in early Roman Christian art.[9] Why David? David and the Harp is relatively obvious. David signifies the assimilation of the Celtic bards into the new Christian faith. The major scenes from the Hebrew Scriptures reflect conflict on the way to the amalgamation of Jesus and the sun. As such, then, these conflict stories reflect the alterations in the new faith. If David the harpist assimilates the bards, then David the fighter assimilates or terminates the Celtic warrior elite class.

David, the warrior type, also fights off the mythological enemies of the faith. What are the mythological opponents? Giants and lions are not a part of the Irish experience or mythology, so it appears that here the biblical narratives control the mythology. David may be a heroic warrior, but David's opponents come from the recorded exploits of great biblical heroes. In the unique Monasterboice scene Goliath, a Celt, has a Celtic circular shield and a helmet above his (decapitated?) head, while David, apparently not a Celt, has a machete in his left hand. The scene is unique because it is a rare multiple narrative. Like the Jonah narrative in early Roman Christian art, there are three Davids. To the left the shepherd boy David has a sling in his hand and a pouch full of stones on his right hip. To the right the victorious David is playing his lyre. That is, David the biblical warrior hero has not only destroyed the ancient Celtic warrior, thereby defeating the famed ferocity of Celtic men and women, but he also replaces ferocity with bard-like music.

The lion is more difficult, of course. Irish artisans could not have known lions, though Picts particularly often utilized monster-type animals as fearsome threats. The lions threaten the biblical hero, David, but cannot really attack him. On the way to the top of the cross, every believer faces such mythological, transmogrified, indefinable conflicts. With David the conflicts can be overcome.

The Daniel Cycle

Daniel in the Lions' Den, one of the more popular scenes, occurs twelve times. But Daniel was no hero. He was a wise man loyal to Jewish traditions. As a wise man he faced death in a lions' den. Daniel Between the Lions was popular both with the early Irish artisans and the early Roman Christians. The Roman Daniel (found six times) has a consistent iconography: Daniel as an Orante between two lions. The iconography makes the meaning clear. Daniel was persecuted for his steadfast loyalty to the Jewish God. The lions of Babylonia could not touch him. As an Orante he had been delivered. The scene was important in early Christian Roman life because they, too, found deliverance from Roman oppression when their faith put them in danger (the Orante).

There was no such oppression in Irish Christianity. There would have been no need to show Daniel delivered from the threat of state persecution. The conflict scenes leading to the head of the cross reflect a past that has been replaced by Christianity. In Cain and Abel animal sacrifice was denied. In Abraham and Isaac human sacrifice was abolished. In Samson headhunting was destroyed. In David and Goliath Celtic ferocity was overcome. In David and the Harp, the bards and music were assimilated. So in Daniel Between the Lions, the wise Celts, the Druids, were absorbed into the procession that led to the Christian faith on the cross head (plate 6). The new Druids, the monks and saints, need not fear such mythological opponents as lions.

The Three Young Men in the Fiery Furnace belongs to the Daniel story. Presumably it does not differ from the Daniel story in either tradition. In Roman art the Three Young Men are portrayed as three Orantes standing in an enclosed fire. Often they are shown in dress other than the customary Roman costumes. Almost always there is a fourth figure in the fire — a dove or a representation of God. Since the three young men were colleagues of Daniel, they too must represent persecution for their faith.

In Irish art the same meaning can be assumed for the Three Young Men as for the Irish Daniel. Using a biblical story the artisans have absorbed the wise Celts or Druids into their narrative. While the Irish scene does not resemble the Roman, the impression of the original narrative is clear. There is a fourth figure who somehow, as an angel, represents a divine blessing on the transformed Druids.

Jonah and the Sea Monster

There are only three examples of Jonah. Two show Jonah coming out of the mouth of the sea monster. One shows Jonah cast out of the boat. These few Jonah pictures occur near the head of the cross. The remarkable portrayal on the Gallen slab actually positions Jonah in the cross with a spiral in the center of the circle. At the bottom an Orante-like Jonah comes out of the mouth of the monster. At the top a Celtic-type head sits in the mouth of another monster. Apparently a few artisans intended to signify a new birth implied by the regurgitation of the prophet Jonah.

While there are fewer than a handful of Jonah scenes in Irish art, Jonah is the major subject of early Christian Roman art. It is difficult to count the number of Jonah stories because it occurs as a cycle, but I estimate fifty portrayals prior to Constantine. The cycle consisted of Jonah thrown from a boat, usually as an Orante; Jonah cast out of the monster mouth, almost always as an Orante; and Jonah reclining under a bush, in exactly the same pose as the Endymion of non-Christian Roman sarcophagi. As noted in chapter 3, in the Hebrew Scriptures the seas and the large animals, for example, Leviathan, represented the powers of evil and especially the powers of imperial states. In Greek mythological thought the symbolism was much the same, though the evil forces were more associated with hostile gods and goddesses than with empires. When early Christian artisans portrayed Jonah cast into the sea, he was not a victim. He was an already delivered Christian thrown into a watery culture inimical to him. He safely emerged from the threatening culture through the mouth of the sea monster. The Jonah cycle was a major motif as long as the faith community was oppressed by the Roman Empire. After that was no longer true, the Jonah cycle disappeared from Roman Christian art.

Summary

When Irish Christian scenes from the Hebrew Scriptures are viewed contextually, the pattern becomes quite clear. Adam and Eve represented that human birth that leads finally to the spiritual birth with Jesus in the solar circle. Cain and Abel signifies the demise of Celtic animal sacrifices. The Sacrifice of Isaac reflects the end of Celtic human sacrifice. Moses with Uplifted Arms refers to the crossing of the Jesus tradition from the Continent to Ireland. Noah and the Ark signifies a safe crossing. David and the Harp indicates the assimilation of the bards into the Christian tradition. Samson marks the end of headhunting. The struggle of David with Goliath and with lions reflects the termination of the fierce warrior class in favor of a peaceful Christian tradition. Pictures of Daniel and the Three Young Men, wise Jews, signify the assimilation of the Druids. And finally the story of Jonah approaches the spiritual rebirth found in the cross circle.

Notes

1. Elizabeth Malbon tried to show a composite meaning where there is no sequence in her *The Iconography of the Sarcophagus of Junius Bassus* (Princeton, N.J.: Princeton University Press, 1990).

2. Robin Jensen, *Understanding Early Christian Art* (London: Routledge, 2000), 64–68.

3. Theodore de Bruyn, *Pelagius's Commentary on St. Paul's Epistle to the Romans* (Oxford: Clarendon Press, 1993), 92–94.

4. André Grabar, *Christian Iconography: A Study of Its Origins* (Princeton, N.J.: Princeton University Press, 1968), 12; Robert Milburn, *Early Christian Art and Architecture* (Berkeley: University of California Press, 1988), 12.

5. So Jensen, *Understanding Early Christian Art,* 178–79. For example, Adam and Eve appear over the baptistery in the house church at Dura-Europos.

6. Robert L. Wilken, *The Myth of Christian Beginnings: History's Impact on Belief* (Garden City, N.Y.: Doubleday, 1971), and *The Christians as the Romans Saw Them* (New Haven: Yale University Press, 1984).

7. Graydon F. Snyder, "Sea Monsters in Early Christian Art," *Biblical Research* 44 (2000): 7–21.

8. Philip Dixon Hardy, *The Holy Wells of Ireland* (Dublin: D. Hardy, 1836). See Harbison, *Pilgrimage in Ireland,* 53–63.

9. There is one fresco of David and Goliath in Dura-Europos, and one with David and his sling in Domitilla. See James Stevenson, *The Catacombs: Life and Death in Early Christianity* (Nashville: Thomas Nelson, 1985), 74.

Chapter 11

The New Testament in Sculptured Art

A contextual basis for the New Testament pictures will not be as easy to discern as the ones from the Hebrew Scriptures were. Those involving Jesus' birth are: The Nativity (2 out of 347); the Wise Men (12); the Massacre of the Innocents (4); and the Flight Into Egypt (2). From the life of Jesus there are: The Presentation at the Temple (1); the Baptism of Jesus (8); the Loaves and Fishes (6); the Feeding of the 5,000 (3); the Wedding at Cana (2); and the Twelve Apostles (4). Scenes from the Passion include: the Betrayal of Jesus (5); the Arrest of Jesus (5); Pilate Washing His Hands (4); the Crucifixion (52; primarily 52 out of 115 crosses); and the Road to Emmaus (2).[1]

In contrast to the contextual nature of the scenes from the Hebrew scriptures, the scenes of Jesus inspired the viewer to reflect on the life of the one who would eventually stand in the center of the crucifix circle. There will be a brief description of each and a comparison with the Roman equivalent.

Infancy Narratives

Not many discernible nativity scenes appear in Irish Christian art and very few nativity scenes turn up in pre-Constantinian Roman art. However, after Constantine a number of such scenes appear on sarcophagi. The iconography is simple in any case: a crib with a baby, Mary and Joseph, and some animals. Sometimes there is a star above the crib (plate 13). Why did nativity scenes not appear until after Constantine, and why did the number of scenes including wise men increase? Interest in the nativity and wise men points to a competitive conflict with Mithraism. The magi of the New Testament story have become, or were (!), magi of the Mithra myth. They were priests of the sun. When in the early Christian art they came to the manger, they were acquiescing to Jesus, the real sun God, born on the winter solstice. So the nativity scene had little importance until later when it reflected the victory of the Christian calendar over sun celebrations.

Since the Irish also had calendar conflicts (see below), it seems strange that the nativity scene occurs so seldom in Irish art. Like the Roman artists, the Irish put more emphasis on the wise men.

It is difficult to tell whether the sculptures of wise men, like the Roman counterpart, have priestesses of the sun, Druids, offering obeisance to the infant Jesus. On the Monasterboice cross the wise men certainly do not resemble Celtic figures, as they might, for example on Kells, West Cross. Given the prominence of sun worship, it appears that the wise men are sun worshipers in some form or another. Like their Roman counterparts they are honoring the true sun God.

The Massacre of the Innocents and the Flight Into Egypt present more problems. Neither one occurs in early Roman Christian art. Any attempt to connect the two Irish scenes with an event or a Celtic motif may seem remote. In Irish Christianity the two scenes remind the viewer that the political leader, Herod, attempted to thwart the Jesus tradition. While there is very little sign of persecution of Christians in the Irish tradition, there is every reason to assume political leaders of the tuath, the kings, resisted the transfer of their power to monastic leaders. The Hebrew Scriptures illustrate how the early Irish Christians dealt with the warrior class, Druids, and bards. Now, their art shows how they dealt with the kingly class. After threats (the Massacre of the Innocents), they avoided any further conflict by flight or peregrination, the Flight into Egypt. And therefore the Jesus tradition survived. In yet another "infancy" scene Jesus appears before the Celtic leaders in the arms of Mary and is accepted by them, as was Jesus when presented at the temple. In early Christian Roman art there are no equivalent scenes that relate the child Jesus to political leaders.

The Baptism of Jesus

The Baptism of Jesus plays a significant role in both Irish (8) and early Roman Christian art (6). The Roman scene certainly is multivalent. It contains some elements of the New Testament narrative, particularly the dove descending. It contains elements of a classical Roman background with a Neptune-like figure performing the baptism while Jesus is portrayed as a young wonderworker, perhaps even Hercules. It contains elements of the conflict with water. Jesus is dipped into the Roman culture (water in early Christian art) in order to redeem it. Even in this multivalent scene Roman Christians surely also saw in the Baptism of Jesus a precedent for their own baptism.

Following the New Testament the Irish scene also shows a dove descending. A larger Celtic figure baptizes the little Jesus in a nondescript forked river. In the Kells scene two adult Celtic figures look on. Unlike the Roman counterpart where Jesus cleanses the water, by the pouring of water over non-Celtic Jesus the Celtic figure is baptizing him into the Irish culture. There could hardly be a more apparent symbol of adapting the Jesus tradition into what became early Irish Christianity. Whether the Baptism of Jesus also references the believer's baptism cannot be determined.

After the baptism the Irish life of Jesus contains two remaining sections: scenes of ministry by Jesus and scenes from the Passion Narrative. The ministry scenes show the Feeding of the 5,000, the Wedding at Cana, and the call of the disciples. These relate specifically to the functions of the church: bread, fish, wine (communion), and the call to serve God (ordination). Because the ministry of Jesus signifies Irish church life, one suspects that the Baptism of Jesus also was a multivalent reference to the believer's baptism.

The Ministry of Jesus

It is surprising, even astounding, that so few scenes from the ministry of Jesus can be found in Irish art. Actually there are not many examples at all, but enough to assume the artisans were aware that the Feeding of the 5,000 related to the presence of loaves and fishes. So the two signify the importance of the communion in the Irish church. In the Kells example of the Feeding of the 5,000, Jesus stands on the lower right as he receives the fish and bread from the boy (Gospel of John rather than the Synoptics). The multitude consists of heads above Jesus and the boy. Strangely enough, David is furnishing dinner music on the lower-left side. The Loaves and Fishes consist of just that — loaves and fishes. The artisan of the Moone Abbey scene sculpted two fish and five circles. The table is set for the communion service, but there is none. On the other hand, there is an occasional production of wine as in the Wedding of Cana. The caterer for the wedding sits in front of Jesus as he transforms the water. Guests and pleading disciples look on.

Roman art has the Feeding of the 5,000, and the symbol of fish with bread. In addition the Roman artisans also portrayed a large number of Agape meals. The meals were indeed based on the Feeding of the 5,000, with two fish and seven baskets of bread, and the Wedding at Cana. Why are meals totally missing from Irish art? The Irish monks certainly ate meals and they celebrated communion, but the epitome of the monastic life was asceticism. Encratic monks could hardly celebrate eating together as the basis for Christian discipleship. To the contrary, they would have preferred to remember the miraculous care of God as they lived the isolated life. And, indeed, that is exactly what they did. As will be discussed later, there are eight out of 347 scenes of Saint Anthony holding out against temptations for food and twelve pictures of Paul and Anthony being fed by the ravens. So there is feeding from God, but there are no common meals pictured in Irish art.

The other part of Jesus' ministry was the call of the disciples. There are no calling scenes as such in either Roman or Irish Christian art. But, in contrast to Roman art, the Irish have at least four examples of the Twelve. In the scene from Moone Abbey there are simply twelve men. Given the references in early Irish literature to the call, one should not be surprised by these scenes. Some people were not only called to be monastics, but were called to a life of asceticism and peregrination. In contrast, there are no calls of the apostles in Roman Christian art. Eventually, especially in Arles, sarcophagi with many apostles appeared, and in Ravenna Jesus the Shepherd with twelve sheep.

On the other hand, the Irish pictures lack scenes very important to the early Roman Christians. Perhaps the lack of meals can be explained by the yearning for asceticism. However, how can the lack of healing scenes be explained? Roman art has multiple scenes of Jesus healing the paralytic, those who can't hear, and those who can't speak (plate 5). The early Irish monks did often heal others. Why, then, doesn't the Irish Jesus heal? There are two reasons. The Roman Christian healing stories appeared because the early church was in conflict with magicians and shamans who claimed to have the divine power to heal (e.g., Acts 8). Some scholars would claim Christianity grew because it won that competition.[2] There was no such conflict in Ireland with healing cults. The assertion that Jesus was a healer was not necessary. Celtic healing as, for example, in sacred pools was automatically assimilated. Second, the Irish portrayals of Jesus' ministry relate to the life of the church (communion and divine call). The satisfactions of the Christian life occur when the faithful are incorporated by Jesus into the solar disc. That is, healing is a function of Jesus the solar Christ, not the historical Jesus. Likewise the joy of music belongs in the spoked wheel. So David plays the harp in the solar disc. Health, music, dance, and poetry are the end result of a satisfactory participation in the Jesus tradition found in the solar spiritual maturity.

The Passion Narrative

In contrast to the ministry of Jesus the Passion Narrative is fairly well represented in Irish Christian art: the Arrest of Jesus (5 out of 347); the Betrayal of Jesus (5); Pilate Washing His Hands (4); and the Crucifixion (52). The *raison d'être* for the Irish crosses lies in the presence of a Jesus with outstretched arms inside a circle, a circle that is interpreted to be a spoked wheel or sun representation. Irish Christian art started with the physical birth of Adam and Eve. Hebrew Scripture scenes were used to describe the assimilation of the Celtic world into the Christian. The birth (arrival) of Jesus caused obeisance on the part of sun worshipers and consternation on the part of displaced political powers. The ministry of Jesus then resulted in two important elements in the life of the Irish church: communion and the call.

Finally, the Passion Narrative itself. Now the situation is reversed. What price did Jesus pay to enter the solar cross? What price does the Irish Christian pay to reach the union of sun and Jesus? The answer is suffering and self-abnegation (a betrayal scene occurs in the head of the cross). The three stories from the Passion Narrative of Jesus admittedly do not match any specific Celtic experience. The artists used the Passion stories to point the way to spiritual maturity for the Irish Christian. The arrest of Jesus, as seen on the Monasterboice cross, shows Jesus as a non-Celtic monk with a staff in his hand. He is submitting to arrest by two soldiers dressed as Romans but with Celtic faces (plate 14).

After the arrest Jesus is bound for trial. As in the picture of the arrest two Roman soldiers tie up a monastic Jesus. Jesus appears as a monastic in the Passion scenes, but there is no reason to see a conflict in Irish history. This deals with the personal history of the faithful as they approach the solar disc. A final Passion scene occurs right on the head of the cross, the mocking of Jesus. Two soldiers change his cloak and another places on his head the crown of thorns.

The scene of Pilate washing his hands simply shows a soldier with a shield pouring water for Pilate to wash his hands. Jesus is not present. The washing of hands is followed by an Ecce Homo scene in which Pilate presents the flogged Jesus to inimical Jews. Though few in number (four), the scene affirms the minimal nature of political activity (persecution) that occurred in the formation of Irish Christianity.

None of these scenes occurred in early Roman Christianity. Far more exist on the ministry of Jesus, such as various types of healing and the resurrection of Lazarus. The progression of the Roman portrayals led to victory over the Roman culture: to healing of diseases found in that culture, to raising people from the death in which they were caught, to commensality for the total family, living and dead. The Roman Christian progression led to a satisfying faith community withdrawn from the Roman culture. The Roman progression did not lead to a suffering Jesus. There was no Passion Narrative. There were no crosses. Only when the cross did appear, after Constantine, were Passion portrayals also created.

The Crucifixion

Of course, the purpose of the 115 crosses and slabs is to portray in some fashion what is later called the crucifixion. There are slabs (e.g., Reask [plate 8] and Whithorn) and many crosses that have spoked wheels, but no Jesus (as in Ahenny) Some even have the ancient symbol of the sun, the spiral, in the center of the head. In the 115 crosses and 347 pictures there are fifty-two spoked wheels with Jesus at the center. Not all crucifixions have been placed inside the spoked wheel. For example, a crucifixion appears on the shaft of a Kells cross, just below the spoked wheel. A soldier crouches on each side, apparently with spear ready. The arms of Jesus are extended at right angles. There is no cross. There is a bird on the left arm and an unknown figure on the right. A dove sits on the head of Jesus as if to pull the crucifixion up into the spoked wheel. In this case the spoked wheel itself portrays a postcrucifixion Jesus in glory.

Nevertheless, the majority of the so-called crucifixions occur within the spoked wheel. While the details differ, essentially the crucifixion consists of Jesus, who may or may not be a Celt, with outstretched arms. Sometimes, as in Monasterboice, a nail can be seen in each hand. There is never a cross per se. On each side of Jesus, under his arms, invariably is a soldier with a spear in his hand. The function of these two spears is never clear. They are not wounding Jesus. Of course, the Irish artisans had never seen a crucifixion and almost certainly had never seen a Byzantine portrayal of one (the Irish pilgrims may have returned with some descriptions). So to ask what is happening in the scenes has little value. This is their formal crucifixion iconography. Instead of a cross the viewer's mind must have seen Jesus' arm stretched out on or as the spokes of the solar wheel (plate 15). The viewer must have seen in the spoked wheel the epitome of Celtic spirituality, maintained for millennia — a oneness with the circular movement of the sun. As a Christian, the viewer must have seen that this spiritual maturity could only be reached by the sacrifice and self-denial taught by Jesus and exemplified by his going to the cross. The viewer may have known such words of Jesus as "taking up your cross and following me" or "those who would save their psyche will lose it and those who lose their psyche for Jesus, will save it." In his passion Jesus had reached the glory of the solar spoked wheel.

There is absolutely no counterpart to these scenes in Roman Christianity. After Constantine, when Christianity became the formal religion, it was possible to show Jesus on the infamous symbol of execution, the cross. Perhaps the earliest can be seen on the wooden door of S. Sabina, though even there (in the fifth century) there is not actually a cross.

Postcrucifixion Narratives

There are several scenes on Irish crosses that reflect Jesus and the Irish experience after the crucifixion scene.

Soldiers Guarding the Tomb

There are four examples of the soldiers guarding the tomb of Jesus. Jesus lies buried under a slab on which the two soldiers, the same images as those at the crucifixion, have fallen asleep. Now that Jesus has entered the spoked wheel, the soldiers are no longer a threat. On the slab sits a woman, with an identifying female hat. She has at her feet a box of spices. A Celtic-type man stands behind her. Most fascinating is the presence of a bird (dove?) that has its beak in the mouth of Jesus. The dove, like the dove above the shaft crucifix, is pulling Jesus into his state of glory. Though difficult to identify, there are at least two scenes of resurrection. In both the Monasterboice example (plate 16) and Clonmacnois, divine figures pull Jesus up from between the two soldiers guarding the tomb.

In early Christian Roman art there are no crucifixes and, appropriately, no tomb scenes. There is the Resurrection of Lazarus, but that is a healing act of Jesus. Tomb scenes first appear in Byzantine art, such as in Apollinare Nuovo, Ravenna.

The Glorified Jesus

There are two examples of Jesus in glory. They occur in the middle of the spoked wheel and at first glance appear to be crucifixions. In the Kells example, instead of soldiers with a spear, Jesus has two long poles in each hand. One ends as a cross and the other ends as a shepherd's crook. Jesus is surrounded by two fantasy animals. Above him is a man holding up a circle or boss with a lamb in it. Some critics call it the Agnus Dei. In terms of Roman art, especially early Byzantine, it does make sense that the glorified Jesus is the Lamb of God who suffered on the way to glorification. Unfortunately, lambs do not otherwise have that symbolic meaning in Irish art, so this unique example may have been borrowed from the Roman Christian world.

Judging the Spiritually Mature

The postcrucifixion Jesus can also shift into the Christ of judgment. Of the 347 scenes there are six so-called judgment portrayals. The iconography of the judgment is the same as the glorification scenes. To his right are persons coming toward him, led by a minstrel and probably David playing the harp. They have clearly reached spiritual maturation. To the left of Christ are persons leaving the center to the edge of the spoke. Clearly they have not reached spiritual maturity, so they cannot stay in the spoked wheel with Jesus. Christ holds in his hands the two staffs associated with the glory scene: one a cross and the other a ceremonial staff. Beneath this scene is a weighing or evaluation of persons to determine whether they could stay in the circle. Speaking theologically, the addition of a weighing scene to the motif of spiritual maturation seems strange. One would not expect glory to shift into judgment. Even in Roman Christian art weighing scenes were not found until well after the post-Constantine period, not before Christians had the authority to make final judgments. How did it come to Irish art? In terms of artistic iconography it could have been described by pilgrims returning to Ireland from the continent. Or it may simply be an illustration of Matthew 25. Neither possibility explains how a creation theology would be capped with a final judgment scene. Normally a creation theology, with its emphasis on the goodness of humanity, would not describe the end of life with a Dante-esque eternal damnation. It would stress achievement or failure to achieve, not condemnation. Yet the scene does indicate that some persons, deceased or not, failed to enter the joy of the spoked wheel. Since they failed to overcome the conflicts and failed to share in Christ's suffering, they failed to share in the spiritual maturity.

Noting the presence of the mature in the solar disc, a very unique cross must not be overlooked. In the circle of the Monasterboice West Cross is a glorified Jesus with both a shepherd's crook and what is seemingly a shield. Jesus would be "protecting" eleven figures who have reached spiritual maturity. Each of the eleven holds a spoked wheel/shield as a sign of reaching the sun circle.

Paul and Anthony

The end result of the Irish spiritual progression does not conclude with a meal, as in the Roman type, but with asceticism. There are eight scenes of the Temptation of Anthony and twelve of Paul and Anthony, some of which include the raven. The Irish monks stressed a severe limitation on food, clothing, and accommodations. As with the early Roman Christians they rejected any temporal show of power and wealth. The Roman Christians rejected banquets and developed a basic menu of bread, fish, and wine. Likewise, the Irish Christians rejected the lavish banquets of the chieftains. They exchanged extravagant robes for simple monastic ones. The Irish were more severe in their simplicity than the Romans. The Roman Christians celebrated their simple meals as a gift of the community, the Irish described their food as a gift, often from an unexpected, perhaps divine, source.

The symbols of this monastic way of life were twofold: Anthony being tempted to follow a more lavish way of life, and Paul and Anthony sitting together as they are fed by a raven. The Irish artisans used these scenes to describe the kind of spiritual maturity available to followers of Jesus. The ascetic experiences of Anthony would have been available to Celtic Christians through Saint Martin of Gaul (325–97). There are no historical reasons to suppose Anthony had a direct influence on Irish Christianity, but Martin and Anthony were well enough known to have been an indirect source, especially through Saint Ninian.[3]

Without being a formal influence, the Jesus tradition might well have been an indirect source for asceticism. To be sure Jesus was accused of being a glutton and a winebibber (Matt. 11:16–19). But he also urged his followers not to store up supplies but, like the lilies of the field and the birds of the air, to accept daily what God gives (Matt. 6:25–34). There is no equivalent teaching in the letters of Paul. He could speak of fasting (Rom. 14:1–4), but there is no hint of a continuing limitation to food intake.[4] So, while the Jesus tradition may have encouraged Irish Christianity to be ascetic, there is no sign of an equivalent asceticism in Paul or early Christian Roman art.

David and the Lyre/Harp

There are at least seven out of 347 examples of David and the Harp/Lyre. They tend to be in the vicinity of the spoked wheel and crucifix. David displaced/incorporated the Celtic warrior class in the formation of the Irish Christian culture. In this scene, David acts as the Celtic bard perhaps, but more important he symbolizes the musical, poetic state of Irish spiritual maturity. Most historians do assume the Celtic love of music and dance passed on into the Irish Christian culture. The rather prominent use of David playing the harp signifies this crucial element in Irish life to this day.

There is no exact equivalent to David Playing the Harp in early Roman Christian art. There are a very few instances of Orpheus playing a lyre. Orpheus sits with his musical instrument amidst several sheep. These few scenes were probably intended to represent the Good Shepherd based on Orpheus rather than on such ancient examples as those found in the Hittite culture.[5] There are extraordinarily few artistic references to music in the Roman Christian art and literature.[6] Even though music must have been integral to early Christian life, there were no bard traditions in the Roman culture that would have passed into the nascent Christian culture. Music was provided to Romans by persons who would have been seen as second-class citizens rather than leaders (bards). While early Christianity accepted everyone into their community, it would have been awkward to assimilate Roman musicians and Roman music into early Christian pictures.

Notes

1. As with the Hebrew Scriptures I have not emphasized scenes where there is only one example or if the scene cannot be clearly identified.

2. Stark, *Rise of Christianity,* 206.

3. McNeill, *The Celtic Churches,* 69–70; Bury, *Life of St. Patrick,* 273–74.

4. O'Neill, "New Testament Monasteries," 126.

5. Jensen, *Understanding Early Christian Art,* 41–44.

6. Stephen G. Wilson, "Early Christian Music," in *Common Life in the Early Church,* ed. Hills, 390–401.

Chapter 12

The Calendar and
Irish Christian Language

If we take seriously the Coligny tablet, the continental Celts followed a solar calendar with subdivisions close to the lunar cycle.[1] So each solar year was divided into six units of twenty-nine days and six units of thirty days. The coming of Christianity radically altered this calendar. How that happened, and when, is as much a question as the advent of Christian language.

Before the first century B.C.E. Rome utilized a lunar calendar. In order to make the calendar seasonal a number of intercalations were required. About 46 B.C.E. Julius Caesar asked the astronomer Sosigenes to develop a more stable system. The result was a solar calendar with twelve months that were only approximately lunar.

The early Christians appropriated the Roman solar calendar at the point of the winter solstice. While it may be true that the early fathers of the church defended the date of Jesus' birth from internal (biblical) data, still the generally assumed explanation cannot be ignored. The church redefined the winter solstice as the birthdate of Jesus rather than the birthdate of the sun god (*natalis solis invicti*).

The vernal equinox and the date of Easter are quite another matter. Some Christians insisted on celebrating the Pascha, the death of Jesus, on the day of the Passover, the fourteenth of Nisan whenever it might occur (Quartodecimians).

The Quartodecimian controversy arises from the Gospel of John where there is no Passover meal. The meal described in 13:1–30, a meal that occurs at the same time (Thursday evening) and with the same personnel as the Passover in the Synoptics, cannot be the Passover in John because, according to John's account, it was the day before the Passover (13:1). So Jesus was crucified at the same time the lambs were slaughtered for Passover meal (i.e., he was crucified on the fourteenth of Nisan). The first Christians celebrated the death of Jesus with a Pascha meal (eucharist) on the lunar date of the Jewish Passover (note 1 Cor. 5:7–8).

At first there was no annual celebration of the resurrection. Eventually, in the gentile world, the day of resurrection was added to the Pascha festival. That day was Sunday. At the Council of Nicea (325) it was ruled that Easter Sunday would be celebrated on the Sunday immediately following that full moon which came after the vernal equinox. At the same time the Council decided that the vernal equinox would be March 21 in the Julian calendar (Eusebius, *Vit. Const.* 3.18). The crucifixion of Jesus would have occurred the Friday before Easter Sunday.

Eventually the system established by the Council of Nicea, essentially a solar system, became the accepted system for the West, though for a while the East kept a form of the lunar Quartodecimian calculation. There was indeed a third system. Some Christians, like the Irish, celebrated Easter on the Sunday after the Quartodecimian date. Because the Jewish date of Nisan 14 was calculated on the basis of a lunar calendar, for the Quartodecimians Easter did not always fall on the first Sunday after the first full moon after the vernal equinox (Nicea's ruling). The Irish, at least, were using this Quartodecimian basis for their Easter Sunday celebration. They had missed the Council of Nicea, so they were unaware of the universal correction. The difference became apparent when the Irish peregrinators landed on the Continent with a date for Easter at variance with the date on the mainland. When the Roman emissaries came to Britain and then to Scotland, they were shocked to find the Irish celebrating this different date for Easter. Attempts to change their practice met with no success. Finally, at the Synod of Whitby (664), the reluctant Irish more or less gave in.[2] By the end of the seventh century most monasteries followed the system decreed at Nicea.

The issues here are critical.

1. The Irish Christian calendar was in place before the Council of Nicea in 325 C.E. The leaders of the pre-Patrick Irish Chris-

tians were unaware of a ruling that would have altered their date for Easter. While some scholars have suggested the aberrant date was taken to Ireland in the fifth or sixth century, that late date hardly accounts for such a well-established practice. And who would have carried to Ireland a calendric system that had been rejected for over a hundred years?[3] In fact, at the Synod of Whitby the Irish representatives defended themselves as Johannine Quartodecimians. Either they were wrong (since they celebrated the Sunday after the fourteenth) or Bede misrepresented the conflict.

2. The Irish leaders simply had no intention of being romanized, either before Patrick or after.

3. The Patrick attempt to bring order failed. Not only did the Irish Christians reject a hierarchical administration and a diocesan organization, but refused to accept the Roman calendar.

4. The Irish calendar did not likely come from North Africa through Spain. The Quartodecimians were primarily in Asia Minor, still somewhat attached to Jewish Christianity. So one suspects the date of the Pascha may have come to Spain and on to Ireland through the same Celtic route described here for Paul's Jesus tradition.

Despite the apparent validity of this argument for the origin of the Irish calendar, there are problems. It was normally the case that the Jewish-based lunar calendar placed in the Julian calendar would have displaced prior non-Christian celebration of the winter solstice to form Christmas and would have displaced prior non-Christian celebration of the vernal equinox to form Easter. That could not have happened in Ireland. The festival closest to Easter was Beltene on May 1. It was not a celebration of the vernal equinox. According to legend, soon after Patrick entered Ireland he engaged the royal power of King Loigaire over the fires of Beltene. Patrick won the magical battle and thereby established Easter. In this way Beltene, with its sun symbols and fires, were assimilated into the Christian calendar.[4]

Of course, that could not have happened and the Christian Easter could not have directly assimilated a Beltene festival so distant from the vernal equinox. It must be that later Irish writers wanted to say that the already intact Christian calendar absorbed the Celtic calendar. Eventually it probably did. But like the relationship of Latin and Old Irish, one must supposes the Celtic calendar existed side by side with the Christian until it was fully assimilated.

Irish Christian Language

The origins of the Celtic languages are uncertain. Equally uncertain is whether there ever was a single language that could be referred to as the language of the Celts. Celtic-language variations exist from Galatia through central Europe, Italy, and on to Gaul. At some time after 600 B.C.E. a variation of what is called goidelic or Gaelic, spoken by Celtiberians and Galicians, became the dialect of Ireland, Gaelic Scotland, and the Isle of Man. The dialect of Gaul, brythonic, became the Celtic language of Cornwall, Wales, and Brittany.[5] Before the Roman expansion Celtic inscriptions found in Gaul were written primarily in Greek alphabet.[6] Because of the proximity of the Romans, Latin had more of an impact on brythonic and hence "English" prior to the formative Anglo-Saxon.

Sometime in the pre-Patrick period Latin also entered the Irish world. The Irish Celts used lines on stones to indicate the Latin letters, cut primarily on the edge of standing slabs. Normally they marked burials or memorials. Ogham stones, as they are called, continued for a short time into the Christian period.[7] The Latin language, then, was used in Ireland before the fifth century. What happened next cannot be clearly determined. By the middle of the sixth century, Latin was the language of the monastic communities. They read Latin, spoke Latin, copied manuscripts in Latin, and wrote poetry in Latin. What they knew and copied in Latin was not simply Christian or biblical. They also used and copied classical literature, so much so that students from Great Britain and the Continent flocked to Ireland for studies. Later, when the great Irish peregrinators traversed the continent, Roman priests and scholars there were amazed at their learning. This love of learning undoubtedly came from a long Druid tradition of oral learning. In this context of oral tradition, how the shift to written Latin from oral Gaelic occurred is not clear.

It has been supposed that Patrick, raised in England and trained in Gaul, must have brought Latin to Ireland and thereby displaced goidelic. Such a presupposition seems highly unlikely. In the first place Patrick wrote and spoke poorly in Latin. He started his *Confession* with a startling statement: "I Patrick, a sinner, and the most rustic and the least of all believers." His poor (rustic) Latin has been identified as the vulgar Latin of Gaul about the fifth century.[8] In any case, there hardly seems time for Patrick to have caused what happened. The early lives and travels of Irish saints, such as Brandon, Columba, Columban, and Wilfred, were written in Latin. Even earlier than Patrick, Pelagius (ca. 350–430) wrote in learned Latin. Clonmacnois was established in 548 and soon after monks were copying biblical and classical texts in Latin. Presumably Columba himself must have copied the *Cathach* and the gospel *Book of Durrow* at the beginning of the seventh century. So by the middle of the sixth century classical Latin must have been known and used. Rustic Patrick could hardly have been the perpetrator of this explosion.

If it weren't for the time issue, it might appear that Latin entered the Irish world through more learned post-Patrick monks. But the evidence does not suggest that. The presence of the Ogham stones indicates otherwise. A minimal Latin must have been known in pre-Patrician times. Even more striking are the comments of Patrick himself. He speaks briefly of Christians in Ireland before he arrived and at least once mentions Latin scholars who criticized him. He calls them *dominicate rhetorici,* or rhetoricians who lorded it over him. The notion that there were Latin scholars in Ireland before Patrick does indeed change the perception of how the Irish Golden Age started. That is even more certain if it is assumed from the evidence that there were pre-Patrician Christian communities in which Latin scholars could have been found.

At the same time Latin did not become the predominant language for Ireland. It was used in the monasteries, but it was not the language of the people. A form of goidelic remained to create the language called Archaic Irish and then Old Irish.[9] It was used side by side with Latin. Monks copied biblical and philosophical materials in Latin. At the same time they copied in Old Irish, often for the first time, ancient Celtic legends and traditions. Such key documents as the Ulster Cycle were copied from the earlier oral traditions, with alterations, no doubt, and with occasional cynical remarks by the Christian copiers. The monks and saints lived in both linguistic worlds. For example, the parents of Columba were Fedelmid mac Ferguso and Eithne. It is likely Columba's birth name was Crimthann. His family, though of royal Celtic lineage, could have been non-Christian. In any case, both languages were operative. The Celts adapted easily to the context in which they found themselves. Throughout northern Europe there were cultural adaptations of the Celts that resulted in the formation of dialects. In Ireland there was no conflict over the intrusion of Latin; it was a case of linguistic inculturation. Without such an infusion Ireland would never have become the great center of learning and copying. Without it peregrinators could not have carried their form of the Christian faith back to the continent. However, there is another side. Fierce as the Celtic warriors may have been, and determined as the Christian peregrinators had to have been, the Irish were not imperialists. They did not force their native language or customs on other peoples.

The early Christian Roman situation was quite different. Jesus spoke in Aramaic, a dialect of Hebrew. The Jesus tradition, while still in oral form, was carried in Aramaic. Very quickly, however, the Aramaic form was translated into the koine Greek, an Attic dialect that had become nearly universal. In that form the developing Jesus tradition was understood in most of the Mediterranean world. The Jesus tradition entered the Roman world at the height of Latin literary tradition (Virgil's *Aeneid,* 29–19 B.C.E.; Livy, 59 B.C.E.– 17 C.E.; Seneca, d. 65 C.E.). Christians writing in Latin appeared first in North Africa. The early Christian defender of Christianity as he knew it, Tertullian of Carthage, was the first major "Father" to write in Latin (writing from 196–212 C.E.). He also used biblical texts in Latin. Around 180, a copy of Paul's letters in Latin must have been available. Later Cyprian, bishop of Carthage (200–257), quotes from an entire Latin Bible. Victor I (ca. 190) was likely the first Latin-speaking bishop of Rome. The great fathers from then on — Ambrose, Jerome, Augustine — expressed themselves in Latin.

Three points need to be considered. Paul may very well have known Latin, but it has to be assumed that he spoke to the Celts of Galatia in Greek. So he passed on the Jesus tradition to them in Greek, the Celts' second language. If the Jesus tradition was carried to Spain by the Galatians, they would have used a Celtic dialect other than what was spoken there (Gaelic). Still the Galatians and the Galicians could have communicated in their basic common language. However, if delegates of Paul or other representatives went to Spain, they would have by necessity spoken in Latin, not Celtic or Greek.

Latin was introduced to Spain well before the time of Jesus and was close to universal in the south, influenced by Latin-speaking North Africa. Strabo noted that Iberian was nearly extinct. Little is known about the use of Latin in the area of northwest Spain. In an area dominated by the Ius Latii, the officials of a town had to know Latin.[10] This is especially true of the northwest where needed minerals were available.[11] There were churches in Galicia by 250 and they considered themselves attached to Carthage. At least they wrote to Cyprian of Carthage to ask about the authenticity of their new bishop, Sabinus.[12] If the Galician Christians were in administrative contact with Carthage (using Latin), there is no reason to doubt they had access to the Carthaginian biblical materials in Latin.

Did Latin cross over to Ireland from Spain? That seems very likely, though, of course, unproven. Did in the latter half of the third century the Latin language, Latin biblical translations, and perhaps even the Jesus tradition from Paul cross over to Ireland at the same time? If so, it would explain many things. It would clarify how Latin and copies of the New Testament in Latin came to Ireland prior to Patrick. In such a case there would be time and opportunity, considering the high intellectual capacity of the Druids, for the scholarly monastic movement to develop. Even more, it would explain why Latin existed alongside early Irish.

Missioners coming from the Roman world had two choices when they came to a linguistically homogeneous area. They could either translate into the local language, as in the case of the Goths, or they could so impact the local language with Latin so that a new dialect was formed (ergo, Spanish, French, or Italian). Ordinarily missioners did not speak Latin — only among themselves. They either altered the local language or translated their Christian materials into the language of the people. Yet that did not happen in Ireland. There can be only one explanation. The persons who brought the Latin scriptures spoke the same language as those already converted. There was no need to translate. The meaning of this is enormous. The Irish were free to develop a Latin academia without ever becoming romanized by an outside colonizing force. The goidelic language, that is, Old Irish, remained the popular language, while the monks and associates spoke and wrote in the international language, the *lingua imperii*. If the monks had spoken only goidelic there would have been no saving of the classical literature and its return to the Continent. If the people of Ireland had shifted to a Latin dialect, they would have become romanized and Irish spirituality as it is now known never would have been realized. In other words, the Latin-speaking monks took to the world a Celtic Christianity that had been maintained and developed in a insular world untouched by Rome.

Second, the Latin Jesus tradition of Rome became the biblical, theological basis for the Holy Roman Empire. Jesus was the *filius dei* killed by Jews and other nonbelievers. As the Son of God he took his place as the mythological head of the universe (shown in apsidial art as the bearded pantocrator). Those who did not accept his reign were not welcome. In contrast, the Jesus tradition of the Irish stressed self-denial, dependence on nature, and spiritual maturation. The Irish Latin tradition never stressed the political power of Jesus. It did not seek hierarchical obedience and creedal unity. Instead it was a missionary good news — not the grace of Augustinian Christianity, to be sure, but the choice of a life pleasing to God.

Notes

1. Ellis, *Ancient World of the Celts*, 33.
2. Bede, III.25.
3. Bury comes to the same conclusion regarding the Easter cycle. The cycle of 532 years (based on the canons of Victorinus) was introduced to the Christian world in 457. The Irish were already using an eight-four-year cycle based on the equinox date of March 25. This system surely preceded the introduction of March 21 (at Nicea in 325 and then general acceptance in 343), over a hundred years before Patrick. The Irish used an Easter cycle which they refused to change until Whitby. In 604 Columbanus wrote, "plus credo traditioni patriae meae, iuxta doctrinam et calculum octoginta quatuor annorum" (*Ep.* 4, 163). See Bury, *Life of St. Patrick*, 371–74.
4. Bury, *Life of St. Patrick*, 108–13.
5. The divisions used by Donald Macaulay, *The Celtic Languages* (Cambridge: Cambridge University Press, 1992). For a summary of the connections see Glanville Price, *Ireland and the Celtic Connection* (Gerrards Cross, England: Colin Smythe, 1987), 7.
6. Ellis, *Ancient World of the Celts*, 27–30.
7. There is an excellent description of Ogham in Philip Freeman, *Ireland and the Classical World* (Austin: University of Texas Press, 2001), 12–27. Another description can be found in Damian McManus, *A Guide to Ogam* (Maynooth, Ireland: An Sagart, 1991).
8. Christine Mohrmann, *The Latin of St. Patrick: Four Lectures* (Dublin: Dublin Institute of Advanced Studies, 1961), 53.
9. Gearóid Mac Eoin, "Irish," in *The Celtic Languages*, ed. Martin J. Ball with James Fife (London: Routledge, 1993), 101–44. He dates Ogham in the fifth to seventh centuries, Archaic Irish in the seventh century, and Old Irish in the eighth and ninth centuries. See p. 102.
10. Ramsay MacMullen, *Romanization in the Time of Augustus* (New Haven: Yale University Press, 2000), 83.
11. Tranoy, *La Galice romaine*, 180, 96–99.
12. Cyprian, *Epist.*; LXVII (CSEL, III2, 735–43); see Tranoy, *La Galice romaine*, 423.

Chapter 12

Hagiography

Sources for early Christianity in Ireland are relatively meager. While sculptured art and symbols, architecture, calendar, and language have been studied here, literary sources are also available. One is the *Vitae Sancti*.[1] While the *Lives* cover saints from the fifth century to the twelfth, some are indeed relatively early.

The most famous are the stories of Brigit, Patrick, and Columba.[2] The earliest known *Vita* is that of Brigit, written by Cogitosus about 680, 105 years after her death. At approximately the same time another Brigit life appeared as *Vita Prima*. There are many legends about Patrick, but the two earliest come from Muirchú of Leinster and Tírechán of Meath (end of the seventh century). While there was likely an earlier hagiographic collection for Columba, the *Vita Columbae* was written by Adomnán, abbot of Iona from 679 to 704.[3] Other helpful *Lives* include "The Voyage of St. Brendan," who was born in Kerry about 484 and made his famous voyages between 565 and 573. Our Latin account, *Navigatio Sancti Brendani*, often translated, was likely written in the ninth century. Even so the stories seem as primitive as any of the *Vitae*. Two seventh-century northern Britain lives, the *Life of Cuthbert* by Bede and the *Life of Wilfred*,[4] are most helpful in supplementing what can be known from the Irish side.[5]

These *Lives* are filled with miracles, fantastic events, incredible voyages, and improbable historical narratives. To utilize them for an understanding of early Celtic Christianity requires considerable sifting.[6] A general word on hermeneutics would be in order here. Legendary material normally involves nonhistorical material and may use nonhuman subjects to create the story. Often the legend will explain the origin of a name, a festival, or a saying (etiological legends). A myth normally appears more historical, and indeed may be, but the action involves divine or metaphysical powers. For the purposes of this study, legendary material may reflect attitudes and practices of the culture, as rooted in its structural foundation, but does not contain historical data. Mythological material will also reflect the basic structures of the cultural, expressed in terms of otherworldly language, and may indeed involve some historical reality.

So the legendary *Vitae* are to be studied and analyzed more for what they say about the developing early Celtic Christianity than for historical data. There are several apparent intentions in the *Vita* material: first, they serve to join the Celtic world with the Jesus tradition.[7] These narratives contain reflections of the Jesus tradition: healing narratives; care for the poor; dependence on God for resources; disregard for military and political power; and suspicion of religious hierarchies. From the Celtic culture the narratives reflect an attachment to nature; a thinness between this life and the other world; events involving transmogrification; the participation of animals in the narrative; an eagerness to travel; and a lack of interest in developing empires.[8] Rejection of the Celtic tradition occurs when the narratives show the elimination of the warrior class (note David and Samson in the art); the assimilation of the Druids into Christian holy people; and the shift of honor from feasts and show of wealth to asceticism and poverty. Rejection of the Jesus tradition occurs in the lack of close community; the diminution of commensality; and a loss of concern for the end-time reign of God.

Second, the *Vitae* demonstrate the inculturation of the Jesus tradition. Some primary evidence exists for Christianity in Ireland, such as the *Confession* written by Patrick as well as his letter to Coroticus. In my opinion, the genuine letters of Pelagius should also be considered primary materials for early Irish Christianity, as in a parallel way, should be Bede's history.[9] The materials reflect the impact of the Jesus tradition. The kinds of legends and myths found in the *Vitae* are not at all confirmed by the primary sources, but they do show the inculturation of the Jesus tradition. Many *Vita* narratives show the conflict with and victory over Celtic practices. How Patrick changed Beltene (May 1) to Easter has already been discussed. Another narrative shows how Patrick changed Imbolc (February 1) to the Christian Candlemas. In all of these *Vitae* Celtic royal power is attacked and ultimate power is granted to the saintly Christian hero of the narrative. None of this appears in the primary material.

Third, and more important, the *Vitae* are political documents. They attempt to place their saint above others and put forward the primacy of their saint's location. So the lives of Patrick make him the primate of Armagh and, by their logic, the father of Irish Christianity.[10] On the other hand the writers for Brigit make her the primate of Kildare. While she might lose the battle for ultimate primacy to Patrick, she certainly became the mother of Irish Christianity. Columba, on the other hand, after founding monasteries on the mainland, crossed over to Iona (563). From that monastery Scotland was won over to Christianity. One might say Columba was the primate of the extra-Irish missions and peregrinations.[11]

The comparison of the Irish experience with the early Christian Roman results in unique insights. The first Roman saints were martyrs. Stephen could be named as the first martyr, followed by Peter, Paul, and nameless others during the Neronic persecution. The Roman martyr/saints resisted the state even to death and then after death demonstrated powers beyond normal followers of Jesus. Martyrs were honored by being placed in special tombs. At these tombs, people could be healed, prayers could be offered to and answered by the saint. Their tombs, and eventually their remains, became a great source of inspiration.

In contrast, the Irish saints were not martyrs and did not engage the state in a life-death struggle. There was no state to oppose the first monks. The Irish became saints by means of their supposed deeds, their leadership, and eventually the *Lives* that circulated about them. The Roman saints also could be ecclesiastical leaders (Ignatius, Polycarp, Cyprian), but need not be. It wasn't until the end of the third century that the bishops of Rome were treated as saints of the church with special tombs (the catacomb of Callixtus).

Nevertheless, as in Armagh and Kildare, major centers on the Continent began to promote their Christian founders and saints. Most obviously Rome claimed Peter and Paul. Venice claimed

Mark. Antioch claimed Matthew. Ephesus claimed John. Two things occurred in the Roman Christian world that parallel what happened in Ireland. The major centers or cities vied for ultimate primacy. Considerable literature was written to advocate the primacy of Peter and the Petrine succession located in Rome. The conflict started remarkably early. The Antioch-based Gospel of Matthew (chapter 16) makes Peter the rock on which the church would be built. Perhaps in response, the Gospel of John deliberately attempts to subordinate Peter to the Ephesus-based Beloved Disciple.[12] In the second century various Acts, not *Vitae*, arose around the chief apostles. These hagiographic Acts served a purpose much like the *Vitae* of Ireland. They incorporated Greco-Roman traditions such as travel, magic, miraculous healing, and control of animals. From the Jesus tradition they brought compassion, gender equality, a Jewish/Christian calendar, a disdain for authorities, lack of fear in the face of persecution and death, and the ability to make personal decisions.

Fortunately, in both Irish and Roman Christianity some literary sources can be considered primary. In early Irish Christianity are the *Confessio* of Patrick and the letter to Coroticus written about 470–80.[13] Possessing this primary material from Patrick, at least, proves that his *Vitae* are mainly legendary.[14] The *Letters of Pelagius* are also primary, but there is no *Vita* for comparison. Another primary document, Bede's *Ecclesiastical History of the English People,* was completed about 731. It deals with both English and Irish matters and is a nearly contemporary account of early Irish Christianity. Bede does recount legendary material and sides with Romano-British concerns. Since at the same time he appears to idealize the first century of Irish Christianity, it can be assumed that he seeks to convey some reliable data.

In contrast to the Irish, Roman Christians do not possess many primary documents. There are no primary documents from Jesus — or even related documents contemporary with Jesus. While the Gospels may well carry authentic oral traditions, they still are community composites, not primary evidence.[15] Regarding other "saints," the Gospel of Matthew, with its Petrine interest, gives basic information about the relationship of the Apostle Peter to

Jesus. It does not correlate with the letter of 1 Peter, nor is there any reason to suppose 1 Peter is a primary source. The same is true of the Gospel of John. The author elevates the Beloved Disciple above Peter, but there is no primary document available about this supposed John, unless one wishes to consider the three letters of John primary documents for the Beloved Disciple.[16]

The closest to Patrick's primary documents would be Paul's seven authentic letters. In addition to these letters, Acts contains a hagiography of Paul. Like the *Confessio* of Patrick and his *Vitae*, the letters of Paul and the hagiographies (Acts, Acts of Paul) often do not describe the same events in the same way. So even now it is not possible to establish the historical veracity of the Book of Acts.

Like the *Vitae* of Columba and Brigit, there is no way to check the historicity of the hagiographies in the Apocryphal Acts (Acts of Peter, Acts of Paul, Acts of John). Only structural realities can be discerned: women play an important role; there is conflict with authorities; individuals are urged to become disciples regardless of family bonds; major figures compete with non-Christian magician/ healers for popular approval; major figures are compassionate; and their message is based on biblical (especially Jesus) traditions.

In the Apocrypha Acts there are few wholesale adaptations of Greco-Roman heroes. Nevertheless, the heroes of the Apocryphal Acts are New Testament heroes who might act in ways understood by the Greco-Roman culture. They were courageous even to death; they were visionary; they acted on the basis of a stated purpose; and they were competitive. In contrast to the Roman Christian Acts, a few of the Irish saints seem like wholesale adaptations of Celtic heroes. The popular and early "Voyage of St. Brendan" appears to be a Christianized form of *Immram Brain, The Voyage of Bran.* Bran responds to a call heard in music and is directed on the voyage by an otherworldly woman. The fantasy voyage of the Celtic hero has him meet Manannán, who is driving a chariot. In fact, Bran himself is rowing above a primeval forest (possibly the garden of Eden). Like the later Brendan, Bran and his companions find remarkable Islands — one of Joy, one of Women, and one of Birds.[17] Of course, the voyage of Brendan has a more Christian purpose, *peregrinari pro Christi,* and the islands sit somewhere between the created world and the paradise of the otherworld. Brendan may have been a historical figure, but then he may be a Christianized Celtic Bran. In any case the *Vitae* gives some basic structures in early Irish Christianity: peregrination, thin places between this world and the other, and submissive piety.

Notes

1. John O'Hanlon, *Lives of Irish Saints* (Dublin: James Duffy, 1875–1903).
2. The various *Vitae* are easily accessible in Davies, ed. and trans., *Celtic Spirituality*, 122–39. The Muirchu life of Patrick, 91–117; the Cogitosus life of Brigit, 122–39; the Irish life of Brigit, 140–54; and the Voyage of Brendan, 155–90.
3. Adomnán of Iona, *Life of St. Columba*.
4. Found in the Penguin edition, *Lives of the Saints,* trans. Webb. For a fine description and evaluation of materials written about Celtic Christianity see Ian Bradley, *Celtic Christianity: Making Myths and Chasing Dreams* (Edinburgh: Edinburgh University Press, 1999). Especially helpful for the earliest material is the chapter on 664–800 (1–38). Regarding a critique of Columba see Máire Herbert, "The Legacy of Colum Cille and His Monastic Community," in *The Cultures of Europe: The Irish Contribution,* ed. James P. Mackey (Belfast: Institute of Irish Studies, 1994), 9–20.
5. Kim McCone, "An Introduction to Early Irish Saints' Lives," *Maynooth Review* 11 (1986): 26–59.
6. Felim Ó Briain, "Irish Hagiography: Historiography and Method," in *Measgra I Gcuimhne Mhichil Ui Chleirigh,* ed. Sylvester O'Brien (Dublin: Assisi Press, 1944), 119–31.
7. Iain Zaczek, *Book of Irish Legends* (Chicago: Contemporary Books, 1998), 120.
8. Thomas Charles-Edwards, "The Social Background to Irish Peregrinatio," *Studia Celtica* 11 (1976): 43–59.
9. Hanson, *Life and Writings of the Historical Saint Patrick;* B. R. Rees, *Pelagius: Life and Letters* (Woodbridge: Boydell Press, 1998).
10. Liam de Paor, "The Aggrandisement of Armagh," *Historical Studies* 8 (1971): 95–110. Kathleen Hughes dates the rise of Armagh and hierarchical organization in the seventh to the ninth centuries; see her *The Church in Early Irish Society* (London: Methuen, 1980), 111–20.
11. E. J. Bowen, "The Cult of Saint Brigit," *Studia Celtic* 8 (1973): 33–47; de Paor, "Aggrandisement of Armagh," 100–101; Marjorie O. Anderson, "Columba and Other Irish Saints in Ireland," *Historical Studies* 5 (1965): 26–36; Byrne, "The Ireland of St. Columba," 37–58.
12. Graydon F. Snyder, "John 13:16 and the Anti-Petrinism of the Johannine Tradition," *Biblical Research* 16 (1971): 1–11.
13. Liam de Paor, *St. Patrick's World* (Dublin: Four Courts Press, 1993). The Latin of the *Confessio* and the *Epistola ad milites Corotici* are to be found in Máire

B. de Paor, ed. and trans., *Patrick the Pilgrim, Apostle of Ireland: St. Patrick's Confessio and Epistola* (Dublin: Veritas Publications, 1998), 220–65, 280–93. She introduces the two documents with extensive commentary. Hanson also offers a scholarly commentary with his edition, *Life and Writings of the Historical Saint Patrick*, 57–121. A more popular rendering of the two documents can be found in *Celtic Spirituality*, ed. Davies, 67–89.

14. Bury, *Life of St. Patrick.*

15. Some early fathers did not rest easy with the absence of a primary document from Jesus. Origen (*Contra Celsum* I:45), Jerome (*Commentarius in Ezechielem* XLIV.29–30, and Augustine (*De Consensu Evangelistarium* I.7.11–12).

16. Snyder, "John 13:16 and the Anti-Petrinism of the Johannine Tradition."

17. Mac Mathúna, *Immram Brain*; A. G. van Hamel, ed., *Immrama* (Dublin: The Stationery Office, 1941).

Chapter 14

Gender and Sexuality

Interpreting culture by means of art, architecture, language, and calendar will challenge the imagination of any historian who normally interprets texts, but the interpreter needs to determine how these data correspond with or alter written documentation. The issue of gender brings yet another set of problems. In Celtic and Irish literature sexuality is seldom addressed directly, and while there may be artifact data in art and language, the mass of evidence derives from indirect allusions known from narratives and legends.

Certainly most of what is known about the volatile world of Celtic sexuality and gender comes from the ancient legends.[1] Some data come from exterior sources such as Roman material. Early Christian information comes from material such as the lives of the saints and annals, all written well after the first years of Christianity in Ireland.

The Romans recorded very strong impressions of Celtic women. They have left the impression that the Celtic women were Amazon-like: independent, promiscuous, and much to be feared. The Romans had a prejudiced view of the Celts because they considered them to be nonliterary and disorganized, though fierce in battle and strange in appearance. There is no particular reason to regard the Roman view of Celtic women as truthful. Diodorus Siculus wrote, "The women of the Gauls are not only like men in their great stature but they are a match of them in courage as well" (5.32). Cassius Dio said of Boudica, "In stature she was very tall, in appearance most terrifying, in the glance of her eye most fierce, and her voice was harsh" (62.2).

However unreliable the Romans' account might be, the Celtic oral traditions leave the impression that some women were as powerful as the men, primarily evidenced in the mythological material. The line between otherworldly beings and humans is not at all clear. Many of the women in the Celtic narratives, whether goddesses or not, had extraordinary powers. Aiofe, third wife of Lir, feared his affection had been estranged because of the two sets of twins borne by her sister, the second wife. So she cursed the children and turned them into swans for 600 years. As told by the monks who wrote it down, the four children were released from the curse by the coming of Patrick to Ireland (actually Saint Kennoch). Or the famous Cattle Raid of Cooley began as a contest of power and wit between Medb, queen of Connacht, and King Ailill. When Medb learned that Dáire owned a Brown Bull twice as powerful as the White-Horned Bull owned by Ailill, she offered cattle, land, a chariot, and her intimate friendship to Dáire for his animal. He could hardly refuse.

A mysterious woman silently entered the home of Crunniuc in Ulster. When at the Ulster races Crunniuc ill-advisedly exclaimed that his wife could outrun the horses, they forced Macha to come to the race and compete with the horses. Being eight months pregnant she pled for mercy. To save the life of her husband she ran the race and won. The effort was so great she gave birth prematurely to twins. In her agony she placed a curse on the Ulster men that whenever their enemies closed in on them they would then feel the same birth pangs a woman would have.

The bridge between the Celtic mythological world and early Christianity lies primarily on Brigid, the goddess who apparently assimilated features associated with Minerva, Mercury, and Vulcan.[2] That collection of attributes made her the goddess of those technical, artistic skills so treasured by the Irish. According to the legends she was the daughter of Dagda, and had two sisters by the same name. This Triple Goddess (threesomes were often found in Celtic gods and goddesses) was responsible not only for technical skills and domestic arts, but also healing, poetry, and fertility. Brigid was often symbolized by cows (the milk of life) or by serpents (the symbol of fertility). Her feast day was Imbolc, February 1, the beginning of new life.

The shift from the goddess Brigid to Saint Brigit has to be one of, if not the, most important shifts from pre-Christian Ireland to early Irish Christianity. Patrick and Columba were legendary saints, but they were not gods. Saint Brigit picked up the myth of Brigid and as such carried with her some of the finest elements of the Celtic world. While Patrick and Columba were surely historical figures, there is less certainty about Saint Brigit. To be sure, her *Vitae* contain many otherworldly elements, like hanging a cloak on a sunbeam, but the *Vitae* of the other saints also tell of otherworldly powers. The important thing is that with the coming of Christianity the Celtic gods died out. Brigid, historicized in the life of Saint Brigit, continued those Celtic attributes that have proved so lasting in the Irish culture. It would appear that the advent of the Jesus tradition terminated those divinities that were antithetical to the new faith. It supported those divinities that were not antithetical. The goddess Brigid is the primary, perhaps the only, survivor.

The Jesus revolution brought an end to warrior ferocity. The *Vitae* of the saints contain no sign of the warrior mentality, revenge, meanness, and quarreling found in the mythological materials. The Jesus tradition, with its rejection of violence, filtered out Celtic ferocity. How did that happen? Were the missioners so powerful they could convert an entire people to another way of life? It seems unlikely. But they could buttress those gods and goddesses whose attributes better matched the Jesus tradition. The triune Brigid did that. Saint Brigit, who may have died about 525 near Kildare, took over the attributes of compassion, healing, poetry, art, and social structure.[3] Even until today these are important characteristics of Irish culture. This is not to say that fighting departed from the Irish soil. Surely there continued to be quarrels among the tuath. But the *Vitae* and the traditions do not reflect Irish ferocity. Tenacity, yes, ferocity, no.

The role of women in Celtic society surely impacted the role of goddesses in the mythology. The women of the myths and legends were not submissive and subordinate to the men. Caesar himself said:

> The men, after due reckoning, take from their own goods a
> sum of money equal to the dowry they have received from

their wives and place it with the dowry. Of each sum account is kept between them and the profits saved; whichever of the two survives receives the portion of both together with the profits of past years. (*Gallic War* 6.19)

Caesar does not at all insinuate that the Celts maintained a matriarchal society. He does say that rights of inheritance could pass to the wife and then to the family through her. There is a hint of a matrilinear structure in these words.[4] Surely women played a significant role. But like most societies where considerable military power is exercised, the Celtic world was patriarchal. The Jesus tradition, as it arrived in Ireland, would have called for more gender equality.[5] Paul's own message to the Celts in Asia Minor would have insisted on dropping destructive distinctions (Gal. 3:28). Given the differences between Celtic and Roman societies, the advent of the Jesus tradition probably did not alter gender in Irish Celtic society as much as it did in the Roman. Even so, among the monastic types there was a sense of gender acceptance. To be sure the *Vitae* portray the monks as celibate, but under the name of Saint Brigit there were also female communities. Her major location was Kildare, where there had been a cult center for Brigid. Her nuns were not at all submissive. They vied with the followers of Patrick for control of Ireland. One of their legends tells of Brendan wanting to meet Saint Brigit. When he found her he offered to hear her confession. She replied that she would prefer to hear his first.[6] Later, it is true, some rather strict rules about sexual encounters developed, but at first men and women both took holy orders, even in the same community. Clerics were not celibate until the twelfth century. Indeed, one of the major complaints about eighth-century church communities was that the office of abbot was inherited by the offspring of the abbot.

The equivalent of Saint Brigit in Roman Christianity was Mary, the mother of Jesus. Unlike Brigit, she may not have had a counterpart in Jewish life. At best it might be Miriam, the sister of Moses (Exod. 15:20–21). According to Luke she did submit to the will of God (Luke 1:38), but she saw in her promised child one who would show mercy, bring down the powerful, feed the hungry, and send away the rich empty (Luke 1:46–55). According to Matthew, Mary had the courage to withstand loss of a betrothed and endure public scandal for having an illegitimate child (Matt. 1:18–19); fearing for the life of Jesus she escaped Bethlehem, and the powerful Herod, by traveling to Egypt (Matt. 1:13–18). Despite the danger, she stayed by Jesus until the end (John 19:25–27). She had met with the community of disciples often enough that she was present with them in an upper room after the ascension (Acts 1:14). There was very little expansion of the Mary image during the pre-Constantinian period, unless one would take the image of the woman clothed with the sun as a mythological counterpart (Rev. 12:1–6). By the third century pictorial representations of Mary and the child began to appear. The iconography of Mary was likely that of Isis and the baby Horus, that is, a standard mythological mother and child. Sometimes the wise men were magi who were giving obeisance to the new master of the Sun. Perhaps due to the increasing Christian encroachment on the birthdate of the sun (winter solstice), Mary played more of a key figure. By the end of the fourth century she was known as the Mother of God (*Theotokos*), as seen in the apse of Maria Maggiore in Rome. According to popular piety Mary was the human entrée to divine power. Over the centuries she gave courage to women who were oppressed.

The Jesus tradition broadened gender equality in the Jewish context. The same was true in the Roman context. Women participated in community worship and meetings. Women held offices and acted as ministers. Women were martyred for their faith and were considered saints.[7] As the church moved more toward a public faith, the leadership of the church became limited to males. In the fourth century attempts surfaced to make the leadership exclusively male celibates, but that did not succeed until the end of the first millennium. The cause for celibacy was much the same as that in Ireland. Without celibacy the land and buildings of the church could have passed to heirs of the leadership rather than revert back to the church.

There was a steady, though not always successful, romanization of the Irish church. Around the twelfth century Irish Christianity began to look more Roman. Saint Brigit then began to appear as the Virgin Mary, but she has never been eliminated from Irish devotion.

Notes

1. Miranda J. Green, *Celtic Goddesses: Warriors, Virgins, and Mothers* (New York: G. Braziller, 1996).

2. According to Caesar, *Gallic Wars*. See MacCana, *Celtic Mythology*, 23, 34–35.

3. D. Ó Cathasaigh, "The Cult of Brigid: A Study of Pagan-Christian Syncretism," in *Mother Worship*, ed. James L. Preston (Chapel Hill: University of North Carolina Press, 1982), 92. Paul Grosjean, "Notes d'Hagiographie Celtique, 4. Une Invocation des Saintes Brigides," *Analecta Bollandiana* 61 (1943): 103–5.

4. Laurence Ginnell, *The Brehon Laws: A Legal Handbook* (London: T. Fisher Unwin, 1894), 211–14. *Ancient Laws of Ireland* [*Senchus Mor*] (Dublin: Alexander Thom, 1869), 2:363–75; Josef Weisweiler, "Die Stellung der Frau bei den Kelten und das Problem des Keltischen Mutter-rechts," *Zeitschrift für Celtische Philologie* 21, no. 2 (1939): 205–79.

5. Kathleen Hughes is of the opinion the Jesus tradition did liberalize gender roles in early Irish Christianity. On the other hand Gearóid Mac Niocaill argues that eventually the Irish legal structure made the Christian ethos more rigid. Both are likely correct. The early Jesus inculturation liberalized the Celtic culture, but, as in Roman Christianity, eventually social and legal structures reversed the initial impact of the Jesus tradition. See Gearóid Mac Niocaill, "Christian Influence in Early Irish Law," in *Irland und Europa*, ed. Próinseás Ní Chatháin and Michel Richter (Stuttgart: Klett-Cotta, 1984), 156, and Hughes, *The Church in Early Irish Society*, 176–77.

6. Mary Condren, *The Serpent and the Goddess: Women, Religion, and Power in Celtic Ireland* (San Francisco: Harper and Row, 1989), 75.

7. Snyder, *Inculturation of the Jesus Tradition*, 175–88.

Chapter 15

Commensality

There is no reason to suppose the first Christians in Ireland lacked for food. The many hunting scenes on the crosses indicate that hunting was a successful venture as well as a pleasurable sport. Archaeological research has discovered the bones of domestic animals, such as oxen, pigs and sheep, in food-refuse pits, as well as the wild animals that would have been caught in the hunt: deer, otter, badger, rabbit, and fox. A poem from the twelfth century lauds a place for its good hunting:

> Your trout out from your banks
> Your wild swine in your wilderness
> The stags of your cliff fine for hunting
> Your dappled red-breasted fawns.[1]

From the data available — archaeology, literature, and poetry — one must conclude that the staple of early Celtic Ireland consisted of a variety of dairy products. In another twelfth-century poem a poet makes fun of the genealogy of an abbot:

Son of mead, son of juice, son of lard,
Son of stirabout, son of pottage, son of fair radiant fruit,
Son of smooth, clustering cream, son of buttermilk, son of
    curds,
Son of beer, glory of liquors, son of pleasant braggart,
Son of twisted leek, son of bacon, son of butter,
Son of full-fat sausage.

Though a late parody, it gives some idea of the food available in Ireland, especially the variety of dairy products.

The ascetic nature of monastic Christianity in Ireland stands in obvious contrast to the food available, which raises two serious issues. First, what is the origin or cause of the asceticism? The *Vitae* indicate the monks ate little, eschewed socializing, and remained celibate. The *Vitae* often describe the saintly monks as hermits. It is hard to believe they existed on a starvation diet, but they probably lived more off the fruit of the immediate land than off prepared or cooked foods. Another poem from the ninth century describes the food:

> Produce of mountain ash, black sloes from a dark blackthorn, berry food bare fruits of a base...
> A clutch of eggs, honey, mast and heath-pease (sent by God), sweet apples, red cranberries, whortleberries.
> Beer and herbs, a patch of strawberries (good to taste in their plenty), haws, yew-berries, nut kernels.
> A cup of excellent hazel mead, swiftly served; Brown acorns, manes of bramble with good blackberries.

Asceticism was not a Celtic value. Perhaps early Irish asceticism derived from some element of the Celtic world that had been buttressed by the Jesus tradition. Unfortunately that cannot be true. There was no Jewish ascetic tradition for the Jesus material to borrow and there was too little ascetic flavor in the Jesus tradition to promote a thoroughgoing monastic life. To be sure, the Jesus tradition recommended that the disciples not worry about tomorrow and depend on God. But otherwise Jesus ate meals, attended banquets, and occasionally danced when the piper played.

Most historians assume an exogenous rather than endogenous influence. Generally it is supposed eastern asceticism, like that of Symeon Stylites, somehow infiltrated Irish Christianity. The impact of Martin of Tours seems even more likely. Bury recalls the legend that Patrick studied in Gaul where Martin was popular. Subsequently Patrick would have brought asceticism with him to Ireland.[2] These theories face the same problem as the introduction of Latin and theological language. Patrick does not seem like a carrier of asceticism. It seems more likely that Palladius and Patrick were sent to take control of a form of Christianity already out of

step with Rome. One of those non-Roman elements would have
been an eremitic lifestyle. Furthermore the middle of the fifth century seems late to start a movement that was in full bloom by the
end of the century.

Early Christian asceticism was not inherent in the Jesus tradition. Ascetic elements in the tradition began as a protest to the
Roman lifestyle. It is very difficult to determine when this happened. In the Gospels Jesus appears to be celibate, though there
are cogent reasons to argue that he must have been married.[3] For a
Jewish man age thirty or more not to be married would surely have
been unusual enough to attract some notice in the tradition. Lack
of any comment almost certainly points to what was the normal
custom. To be sure, it is possible Jesus took on a type of voca-
tional celibacy based on some unknown relationship to the Qumran
community.[4]

When Constantine made Christianity the accepted religion of
the Roman Empire, the general population continued as pagan
Romans but with a new divinity. The Christian community made
serious and successful attacks on opulent displays of wealth and
extravagant meals. The church meal (Agape) consisted primarily
of fish and bread, the menu of the lower classes. Despite the suc-
cesses, after Constantine practice of the Christian faith split. Put in
terms of Ernst Troeltsch, the radical love ethic went into the monastic movement (sect), while the population as a whole adapted the
institutional form of the church.[5] Such a division may be too simplistic, but some such pattern must have emerged. Monks, acting
either as individuals (anchoritic monasticism) or living in communities (cenobitic monasticism), replaced the martyrs as saints.
Monks were the ones who were willing to deny the pleasures of
this life (food, clothing, sexuality) in order to follow Jesus. Egypt is
normally considered the place of origin for the ascetic movement.
Indeed, the beginnings there almost coincide with the formation of
Christianity as a state religion. Anthony, made famous by Athanasius' *Life of Anthony*, must have lived between 251 and 356. Others
in Egypt would include Ammun, who died about 350; Macarius the
Great, from about 300 to 390; and Pachomius, who lived about
292–346. In Syria Symeon Stylites, who dwelt on his famous col-

umn, lived from 388 to 459. Further west, Martin of Tours, who founded the monastery at Marmoutier, lived about 316–97. In other words, while Egyptian asceticism may be the earliest, there would be no reason to suppose it started after it was copied in other Christian regions. Monasticism was an endogenous reaction of some persons to the Constantinian formation of Christianity as a national religion.

The early Irish Christians may not have specifically borrowed or copied monasticism from some other part of the Christian world. There is no obvious point of contact between the ascetic world and pre-Patrician Ireland. Of course, there might be other routes. Monasticism might have crossed from Gaul to Britain and on to Ireland. Britain would simply have been a pipeline, in such a case.

Far more important is the nature of early Irish monasticism. While all continental monasticism may have been a subtle, or even apparent, form of discontinuity with the Roman world, for the most part it also occurred as a denigration of the natural world. In other words, it had a tinge of Gnosticism, Docetism, even of Manicheeism. The object of asceticism was to deny the natural, control the natural, suppress the natural, or do penance for the natural. That could not be true for the Atlantic Celts, or, at least, for the early Irish Christians. The Celtic world had a love and enjoyment of nature. The boundary between nature and human was quite thin. It would be highly unlikely that Celtic Christians, coming from a naturalistic Celtic heritage, would have altered that centuries-old tradition.

Asceticism in Ireland most likely started as nondualistic. At about the same time the monastic movement started on the Continent, there arose in Ireland a theologian by the name of Pelagius (about 350–425). His life and theology will be featured in a later chapter, but now the focus is on his major conflict with Rome and Augustine, exactly at the issue of dualism. Pelagius believed in the goodness of creation and the sinlessness of the newborn child. There was no need to escape this evil world (Manicheeism) or any need for grace (baptism) to save the newborn child. Instead, for Pelagius, the Christian would live a life pleasing to God. That life did not involve the consumption of lavish foods, extravagance, or time wasted on sexual dalliance. The good life would be a natural life, often alone with God.

Irish asceticism, then, was not necessarily exogenous. It actually had little in common with Mediterranean asceticism. In early Irish history there was no nation-state that adopted Christianity. There was no need for a "dedicated small group" to carry on the vision of the first Christians over against an institutionalized church. Furthermore, when asceticism did appear, it promoted the natural as the good life. Irish monasticism had no real counterpart in the history of the Christian church.

In regard to commensality another problem appears. The monastic communities had meals. The monks of all orders ate some type of food. Why is so little mentioned about their meals? Why are not meals together seen as building community? What happened to the Agape meal? I have shown elsewhere that the early Christians ate the Agape as a meal of community formation.[6] The Agape was normally, though not always, attached to the Eucharist. Sometime by the beginning of the third century the Agape, enhanced by the Greco-Roman meal for the dead, notably special dead, shifted to a refrigerium for the dead and their family. Martyrs were buried in special places where larger celebrations could be held. Eventually the refrigerium was joined with the ecclesiastical Eucharist (fifth century). From that time on the Agape/refrigerium was essentially contained in the Roman mass.

No such development can be seen in Ireland. There is no community-forming meal. There is no celebrative meal for the dead. Meals did not perform a community-building function in the Celtic world. So even though the Jesus tradition would have enhanced communal meals, as it did in the Roman tradition, that didn't occur in Ireland. The issue is theological. The goal of Roman Christians was community. The goal of Irish Christians was spiritual maturity. The Roman Christians progressed as a community that enhanced its members and infiltrated the Roman world. The Irish Christians were individuals who overcame conflicts and arrived with Jesus in the sun circle. The Irish enjoyed nature. They affirmed life. They sought unity with Jesus. They did not find that unity in family or church. So they appear to us to be ascetic.

While some of the earliest extant Latin eucharistic prayers can be found in the *Vitae,* celebrating the suffering of Christ still remains at issue. The Irish didn't use much wine. Actually Columba had to change water into wine in order to have the Eucharist.[7] The ubiquitous mead and beer gives one the sense that joyful spiritual maturity was more important than celebrating the spilled blood of Jesus.

In regard to commensality, perhaps the development of hagiography is misleading. The transmitters of the *Vitae* wanted readers to know that the saints were clairvoyant and prophetic, workers of miracles, living a thin line between this world and the otherworld, travelers, ascetics, or even hermits. These characteristics have been highly exaggerated in order to type the person as a saint. Presumably asceticism has also been highly exaggerated. Nevertheless Pelagius, though a large man, was described by his opponents as an ascetic. Likewise the Irish monks who traveled to the continent were known as stern ascetics.[8] A few Irish Christians, some of those who were associated with monasteries, did indeed live a life with strict disciplines regarding food, but it was not a lifestyle generally practiced in Ireland.

Notes

1. Jackson, *A Celtic Miscellany* (London: Routledge and Kegan Paul, 1967), 136; de Paor and de Paor, *Early Christian Ireland,* 89.

2. Bury, *Life of St. Patrick,* 273–74.

3. William E. Phipps, *Was Jesus Married? The Distortion of Sexuality in the Christian Tradition* (New York: Harper and Row, 1973), 61–70.

4. Meier, *A Marginal Jew,* 1:332–45.

5. Ernst Troeltsch, *The Social Teaching of the Christian Churches,* vol. 1, trans. Olive Wyon (New York: Macmillan, 1931), 162.

6. Snyder, *Inculturation of the Jesus Tradition,* 156–57.

7. *Life of St Columba,* I.1.

8. Tomás Ó Fiaich, "Irish Monks on the Continent," in *An Introduction to Celtic Christianity,* ed. James P. Mackey (Edinburgh: T. & T. Clark, 1989), 108–10.

Chapter 16

Theology

The Jesus tradition, while still in an oral form, first came to the Celts when Paul preached to them in Galatia. That tradition was carried orally, in goidelic, to Ireland through the Celts of Spain. Other elements of the new faith may also have passed through the Iberian pipeline, but strictly Pauline elements, such as apocalypticism and eschatology, seem not to have influenced Irish Christianity. By the mid-third century, written sections of the New Testament were available in Latin from Africa to the Galician Celtic Christians, and therefore also to Irish Christians. Sometime around the beginning of the fourth century, complete Latin texts were available in Ireland, where certain learned Christians began to use them and perhaps even copy them. By the end of the fourth century, knowledge of Latin and the New Testament was sufficient to train biblical and theological scholars. In such a milieu arose at least one great scholar — Pelagius.

Pelagius

Pelagius, so often called by some form or another Pelagius Britto, must have been born in a Celtic area about 350 or 360. I would prefer to agree with Zimmer that he was born and raised in Ireland. Jerome, who called him many names, referred to him as Scotus.[1] Failing to make Ireland his birthplace, at least something in the area of Wales is likely. In any case he was Celtic; he was extraordinarily popular in Ireland; and he expresses admirably the theology that is associated with Irish thought. He was well trained in Latin and apparently in biblical studies. Around 380 Pelagius went to Rome to study law but soon shifted his interests to theology and the church. He became immensely popular. His adversary, Jerome, speaks of him as one made stupid and stout by Irish porridge (*stolidissimus et Scottorum pultibus praegravatus*). Apparently he was large, strong, and stout. In any case, many were eager to hear him. It needs to be noted that he dealt equally well with men and women. Jerome, himself something of a misogynist, referred to the women as Pelagius's Amazons.[2]

Pelagius wrote as well as taught, as evident by his Commentary on the Epistles of Paul and eighteen letters or fragments thereof.[3] Though Jerome often attacked Pelagius with ridiculous epithets, it is difficult to see why the great biblical scholar was so incensed. The real conflict for Pelagius came not with Jerome but with Augustine of Hippo. Most agree that it started when Pelagius heard someone (possibly Paulinus of Nola) quote a well-known sentence from Augustine's *Confessions* (Book 10): *da mihi quod iubes, et iube qoud vis* [give me what you command, and command what you will]. Pelagius was deeply offended, even angry, at this apparent denial of free will. In his commentary on the Pauline epistles, written while in Rome, Pelagius made clear his positions on human nature, free will, and grace.

In 409 Pelagius left Rome for Syria, where he wrote various letters, many of which addressed the debate with Augustine. The central issue was *impeccantia* or sinlessness. Pelagius denied the doctrine of original sin. He argued it was possible to make choices that would leave one sinless (though that was not likely to happen). God's grace was manifest in creating us with the possibility to choose the good. Augustine, on the other hand, insisted on human sinfulness from birth. God's grace gave men and women the opportunity to live in righteousness, even though born in sin. In the heat of the debate Augustine had to reject free will by asserting the omniscience and even omnipotence of God. Though Augustine denied it, it was, and is, difficult to see how divine omniscience can leave any freedom of choice for humans. God knows what will happen and has the power to confirm it. Eventually Pelagianism was rejected as heresy (418) and Augustine's doctrine of grace became the basic theology of Western Christianity.

The struggle between Pelagius and Augustine has been thoroughly researched, so it need not be repeated here.[4] The important

issues are: What was the relationship of Pelagius's theology to the
Celtic tradition? And why was Pelagius so popular in Ireland? In
the letters of Pelagius it is easy to discern why he was popular in
the Celtic world, and why his theology was not acceptable to Au-
gustinians. His letter to Demetrias is an excellent resource.[5] In it he
advises a young wealthy Roman girl (fourteen years of age) about
her decision to take vows as a virgin. Some theological elements
commensurate with a Celtic tradition would be:

Goodness of creation

> First then you ought to measure the good of human nature
> by reference to its creator, I mean God, of course: if it is he
> who, as report goes, has made all the works of and within the
> world good, how much more excellent do you suppose that he
> has made man himself, on whose account he has clearly made
> everything else. (Dem. 2,2)

Born without sin

> And before actually making man, he determines to fashion
> him in his own image and likeness and shows what kind of
> creature he intends to make him. (Dem. 2,2)

> And God created man in his own image and likeness (Gen.
> 1.27). And justifiably so, for God had created him free from
> corruption. (On Chastity 3,5)

Sin as habit

> Nor is there any reason why it is made difficult for us to do
> good other than that long habit of doing wrong which has
> infected us from childhood and corrupted us little by little
> over many years. (Dem. 8,3)

Freedom of will

> It was because God wished to bestow on the rational creature
> the gift of doing good of his own free will and the capacity
> to exercise free choice, by implanting in man the possibility of
> choosing either alternative, that he made it his peculiar right

to be what he wanted to be, so that with his capacity for good and evil he could do either quite naturally and then bend his will in the other direction too. (Dem. 3,2)

Nor would there be any virtue at all in the good done by the man who perseveres, if he could not at any time cross over to the path of evil. (Dem. 3,1)

Moral and just behavior

There is, I maintain, a sort of natural sanctity in our minds which, presiding as it were in the mind's citadel, administers judgement equally on the evil and the good and, just as it favours honorable and upright actions, so too condemns wrong deeds and, on the evidence of conscience, distinguishes the one side from the other. (Dem. 4,2)

Spiritual maturity

She [Demetrias] wants her conduct to become no less an object of wonder than her conversion has been: already noble in this world, she desires to be even nobler before God and seeks in her moral conduct values as precious as the objects which she spurned in this world. What outpouring of talent will even satisfy a mind so enthusiastic and dedicated, so thirsty for a high degree of perfection? (Dem. 1,2)

Waiting the Spirit

But the path that you [Demetrias] have to tread is far different, you who have trampled under foot the love of this world and, by always considering the things which are of God, wish to show yourself a virgin of the apostles, you who await the Lord's coming as holy in spirit as you are in body and, continually pouring the oil of holy works into the lamp of your soul, are prepared to meet the bridegroom in the company of wise virgins. (Dem. 10,3)

The letters underscore some differences between Pelagius and his Celtic background. For example, there is no trace of Celtic religious ceremonies (calendar) in the extant works of Pelagius. Nor is there any reason to suppose that the moral goals of the Druids included asceticism. Yet it stands to reason that if Pelagius was raised and educated in Celtic Ireland or even Wales, then he would share some of the tradition of the Celtic world. While there is no direct connection between Pelagius and the theological environment in which he was raised, how could it have been otherwise? Some similarities are self-evident: the Celts were not dualistic; they loved nature; error (sin) was not caused by opposing evil sources; the goal of life was increased·spiritual maturity; the line between this world and the other world was very thin. The critics are correct: Pelagius differed from Augustine and Jerome because he came from the Celtic tradition rather than the Greco-Roman. Furthermore, Pelagius had much in common with the Jesus tradition. In "On the Christian Life" he writes:

> How can you then be called a Christian, if there is no Christian act in you? Christian is the name for righteousness, goodness, integrity, forbearance, chastity, prudence, humility, kindness, blamelessness, godliness. How can you defend and appropriate that name, when not even a few of these many qualities abide in you? He is a Christian who is one not only in name but in deed, who imitates and follows Christ in everything, who is holy, guiltless, undefiled, unstained, in whose breast malice has no place, in whose breast only godliness and goodness reside, who does not know how to hurt or harm anyone, but only how to help everyone. He is a Christian who does not know how to hate even his enemies but rather to do good to his adversaries and pray for his persecutors and enemies, following Christ's example; for anyone who is ready to hurt and harm someone else lies when he declares he is a Christian. The Christian is one who is able to make the following claim with justification: I have harmed no man, I have lived righteously with all. (6,2)

To be sure, some of these "qualities" or virtues could have derived from philosophical ethics, especially Stoic, and virtues in general do not match the Jewish/Jesus perception of ethics as attitudes deriving from the total psyche. Whether or not his virtues are specifically

Christian, he does base them on the imitation of Jesus as seen in the Jesus tradition:

> He called the crowd with his disciples, and said to them, "If any want to become my followers, let them deny themselves and take up their cross and follow me." (Mark 8:34)

Humility would be another apparent attitude based on the Jesus tradition:

> For those who want to save their life will lose it, and those who lose their life for my sake, and for the sake of the gospel, will save it. For what will it profit them to gain the whole world and forfeit their life? (Mark 8:35–36)

Most of the characteristics of Pelagian theology can be seen in the Jesus tradition. Nature is good. Jesus denied the kashrut laws that declared some parts of God's creation unclean:

> He said to them, "Then do you also fail to understand? Do you not see that whatever goes into a person from outside cannot defile, since it enters, not the heart but the stomach, and goes out into the sewer?" (Thus he declared all foods clean.) (Mark 7:18–19)

Evil does not come from something outside, but what is inside the person:

> And he said, "It is what comes out of a person that defiles. For it is from within, from the human heart, that evil intentions come: fornication, theft, murder, adultery, avarice, wickedness, deceit, licentiousness, envy, slander, pride, folly. All these evil things come from within, and they defile a person." (Mark 7:20–23)

For Jesus, as for Pelagius, children are not evil. They may be the purest examples of faith:

> But Jesus called for them and said, "Let the little children come to me, and do not stop them; for it is to such as these that the kingdom of God belongs. Truly I tell you, whoever does not

receive the kingdom of God as a little child will never enter it." [Q] (Luke 18:16–17)

Most important, however, is the love commandment. Pelagius not only makes it the central virtue of the Christian life, but, like Jesus, he also raises love to an ultimate level, the love of enemies:

> You have heard that it was said, "You shall love your neighbor and hate your enemy." But I say to you, Love your enemies and pray for those who persecute you. (Matt. 5:43–44)

Love of neighbor creates a caring community while love of enemy undermines any sense of nationalism and patriotism. Consequently, it is seldom found in other philosophers or religious thinkers.[6] In 415 Pelagius was accused of heresy. Whatever Pope Innocent I might have done will remain unknown since he died and was replaced by Zosimus. Finding no fault with Pelagius's theology, Zosimus condemned and excommunicated Heros and Lazarus, the two bishops who had made the original charge against Pelagius. In his statement of September 17, 417, regarding the two bishops, Zosimus himself penned a statement deeply empathic to Pelagius and the Jesus tradition: "Love peace, value charity, pursue harmony. For it is written: Love your neighbor as yourself."[7] Pelagius may have been at the wrong place at the wrong time. The conflict with Augustine over original sin was real, yet ultimately neither could claim to be absolutely correct. Both discerned a critical element in human nature and in the Christian faith.

Both Pelagius and Augustine had a common failure. They wrote of the life pilgrimage of the individual believer. Their theology tends to be in terms of God/person rather than God's people/person. So they did not write as succinctly about the development of the believer in the faith community as they did about the spiritual journey of each individual. In many respects, that is a fatal error for both.

Pelagius was not a heretic. The movement he spawned was so popular that it threatened to divide the newly developing Roman Empire. His theological ethics, love, and love of enemy made him a danger to the growing state. On April 30, 418, Emperor Honorius condemned Pelagius and his supposed cohort, Celestius, because they were affecting the peace of Rome. Nicholson notes how closely the condemnation matches an earlier condemnation of the Druids: "against public tranquility, and the authority of the Roman people."[8]

Pelagius was a Celtic theologian who fed the soul of early Irish Christianity. Clearly his theology and ethics matched much of the Celtic tradition and much of the Jesus tradition. The Jesus tradition must have, at least at a theological or elite level, eradicated the violence of the Celtic tradition and replaced it with love, even love of enemy. It exchanged the worldly values of wealth and accompanying honor for spiritual maturity and perfection. On the other hand, there is little in Pelagius regarding the family of faith as it is found in the Jesus tradition. There is no real parallel to anticipation of the coming kingdom of God. Pelagius, like Augustine, concentrated on the spiritual development of the individual. While no doubt there was communality in the Celtic tuath or the early monasteries, all the Irish *Vitae* stress the faith, morality, and religious expressions of the individual "saint." Lacking a specific interest in the community of saints, the spiritual maturity of the "saint" took on an ascetic appearance — a life unhampered by the pursuit of wealth, family relationships, and special foods. Spiritual maturity was simple. While the Jesus tradition called for a simple life, it did not reward striving for unusual abstinence.

Patrick

The basic facts about Patrick are relatively clear. As a way of controlling the extravagant claims of the *Vitae,* there is from him a letter to Coroticus and his own *Confession.* In addition a variety of *Annals,* especially the *Annals of Ulster,* purport to give information about Patrick. From all this some minimal outline seems to be clear. He was born of an upper-class family in England. When he was about 16, pirates carried him to Ireland. After six years as a slave on a sheep farm, he escaped. In 432 he returned to Ireland as bishop and served there until he died. Despite the massive research, and sifting through evidence, nothing else can be said for certain, not his date or place of birth, or the date of his death. All of these are important, but the place of birth most affects this thesis. In *Confession* 1 Patrick says: "My father was Calponius, a deacon, a son of Potitus, a presbyter, who was at the village of Bannavem Taberniae."[9]

Clearly Patrick was raised in a Christian family somewhere in Britain. But where? There is no known place, even when linguistic variations of the name are taken into consideration. Historians are likely correct in saying it was west Britain, since it was Irish pirates who made the raid. If that is true, like Pelagius Patrick spent his childhood and adolescence in a Celtic environment, presumably of parents who held offices in a British Celtic church.

He appears to have had an abortive education. His Latin was poor; in fact, it is a good example of Vulgar Latin. He constantly apologized for his language and education. While it may seem he was overly apologetic, nevertheless he did not write with the skill that might be expected of a bishop. He must have spent his formative time tending sheep. Despite exhaustive efforts by historians to find evidence of his education, it seems he did not spend considerable time, if any, being trained as a priest/scholar in Gaul.

The Ireland to which Patrick returned sounds very much like the Celtic world. He mentions kings and sub-kings, but no overall rulers (*Confession* 52). He mentions officials that administer justice, that is, brehons (*Confession* 53). Nothing indicates Ireland has been romanized or even briticized. In an oblique way he refers to Christians in Ireland prior to his arrival when he speaks of evangelizing in places where no missioner had ever penetrated (*Confession* 51). Yet he claims to have baptized thousands and ordained many priests (*Confession* 50).

If the *Vitae* are discounted, it appears that Patrick was a humble, caring, and courageous person. While he often apologized for his shortcomings, just as often he gave thanks to God for pardoning his weaknesses (*Confession* 46). Details of his faith are nonexistent; it is possible he was unaccustomed to writing about his theology. *Confession* 4 has a Rule of Faith, obviously taken from an earlier tradition and written in a Latin different from the rest of the *Confession*. Used as a Rule in Britain, it may go back to Victorinus of Pettau (d. ca. 304). The Rule is distinctly Trinitarian with a taste of end-time expectation (in the fifth century the works of Victorinus were condemned as too millenarian). The literary critic always wonders how much faith to put in a creedal insertion. One suspects *Confession* 4 was not an example of Patrick's living faith.

Even though Pelagius wrote as a learned theologian and Patrick did not, some would say that their theologies do not differ that much.[10] Both share the Celtic traditions, both infused that rich heritage with the Jesus tradition. Both produced a gentle Christianity with deep spiritual dimensions. Both sought individual perfection. It may be Patrick was sent by the British (Roman) church to bring the Irish into line. If so, he failed. When he died there were no parish organizations and no bishops to lead them. The monastic structure, following the structure of the tuath, had prevailed. Abbots ruled in the place of local kings.[11]

We know of at least one time when Patrick lost his gentleness. When the British king Coroticus captured, murdered, and enslaved a group of Irish Christians recently baptized by Patrick, he wrote a scathing letter to Coroticus. He was furious that the king, even though a Christian, had been so violent, especially against other Christians (Letter 2). He was furious at the British for considering the Irish second-class citizens who could be enslaved (Letter 16). Like Pelagius, he had severely rejected the violence of his Celtic tradition. Because of Coroticus's violence Patrick formally excommunicated him (Letter 7). There is no evidence of what happened.

A study of Patrick is not complete without looking at his breastplate. A breastplate was a creedal statement used as a protective statement. The famous Breastplate of Patrick, or the *Lorica Sancti Patritii*, in its extant form dates back to the eighth century. No one would care to say that Patrick wrote it, yet it reflects in some respects an early Irish Christian faith saved in Old Irish, except for the final lines in Latin.[12]

This poem has been translated into many languages and to this day appears in most hymnbooks of the western world. In some respects it reflects a standard faith, and in other ways it reflects the unique, beautiful world of early Celtic Christianity. The first stanza expresses the Trinitarian faith found in Pelagius and, to a lesser extent, in Patrick.[13] The second stanza is an abbreviated form of the early Christian kerygma. Otherworldly persons and power are called upon for protection in stanza 3. In stanza 4 the divine powers of God's creation, including the sun, are asked to protect the person offering the prayer. The faith here is strictly Celtic. In stanza 6 the prayer lists those forces and persons that could be destructive because they reflect the conflict with the Celtic world. Druids are yet to be absorbed. Fine Celtic blacksmiths (artisans) could create designs that could pull the viewer back into the Celtic spiritual world. Above all stanza 7 contains the great beloved description of the Irish spiritual experience. Christ is everywhere around the person praying, and the request is made that the same spiritual maturity be passed on to others.

Columba

While Pelagius may be the theologian of Irish Christianity, Patrick the father and Brigit the mother, the real founder would be Columba. It is not known when Columba was born, but according to Adomnán, the author of his *Vita,* Columba died on June 9, 597. Some of the *Annals* say he was seventy-five years of age, so 521 might be the year of his birth. According to Adomnán Columba came from a royal family, Uí Néill, at a time when high kings existed. As a child, Columba was fostered to a priest named Cruith-nechán.[14] The key moment in the life of Columba, perhaps even in the history of Ireland, was the decision to do a peregrination. It is not clear why he made that decision. Some accounts say he fell into political disfavor by seeking God's favor for his family. Other legends say this disfavor occurred because he copied a manuscript that did not belong to him.[15] In any case he sailed north to Iona, an Island in the Scottish Dalraida (counterpart of the Irish Dál Riata, the northern part of Ireland).

Columba founded the community at Iona where incredible learning and copying (e.g., the Book of Kells) occurred. From Iona the continental peregrinations originated. From Iona much of the destroyed classical literature was returned to the Continent. The theology of Columba cannot be discerned from Adomnán's life. What Adomnán wanted us to believe about a saint is clear. Columba was spiritual and believed in the providence of God; he was kind, yet firm as a leader, and very stern with malicious persons. The *Vita* has three sections.[16] In the first Columba demonstrates the power to predict coming events or see events occurring from afar.[17] In fact, this may have been the source of the story about his leaving Ireland, that is, using psychic powers he interfered with a struggle in northern Ireland. The second section tells of the miraculous powers of Columba. Not a few of these stories have some overtones of the Jesus tradition. As could be expected in an island habitat, there are frequent storms, with boats in danger. Columba, like Jesus, could still the storm (II.12.45). He could guide fishermen to make a catch (II.19). He raised a boy from the dead, in the name of Jesus (II.32). He frequently healed the sick (II.30). In the third section Adomnán records the many times Columba was in touch with the Otherworld. Like the Celts the line between this world and the Otherworld was very thin, though in the case of Columba there was little transmogrification.

Notes

1. Zimmer, *Pelagius in Irland,* 19–20; Rees, *Pelagius: Life and Letters,* 1:xiii.
2. So Jerome in his commentary on Jeremiah. M. Forthhomme Nicholson, "Celtic Theology: Pelagius," in *Introduction to Celtic Christianity,* ed. Mackey, 388–89.
3. Rees, *Pelagius: Life and Letters,* 1:133–34.
4. Ibid., 1:1–124, 2:1–250.
5. Translations from Rees, *Pelagius: Life and Letters,* vol. 2.
6. Musonius Rufus would be an exception. Martin Percival Charlesworth, *Five Men: Character Studies from the Roman Empire* (Cambridge: Harvard University Press, 1936), 33–62.
7. Zosimus Papa, *Epistola ad Aurelium* III, sec. 4 (Migne, XX, 658). See Nicholson, "Celtic Theology," 391.
8. Quoted by Nicholson, "Celtic Theology," 391.
9. Translations from Hanson, *Life and Writings of the Historical Saint Patrick.*
10. Stefan Czarnowski, *Le culte des héros et ses conditions sociales: Saint Patrick, héros national de l'Irlande* (1919; New York: Arno Press, 1975), 40–42.
11. Charles Doherty, "The Monastic Town in Early Medieval Ireland," in *The Comparative History of Urban Origins in Non-Roman Europe,* ed. Howard Clark

and Anngret Simms, BAR International Series 255 (Oxford: British Archaeological Reports, 1985), 45–75.

12. N. D. O'Donoghue, "St. Patrick's Breastplate," in *Introduction to Celtic Christianity*, ed. Mackey, 45–63.

THE HYMN OF PATRICK

I
For my shield this day I call:
A mighty power:
The Holy Trinity!
Affirming threeness,
Confessing oneness,
In the making of all
Through love.

II
For my shield this day I call:
Christ's power in his coming
and in his baptising,
Christ's power in his dying
On the cross, his arising
from the tomb, his ascending;
Christ's power in his coming
for judgment and ending.

III
For my shield this day I call:
strong power of the seraphim,
with angels obeying,
and archangels attending,
in the glorious company
of the holy and risen ones,
in the prayers of the fathers,
in visions prophetic
and commands apostolic,
in the annals of witness,
in virginal innocence,
in the deeds of steadfast men.

IV
For my shield this day I call:
Heaven's might,
Sun's brightness,
Moon's whiteness,
Fire's glory,
Lightning's swiftness,
Wind's wildness,
Ocean's depth,

Earth's solidity.
Rock's immobility.

V
This day I call to me:
God's strength to direct me,
God's power to sustain me,
God's wisdom to guide me,
God's vision to light me,
God's ear to my hearing,
God's word to my speaking,
God's hand to uphold me,
God's pathway before me,
God's shield to protect me,
God's legions to save me:
from snares of the demons,
from evil enticements,
from failings of nature,
from one man or many
that seek to destroy me,
anear or afar.

VI
Around me I gather
these forces to save
my soul and my body
from dark powers that assail me:
against false prophesyings,
against pagan devisings,
against heretical lying
and false gods all around me.
Against spells cast by women
by blacksmiths, by Druids,
against knowledge unlawful
that injures the body,
that injures the spirit.

VII
Be Christ this day my strong protector;
against poison and burning,
against drowning and wounding,
through reward wide and plenty....
Christ beside me, Christ before me;
Christ behind me, Christ within me;
Christ beneath me, Christ above me;
Christ to right of me, Christ to left of me;
Christ in my lying, my sitting, my rising;
Christ in heart of all who know me,

Christ on tongue of all who meet me,
Christ in eye of all who see me,
Christ in ear of all who hear me.

VIII
For my shield this day I call
a mighty power:
the Holy Trinity!
affirming threeness,
confessing oneness
in the making of all —
through love

IX
For to the Lord belongs salvation,
and to the Lord belongs salvation
and to Christ belongs salvation.

May your salvation, Lord, be
with us always.
(Domini est salus, Domini est salus,
Christi est salus;
Salus tua, Domine, sit semper nobiscum.)

13. The Celts were famous for their triadic representations of gods and goddesses. See James, *The World of the Celts*, 89.

14. Fostering was a Celtic tradition among leadership families. It served to hold together crucial families. See Charles-Edwards, *Early Christian Ireland*, 115–17.

15. Byrne, "Ireland of St. Columba," 37.

16. Adomnán of Iona, *Life of St. Columba.*

17. Adomnán wanted to identify the psychic Columba with the gifts of the Druids. Indeed, apparently Columba succeeded in protecting Celtic leadership, especially the bards (the Convention of Druin Cett). See Byrne, "Ireland of St. Columba," 37.

Conclusions

The Celts

In the first millennium before Christ a culture appeared in middle Europe, resulting from the migration of eastern Indo-Europeans. Although details are sparse, our first extant knowledge of the Celts comes from a find in Hallstatt that dates back to the seventh century. A rather similar culture called proto-Celtic must have existed even two millennia prior in such areas as Ireland and Britain. The great monuments Stonehenge, Newgrange, and those in the Boyne Valley point to a culture deeply invested in the sun with symbols signifying the circular movement of life. The Celts did not form an empire, for they were more interested in the process of life than structural goals. Consequently, on the Continent they tended to merge with local tribes to form diverse lifestyles and languages. With a famous and much feared ferocity, they defended themselves when attacked. When they originated the conflict it was normally for plunder.

In the third century several tribes from Gaul raided Delphi for its treasures. A major result of this raid was the migration of three tribes into northern Asia Minor. These Celtic tribes gave their name to the region — Galatia.

Paul

According to Acts 16:6, Paul made his second missionary journey through Galatia on the way to Mysia and eventually Troas. According to his later letter to the Galatians, he must have developed eye problems so severe they caused him to stop in the territory of the Galatian tribes. He found a satisfactory cure at one of their several spas before moving on. During his stay he brought the gospel to a few groups. House churches were established. Later, on his third missionary journey, he returned to the territory of the Celtic tribes (Acts 18:23). He was dismayed by what he found, for they had reverted to Celtic cultural customs. His well-known letter (written about 55) addressed to the "foolish Celts" speaks directly to them in their cultural context about their dangerous return to Celtic ways.

The Jesus Tradition

While it is not known precisely what Jesus tradition Paul delivered to the Galatians on his first trip, some reliable assumptions can be made. Paul surely had in hand the Jesus tradition in oral form. In the gospels (including the Gospel of Thomas) those elements of the tradition that would have been circulating orally when Paul started his missionary journeys show how the Jesus tradition dealt with language, divine authority, religious authority, political authority, calendar, time, good and evil, healing, commensality, and family. These traditions must have been a part of Paul's preaching to the Galatians as well as other letter recipients.

The Jesus tradition, however, did not first enter the Celtic world through written letters.[1] Quite the contrary, the Celts maintained a highly sophisticated system of oral tradition, led by Druids, bards and brehons. The oral tradition of Jesus no doubt first entered the Celtic oral tradition through Paul in Galatia.

Spain

The point of departure for Ireland from the continent was Spain, or more specifically from the Celtic region called Galicia in northern Spain and what is now Portugal. Several types of data show that connection. If Gaul had been the point of departure, then surely the Celtic tradition would have gone through Britain, which for its part had a Celtic dialect (brythonic) different from that of Ireland, and which eventually added a strong Roman quality to its former Celtic culture. Ireland lacked that romanization.

Besides being the point of departure from the Continent to Spain,

Galicians spoke the same dialect found in Ireland, Scotland, and the Isle of Man (goidelic or Gaelic). Even though the pipeline between Galicia and Ireland has been established, there is little hard evidence for early (first- and second-century) Christianity in Galicia. By the third century the churches there were in contact with Christian centers in North Africa. There was a strong tradition regarding Paul in Spain. While there is no room in the life of Paul for such a missionary trip, the tradition cannot be meaningless. Someone or some group attached to Paul was responsible for taking the gospel to Spain, perhaps because Paul was indeed the apostle to the Celts. The written gospel entered Ireland from North Africa via Galicia by the middle of the third century, though the oral tradition probably arrived via the Celts (the Paul tradition) much earlier.

Early Irish Christianity

Early Celtic/Irish writers like Pelagius had access to this written New Testament. While there was knowledge of Paul's writing, it was the oral Jesus tradition that most impacted the Celtic culture of Ireland. It can be seen not only in Pelagius, Patrick, and Columba, but also in the later art of the Irish crosses. Humans were created to be good and placed in a creation that was both good and wonderful. People grew up in some conflict, but eventually they could reach a level of spiritual maturity signified in the art by Jesus with outstretched hands in the sun circle. There were four significant results. First, monastic communities were formed with the intent of seeking that spiritual maturity. At the same time, the various orders of monks stressed the copying of the New Testament and classic documents. Since they had the learning and the texts, the Irish monks became world-famous teachers. Because the monks were peregrinators, they carried the biblical and classical materials back to a ravaged continent. In that sense they "saved civilization." At the same time they developed a lifestyle based on the Jesus tradition as it joined with the ancient Celtic tradition.

In 664, at Whitby, where Irish church leaders agreed to follow what was generally accepted elsewhere, the process of romanization began. So there was an early Irish Christianity, free of romanization and briticization, that lasted from the third century to 664. It was the Golden Age of Ireland. Following the tradition of the Druids, a highly skilled and intelligent Christian leadership developed; following the bards, a highly imaginative poetic and narrative tradition emerged. In contrast to the Celtic legends, violence was eliminated in favor of caring, healing, and moral development. While the monastic people, men and women together, sought spiritual maturity, copied texts, and ran schools, the Celtic people only gradually accepted the Jesus tradition. There was little conflict and there were no martyrs. It was indeed a golden age. Even though Bede wanted the Irish to fall in line with the Roman church, he looked back with longing for the days when Irish Christianity was the shining star in Western Christianity.

Early Roman Christianity

A few centuries earlier the Jesus tradition left Palestine and moved into the Greco-Roman world, bringing together people of different races, creating an atmosphere of gender equality, bringing a sense of caring and healing, and celebrating the new faith family with worship and common meals. They expressed much of their faith in iconographic and rhetoric forms already present in the Greco-Roman world. Despite the gentle means of inculturation, the first Christians were sharply resisted by the Roman Empire. Persecutions and martyrdoms resulted. By 300 it became clear that the Roman Empire would profit by adopting the nascent Christian faith rather than attempting to destroy it. After Constantine (313), the romanization of Mediterranean Christianity occurred more rapidly. Many of the early symbols of earlier Christianity disappeared; the power of the Jesus tradition waned. Art and texts showed more interest in the ecclesiastical organization of the Mediterranean world than in the powerful Jesus tradition. Theology moved toward an exaggerated Paulinism, which, though not dualistic, saw this world in need of present and end-time redemption.

This progression stands in sharp contrast to early Irish Christianity. There the Jesus tradition entered a Celtic world in which nature was good and humans knew no sin. The Jesus tradition flourished in this environment. To be sure, Paul was well known, but his theology was not exaggerated. If anything his faith was adapted to the more dominant Jesus tradition. As a result the greatest conflict between the two styles came in the Augustine-Pelagius debates, or later between the Irish peregrinators and continental representatives of Rome in the sixth and seventh centuries.

The intent of this study was to show that there were at least two occasions when the Jesus tradition entered a powerful culture, one Roman, the other Celtic.[2] Two different Christianities resulted. Both are valid. However, if the Irish Christians had been expansive, the Christian world might well have been Irish rather than Roman. It would have been an Irish Jesus rather than a Roman Jesus. That possibility should make all Christians pause — pause before insisting that Roman (Western) Christianity is the only orthodox faith, and pause before promoting Roman (Western) Christianity as the true faith among non-Christian cultures. The vital mission roots of Christianity belong in the Jesus tradition. Both Irish and Roman Christianity are simply great cultural expressions of the original vitality.

Notes

1. In the language of current parlance, it might be argued that the oral Jesus of tradition entered into a culture that was right-brain oriented, that is, oral and musical (Celtic). The letters of Paul entered into a left-brain culture that stressed writing and expansion (Roman).

2. As mentioned before, the inculturation of the Jesus tradition in Ethiopia and India would have been equally valid studies.

The Jesus Tradition
Utilized by Paul

Q Used by Paul

Q has been constructed from those passages in Matthew and Luke that agree but are not taken from the Gospel of Mark. The two-document hypothesis proposes that Matthew and Luke are essentially a combination of the Gospel of Mark with Q. It is generally assumed that the community of Q could be located in Galilee.[1] It does not contain the theological or apocalyptic elements found in Mark and Paul. Nevertheless, elements of Q can indeed be found in the letters of Paul, evidence that Paul passed on to his listeners sayings of Jesus that came from that source.[2] They are:

1 Thess. 2:14–16: Killing the Prophets

> For you, brothers and sisters, became imitators of the churches of God in Christ Jesus that are in Judea, for you suffered the same things from your own compatriots as they did from the Jews, who killed both the Lord Jesus and the prophets, and drove us out; they displease God and oppose everyone by hindering us from speaking to the Gentiles so that they may be saved. Thus they have constantly been filling up the measure of their sins; but God's wrath has overtaken them at last.

Q Parallel (QS 34)

> Therefore also the Wisdom of God said, "I will send them prophets and apostles, some of whom they will kill and persecute," so that this generation may be charged with the blood

of all the prophets shed since the foundation of the world, from the blood of Abel to the blood of Zechariah, who perished between the altar and the sanctuary. Yes, I tell you, it will be charged against this generation. Woe to you lawyers! For you have taken away the key of knowledge; you did not enter yourselves, and you hindered those who were entering. (Luke 11:49–52)

1 Thess. 5:2: Like a Thief in the Night

For you yourselves know very well that the day of the Lord will come like a thief in the night.

Q Parallel (QS 38)

But know this: if the owner of the house had known at what hour the thief was coming, he would not have let his house be broken into. (Luke 12:39)

1 Cor. 1:19: Wisdom of the Wise (common source from Isa. 29:14)

For it is written, "I will destroy the wisdom of the wise, and the discernment of the discerning I will thwart."

Q Parallel (QS 24)

because you have hidden these things from the wise and the intelligent and have revealed them to infants; yes, Father, for such was your gracious will. (Luke 10:21b)

1 Cor. 4:5: Nothing Hidden

Therefore do not pronounce judgment before the time, before the Lord comes, who will bring to light the things now hidden in darkness and will disclose the purposes of the heart. Then each one will receive commendation from God.

Q Parallel (QS 35)

Nothing is covered up that will not be uncovered, and nothing secret that will not become known. (Luke 12:2)

Gospel of Thomas Parallel

(5) for there is nothing hidden which shall not be made manifest. (6) For all things are revealed before heaven. For there is nothing hidden which shall not be manifest, and there is nothing covered which shall remain without being uncovered.

1 Cor. 5:6: Yeast Leavens

Your boasting is not a good thing. Do you not know that a little yeast leavens the whole batch of dough?

Q Parallel (QS 46)

It is like yeast that a woman took and mixed in with three measures of flour until all of it was leavened. (Luke 13:21)

1 Cor. 9:14: The Laborer Deserves to Be Paid

In the same way, the Lord commanded that those who proclaim the gospel should get their living by the gospel.

Q Parallel (QS 20)

Remain in the same house, eating and drinking whatever they provide, for the laborer deserves to be paid. Do not move about from house to house. (Luke 10:7)

1 Cor. 13:2: Power of Faith

And if I have prophetic powers, and understand all mysteries and all knowledge, and if I have all faith, so as to remove mountains, but do not have love, I am nothing.

Q Parallel (QS 59)

> The Lord replied, "If you had faith the size of a mustard seed, you could say to this mulberry tree, 'Be uprooted and planted in the sea,' and it would obey you." (Luke 17:6)

Gospel of Thomas Parallel

> (48) Jesus said: If two make peace with one another in this one house, they shall say to the mountain: Be moved, and it shall be moved.

Rom. 2:1–2, 14:10: Passing Judgment

> Therefore you have no excuse, whoever you are, when you judge others; for in passing judgment on another you condemn yourself, because you, the judge, are doing the very same things. You say, "We know that God's judgment on those who do such things is in accordance with truth." (Rom. 2:1–2)

> Why do you pass judgment on your brother or sister? Or you, why do you despise your brother or sister? For we will all stand before the judgment seat of God. (Rom. 14:10)

Q Parallel (QS 10)

> Do not judge, and you will not be judged; do not condemn, and you will not be condemned. Forgive, and you will be forgiven. (Luke 6:37)

Rom. 12:14: Bless Those Who Persecute You

> Bless those who persecute you; bless and do not curse them.

Q Parallel (QS 9)

> bless those who curse you, pray for those who abuse you. (Luke 6:28)

Rom. 13:10, 12:17; Gal. 5:14: The Law of Love

Love does no wrong to a neighbor; therefore, love is the fulfilling of the law. (Rom. 13:10)

Do not repay anyone evil for evil, but take thought for what is noble in the sight of all. (Rom. 12:17)

For the whole law is summed up in a single commandment, "You shall love your neighbor as yourself." (Gal. 5:14)

Q Parallel (QS 9)

Do to others as you would have them do to you. (Luke 6:31)

Rom. 14:17: Seeking the Kingdom

For the kingdom of God is not food and drink but righteousness and peace and joy in the Holy Spirit.

Q Parallel (QS 39)

Instead, strive for his kingdom, and these things will be given to you as well. (Luke 12:31)

Gal. 6:1: Forgiveness

My friends, if anyone is detected in a transgression, you who have received the Spirit should restore such a one in a spirit of gentleness. Take care that you yourselves are not tempted.

Q Parallel (QS 58)

and if there is repentance, you must forgive. (Luke. 17:3b)

Phil. 2:8–9: Being Humble

he humbled himself and became obedient to the point of death even death on a cross. Therefore God also highly exalted him and gave him the name that is above every name.

Q Parallels (QS 50)

> For all who exalt themselves will be humbled, and those who humble themselves will be exalted. (Luke 14:11)

> I tell you, this man went down to his home justified rather than the other; for all who exalt themselves will be humbled, but all who humble themselves will be exalted. (Luke 18:14)

Paul's Q deals primarily with the function of the reign of God, those qualities of life expected for those anticipating the reign (humility, faith, forgiveness, love, lack of anxiety). Paul uses the Q warning about killing the prophets as a type for the death of Jesus, and indicates by it who can receive the revelation of God. As an added, unexpected item, he also uses Q to defend and support the first Christian missionaries.

It is not at all clear how Paul came in contact with the Q community or how he received the sayings source. Even though Q is Galilean, there is no reason to suppose the sayings were limited to a geographical region. Perhaps the location of Paul's headquarters in Antioch will suffice to establish the contact (Gal. 2:11). In any case it is certain he did not know Q from time spent in Jerusalem (Gal. 1:22).

Even more difficult is the matter of language. Because the Q of Matthew and Luke so frequently agree with each other, one is forced to say there was a Greek form of Q that each one used. Because of the striking verbal similarities, most would argue for a written document that no longer exists. Since Paul used a Greek Q and undoubtedly passed it on to his listeners in Greek, what was the original language? Demonstrating through archaeology the strong influence of Hellenism in Galilee, it is popular to assume Greek was the primary language. Assuming Jesus walked every day to Greek-speaking Sepphoris, it is sometimes projected that his Greek could have been of such a quality to address assembled crowds. If so, he might indeed have delivered the Q sayings in Greek. Though an attractive hypothesis, the idea that Jesus was a fairly accomplished speaker in Greek has not been widely accepted. Q shows clear signs of translation, so the Greek redactor of Q may have had

Aramaic as a primary language. In addition, the archaeological evidence does not support such a hellenistic society. There are too many synagogues, Jewish houses, and signs of a Jewish lifestyle.[3] So the general consensus is that Jesus delivered the sayings in Aramaic and they were soon translated, section by section, into Greek for the Galilean and northern listeners.[4]

Scholars have identified at least three layers in Q. The first reflects wisdom traditions, while the later levels incorporate more Christology and eschatology. Paul's Q comes primarily from the first level, Q1. One would suspect, then, that Paul possessed an oral form of primarily Q1. Dale Allison argues that the presence of QS 34 in 1 Thess. 2:14–16 indicates that by 50 C.E. Paul knew a complete Q.[5] Either way, Paul did have access to a Q tradition. That tradition was a single source, of course. Two sources are known because Luke and Matthew each have one. Some scholars have attempted to recreate the single source, that is, QS. One of the more successful attempts is that by Burton Mack.[6]

Given the above data, Paul's oral Q source would have looked like this:

QS 9: On Responding to Reproach

> I am telling you, love your enemies, bless those who curse you, pray for those who mistreat you. If someone slaps you on the cheek, offer your other cheek as well. If anyone grabs your coat, let him have your shirt as well. Give to anyone who asks, and if anyone takes away your belongings, do not ask to have them back. As you want people to treat you, do the same to them. If you love those who love you, what credit is that to you? Even tax collectors love those who love them, do they not? And if you embrace only your brothers, what more are you doing than others? Doesn't everybody do that? If you lend to those from whom you expect repayment, what credit is that to you? Even wrongdoers lend to their kind because they expect to be repaid.
>
> Instead, love your enemies, do good and lend without expecting anything in return. Your reward will be great, and you

will be children of God. For he makes his sun rise on the evil and on the good; he sends rain on the just and on the unjust. (Luke 6:27–35)

QS 10: On Making Judgments

Be merciful even as your Father is merciful. Don't judge and you won't be judged. For the standard you use [for judging] will be the standard used against you. (Luke 6:36–38)

QS 20: On Working for the Kingdom of God

He said, "The harvest is abundant, but the workers are few; beg therefore the master of the harvest to send out workers into his harvest. Go. Look, I send you out as lambs among wolves. Do not carry money, or bag, or sandals, or staff; and do not greet anyone on the road. Whatever house you enter, say, 'Peace be to this house!' And if a child of peace is there, your greeting will be received [literally, 'your peace will rest upon him']. But if not, let your peace return to you. And stay in the same house, eating and drinking whatever they provide, for the worker deserves his wages. Do not go from house to house.

"And if you enter a town and they receive you, eat what is set before you. Pay attention to the sick and say to them, 'God's kingdom has come near to you.' But if you enter a town and they do not receive you, as you leave, shake the dust from your feet and say, 'Nevertheless, be sure of this, the realm of God has come to you.' " (Luke 10:2–11)

QS 24: On the One Who Receives Revelation

Jesus declared, "I am grateful to father, master of heaven and earth, because you have kept these things hidden from the wise and understanding and revealed them to babies.

"Truly I am grateful, father, for that was your gracious will. Authority over all the world has been given to me by my father. No one recognizes the son except the father; and no one knows who the father is except the son and the one to whom the son chooses to reveal him." (10:21–22)

QS 34: O You Pharisees

Shame on you Pharisees! for you are scrupulous about giving a tithe of mint and dill and cumin to the priests, but you neglect justice and the love of God. These things you ought to have done, without neglecting the others. Shame on you Pharisees! for you clean the outside of the cup and the dish, but inside are full of greed and incontinence. Foolish Pharisees! Clean the inside and the outside will also be clean. Shame on you Pharisees! for you love the front seats in the assemblies and greetings in the marketplaces. Shame on you! for you are like graves, outwardly beautiful, but full of pollution inside.

Shame on you lawyers! for you load people with burdens heavy to bear, but you yourselves refuse to carry even a light load. Shame on you! for you erect memorials for the prophets, the prophets your fathers killed. Thus you witness and consent to the deeds of your fathers; for they killed the prophets and you build monuments to them.

For this reason the wisdom of God said, 'I will send them prophets and wise men, some of whom they will kill and prosecute,' in order to hold this generation accountable for the blood of all the prophets shed from the foundation of the world, from the blood of Abel to the blood of Zechariah who perished between the altar and the sanctuary. Truly, I tell you, this generation will be held accountable.

Shame on you lawyers! for you have taken the key of knowledge away from the people. You yourselves do not enter the kingdom of God, and you prevent those who would enter from going in. (Luke 11:39–52)

QS 35: On Speaking Out

Nothing is hidden that will not be made known, or secret that will not come to light. What I tell you in the dark, speak in the light. And what you hear as a whisper. (Luke 12:2–3)

QS 38: This Very Night

Someone from the crowd said to him, "Teacher, tell my brother to divide the inheritance with me." But he said to him, "Sir, who made me your judge or lawyer?"

He told them a parable, saying, "The land of a rich man produced in abundance, and he thought to himself, 'What should I do, for I have nowhere to store my crops?' Then he said, 'I will do this. I will put down my barns and build larger ones, and there I will store all my grain and my goods. And I will say to my soul, 'Soul, you have ample goods stored up for many years. Take it easy. Eat, drink, and be merry.' But God said to him, 'Foolish man! This very night you will have to give back your soul, and the things you produced, whose will they be?' That is what happens to the one who stores up treasure for himself and is not rich in the sight of God." (Luke 12:13–21)

QS 39: On Food and Clothing

I am telling you, do not worry about your life, what you will eat, or about your body, what you will wear. Isn't life more than food, and the body more than clothing? Think of the ravens. They do not plant, harvest, or store grain in barns, and God feeds them. Aren't you worth more than the birds? Which one of you can add a single day to your life by worrying?

And why do you worry about clothing? Think of the way lilies grow. They do not work or spin. But even Solomon in all his splendor was not as magnificent. If God puts beautiful clothes on the grass that is in the field today and tomorrow is thrown into a furnace, won't he put clothes on you, faint hearts? So, don't worry, thinking, "What will we eat," or "What will we drink," or, "What will we wear?" For everybody in the whole world does that, and your father knows that you need these things. Instead, make sure of his rule over you, and all these things will be yours as well. (Luke 12:22–31)

QS 46: The Mustard and the Yeast

> He said, "What is the kingdom of God like? To what should I compare it? It is like a grain of mustard which a man took and sowed in his garden. It grew and became a tree, and the birds of the air made nests in its branches."
>
> He also said, "The kingdom of God is like yeast which a woman took and hid in three measures of flour until it leavened the whole mass." (Luke 13:18–21)

QS 50: On Humility

> Everyone who glorifies himself will be humiliated, and the one that humbles himself will be praised. (Luke 14:11, 18:14)

QS 58: On Forgiveness

> If your brother sins, warn him. If he listens to you, forgive him. Even if he sins against you seven times in a day, you must forgive him. (Luke 17:3–4)

QS 59: On Faith

> If you have faith like a grain of mustard, you could say to this mulberry tree, "Begone and plant yourself in the sea," and it would obey you. (Luke 17:6)

Gospel of Thomas Used by Paul

The Gospel of Thomas presents so many difficulties that the question of its use by Paul actually may seem much simpler than that about his use of Q. In other words, there is little room for speculation. While it was known that the Gospel of Thomas existed, modern scholars did not know its content until the discovery of a Coptic copy in the Nag Hammadi finds. The Gospel of Thomas purports to come from Didymos Judas Thomas, a name used for Thomas in Syria. There is no reason to doubt that the sayings of Jesus in Thomas were indeed collected in Syria. Many of the sayings are patently not from the mainline Jesus tradition. They tend to be more philosophical, docetic, even Gnostic, and were not often used by the later fathers as a source for the sayings of Jesus. Thomas was probably formed late in the first century, or early second century, at a time when docetic theology was more probable. Yet Paul has access to the some of the sayings of Thomas, so some of the material had to be much earlier than the actual collection.[7] Like Q the sayings are in Greek but reflect an Aramaic background. The Thomas sayings used by Paul are:[8]

1 Cor. 2:9: Not of Human Origin

But, as it is written, "What no eye has seen, nor ear heard, nor the human heart conceived, what God has prepared for those who love him."

Gospel of Thomas Parallel

(17) Jesus said: I will give you that which eye has not seen, an ear has not heard, and hand has not touched, and which has not entered into the heart of man.

Q Parallel

Then turning to the disciples, Jesus said to them privately, "Blessed are the eyes that see what you see! For I tell you that many prophets and kings desired to see what you see, but did not see it, and to hear what you hear, but did not hear it." (Luke 10:23–24)

1 Cor. 10:17: Commensality

Because there is one bread, we who are many are one body, for we all partake of the one bread.

Gospel of Thomas Parallel

(14) Jesus said to them: If you fast, you will beget a sin for yourselves; and if you pray, you will be condemned; and if you give alms, you will do an evil to your spirits. And if you go into any land and travel in its regions, if they receive you eat what they set before you. Heal the sick among them. For that

which goes into your mouth will not defile you, but that which comes forth from your mouth, that is what will defile you.

Q Parallel

Whenever you enter a town and its people welcome you, eat what is set before you; cure the sick who are there, and say to them, "The kingdom of God has come near to you." (Luke 10:8–9)

1 Cor. 8:6: Creation

yet for us there is one God, the Father, from whom are all things and for whom we exist, and one Lord, Jesus Christ, through whom are all things and through whom we exist.

Rom. 11:36 Parallel

For from him and through him and to him are all things. To him be the glory forever. Amen.

Gospel of Thomas Parallel

(77) Jesus said: I am the light that is over them all. I am the All; the All has come forth from me, and the All has attained unto me. Cleave a (piece of) wood: I am there. Raise up the stone, and ye shall find me there.

1 Cor. 13:2: Faith Moves Mountains

And if I have prophetic powers, and understand all mysteries and all knowledge, and if I have all faith, so as to remove mountains, but do not have love, I am nothing.

Gospel of Thomas Parallels

(48) Jesus said: If two make peace with one another in this one house, they shall say to the mountain: Be moved, and it shall be moved.

(106) Jesus said: When you make the two one, you shall become sons of man, and when you say: Mountain, be moved, it shall be moved.

2 Cor. 4:6: Light in the Face

For it is the God who said, "Let light shine out of darkness," who has shone in our hearts to give the light of the knowledge of the glory of God in the face of Jesus Christ.

Gospel of Thomas Parallel

(24) His disciples said: Teach us concerning the place where thou art, for it is necessary for us to seek after it. He said to them: He that hath ears, let him hear. There is a light within a man of light, and it gives light to the whole world. If it does not give light, there is darkness.

Q Parallel

Your eye is the lamp of your body. If your eye is healthy, your whole body is full of light; but if it is not healthy, your body is full of darkness. Therefore consider whether the light in you is not darkness. (Luke 11:34–35)

Gal. 3:27–28: Male and Female

As many of you as were baptized into Christ have clothed yourselves with Christ. There is no longer Jew or Greek, there is no longer slave or free, there is no longer male and female; for all of you are one in Christ Jesus.

Gospel of Thomas Parallel

(22:5b) and when you make the male and the female into a single one, that the male be not male and the female female; when you make eyes in the place of an eye, and a hand in place of a hand, and a foot in place of a foot, an image in place of an image, then shall you enter [the kingdom].

Gal. 5:16–18: Flesh and Spirit

> Live by the Spirit, I say, and do not gratify the desires of the flesh. For what the flesh desires is opposed to the Spirit, and what the Spirit desires is opposed to the flesh; for these are opposed to each other, to prevent you from doing what you want. But if you are led by the Spirit, you are not subject to the law.

Gospel of Thomas Parallels

> (29) Jesus said: If the flesh has come into being because of the spirit, it is a marvel; but if the spirit (has come into being) because of the body, it is a marvel of marvels. But as for me, I marvel at this, how this great wealth has settled in this poverty.

> (87) Jesus said: Wretched is the body which depends upon a body, and wretched is the soul which depends on these two.

> (112) Jesus said: Woe to the flesh which depends upon the soul; woe to the soul which depends upon the flesh.

Rom. 2:29 et al.: Circumcision of the Heart

> Rather, a person is a Jew who is one inwardly, and real circumcision is a matter of the heart — it is spiritual and not literal. Such a person receives praise not from others but from God. (Rom. 2:29)

> For it is we who are the circumcision, who worship in the Spirit of God and boast in Christ Jesus and have no confidence in the flesh. (Phil. 3:3)

> Circumcision is nothing, and uncircumcision is nothing; but obeying the commandments of God is everything. (1 Cor. 7:19)

> For neither circumcision nor uncircumcision is anything; but a new creation is everything! (Gal. 6:15)

Gospel of Thomas Parallel

> (53) His disciples said to him: Is circumcision profitable or
> not? He said to them: Were it profitable, their father would
> beget them from their mother circumcised. But the true cir-
> cumcision in spirit has proved entirely profitable (*lit.:* has
> found usefulness altogether).

Paul uses Thomas for some very important elements of his writing: the divine goodness of creation, divine revelation to the faithful,
the importance of eating together, eradication of the distinction between male and female, the power of the Spirit over flesh, and the
nature of true circumcision. Thomas becomes even more important when reading Galatians, where Paul was dealing with exactly
these issues: eating together (kashrut), circumcision, and community oneness. The calendar is not directly mentioned in either Q
or Thomas, an indication that for Christians in a Greek-speaking
hellenized world the Sabbath laws were already considered inap-
propriate. Indirectly, Paul's use of QS 38 in 1 Thess. 5:2, the Thief
in the Night, indicates Paul has used the Jesus tradition to support
his relativization of timekeeping.

Given the above list it is plausible to believe that Paul had this
minimal Gospel of Thomas:

> (14) Jesus said to them: If you fast, you will beget a sin for
> yourselves; and if you pray, you will be condemned; and if
> you give alms, you will do an evil to your spirits. And if you
> go into any land and travel in its regions, if they receive you eat
> what they set before you. Heal the sick among them. For that
> which goes into your mouth will not defile you, but that which
> comes forth from your mouth, that is what will defile you.

> (17) Jesus said: I will give you that which eye has not seen, an
> ear has not heard, and hand has not touched, and which has
> not entered into the heart of man.

> (22) Jesus saw some infants at the breast. He said to his dis-
> ciples: These little ones at the breast are like those who enter
> into the kingdom. They said to him: If we then be children,

shall we enter the kingdom? Jesus said to them: When you make the two one, and when you make the inside as the outside, and the outside as the inside, and the upper side as the lower; and when you make the male and the female into a single one, that the male be not male and the female female; when you make eyes in the place of an eye, and a hand in place of a hand, and a foot in place of a foot, an image in place of an image, then shall you enter [the kingdom].

(24) His disciples said: Teach us concerning the place where thou art, for it is necessary for us to seek after it. He said to them: He that hath ears, let him hear. There is a light within a man of light, and it gives light to the whole world. If it does not give light, there is darkness.

(29) Jesus said: If the flesh has come into being because of the spirit, it is a marvel; but if the spirit (has come into being) because of the body, it is a marvel of marvels. But as for me, I marvel at this, how this great wealth has settled in this poverty.

(48) Jesus said: If two make peace with one another in this one house, they shall say to the mountain: Be moved, and it shall be moved.

(53) His disciples said to him: Is circumcision profitable or not? He said to them: Were it profitable, their father would beget them from their mother circumcised. But the true circumcision in spirit has proved entirely profitable (lit.: has found usefulness altogether).

(77) Jesus said: I am the light that is over them all. I am the All; the All has come forth from me, and the All has attained unto me. Cleave a (piece of) wood: I am there. Raise up the stone, and ye shall find me there.

(87) Jesus said: Wretched is the body which depends upon a body, and wretched is the soul which depends on these two.

(106) Jesus said: When you make the two one, you shall become sons of man, and when you say: Mountain, be moved, it shall be moved.

(112) Jesus said: Woe to the flesh which depends upon the soul; woe to the soul which depends upon the flesh.

There is no way to know if he had more than this. Paul's version of these sayings did not match the later written document from Nag Hammadi.

Gospel of Mark Used by Paul

Most likely Paul had much of the Gospel of Mark at his disposal. The Gospel of Mark became a document about 65 C.E., well after Paul had stopped preaching and writing. There was, of course, an oral Good News before Mark was written down. No consensus has been reached in multiple attempts to determine just what elements were available prior to Mark and when they took formal shape. That leaves the critic with an impossible task. Paul twice refers directly to a saying of Jesus. Altogether there are three references to the Gospel of Mark: two regarding commensality and one regarding marriage and divorce. Missing are any references to the parables, to healing stories, and to conflict narratives. Beyond these three "quotes" there are some thematic references to the gospel, such as the death of Jesus. But if Mark was the source for Paul's kerygma, then some themes (such as the resurrection statement in 1 Cor. 15:3–8) cannot be accounted for. The uses of Mark are:

1 Cor. 10:27: Accept the Offer to Eat Together

If an unbeliever invites you to a meal and you are disposed to go, eat whatever is set before you without raising any question on the ground of conscience.

Mark Parallel

He said to them, "Wherever you enter a house, stay there until you leave the place. If any place will not welcome you and they refuse to hear you, as you leave, shake off the dust that is on your feet as a testimony against them." (Mark 6:10–11)

Q Parallel

Whatever house you enter, first say, "Peace to this house!" And if anyone is there who shares in peace, your peace will rest on that person; but if not, it will return to you. Remain in the same house, eating and drinking whatever they provide, for the laborer deserves to be paid. Do not move about from house to house. Whenever you enter a town and its people welcome you, eat what is set before you; cure the sick who are there, and say to them, "The kingdom of God has come near to you." But whenever you enter a town and they do not welcome you, go out into its streets and say, "Even the dust of your town that clings to our feet, we wipe off in protest against you. Yet know this: the kingdom of God has come near." I tell you, on that day it will be more tolerable for Sodom than for that town. (Luke 10:5–12)

1 Cor. 7:10: The Finality of Marriage

To the married I give this command — not I but the Lord — that the wife should not separate from her husband.

Mark Parallel

He said to them, "Whoever divorces his wife and marries another commits adultery against her; and if she divorces her husband and marries another, she commits adultery." (Mark 10:11–12)

1 Cor. 11:23–25: The Bread and the Cup

For I received from the Lord what I also handed on to you, that the Lord Jesus on the night when he was betrayed took a loaf of bread, and when he had given thanks, he broke it and said, "This is my body that is for you. Do this in remembrance of me." In the same way he took the cup also, after supper, saying, "This cup is the new covenant in my blood. Do this, as often as you drink it, in remembrance of me."

Mark Parallel

While they were eating, he took a loaf of bread, and after blessing it he broke it, gave it to them, and said, "Take; this is my body." Then he took a cup, and after giving thanks he gave it to them, and all of them drank from it. He said to them, "This is my blood of the covenant, which is poured out for many. Truly I tell you, I will never again drink of the fruit of the vine until that day when I drink it new in the kingdom of God." (Mark 14:22–25)

Rom. 12:18; 1 Thess. 5:13: Live Peaceably

If it is possible, so far as it depends on you, live peaceably with all. (Rom. 12:18)

Mark Parallel

Salt is good; but if salt has lost its saltiness, how can you season it? Have salt in yourselves, and be at peace with one another. (Mark 9:50)

Rom. 13:7: On Paying Taxes

Pay to all what is due them — taxes to whom taxes are due, revenue to whom revenue is due, respect to whom respect is due, honor to whom honor is due.

Mark Parallel

Then they sent to him some Pharisees and some Herodians to trap him in what he said. And they came and said to him, "Teacher, we know that you are sincere, and show deference to no one; for you do not regard people with partiality, but teach the way of God in accordance with truth. Is it lawful to pay taxes to the emperor, or not? Should we pay them, or should we not?"

But knowing their hypocrisy, he said to them, "Why are you putting me to the test? Bring me a denarius and let me see it."

And they brought one. Then he said to them, "Whose head is this, and whose title?"

They answered, "The emperor's."

Jesus said to them, "Give to the emperor the things that are the emperor's, and to God the things that are God's." And they were utterly amazed at him. (Mark 12:13–17)

Rom. 14:13: Avoid Being a Stumbling Block

Let us therefore no longer pass judgment on one another, but resolve instead never to put a stumbling block or hindrance in the way of another.

Mark Parallel

If any of you put a stumbling block before one of these little ones who believe in me, it would be better for you if a great millstone were hung around your neck and you were thrown into the sea. (Mark 9:42)

Rom. 14:14: Nothing Is Unclean

I know and am persuaded in the Lord Jesus that nothing is unclean in itself; but it is unclean for anyone who thinks it unclean.

Mark Parallel

there is nothing outside a person that by going in can defile, but the things that come out are what defile. (Mark 7:15)

See Table A.1 for a complete summary of the topics used by Paul from the Jesus tradition available to him.

There is a tendency for the Q material to deal with the life of a congregation. There are sayings regarding forgiveness, not passing

Table A.1. Summary of the Topics Used by Paul from the Jesus Tradition

SOURCE		TOPIC
Q	1 Thess. 2:14–16	Killing the Prophets
	1 Thess. 5:2	Like a Thief in the Night
	1 Cor. 1:19	Wisdom of the Wise
	(common source from Isa. 29:14)	
	1 Cor. 4:5	Nothing Hidden
	1 Cor. 5:6	Yeast Leavens
	1 Cor. 9:14	The Laborer Deserves to Be Paid
	1 Cor. 13:2	Power of Faith
	Rom. 2:1–2; 14:10	Passing Judgment
	Rom. 12:14	Bless Those Who Persecute You
	Rom. 13:10; 12:17; Gal. 5:14	The Law of Love
	Rom. 14:17	Seeking the Kingdom
	Gal. 6:1	Forgiveness
	Phil. 2:8–9	Being Humble
Gospel of Thomas	1 Cor. 2:9	Not of Human Origin
	1 Cor. 10:17	Commensuality
	1 Cor. 8:6	Creation
	2 Cor. 4:6	Light in the Face
	Gal. 3:27–28	Male and Female
	Gal. 5:16–18	Flesh and Spirit
	Rom 2:29 et al.	Circumcision of the Heart
Gospel of Mark	1 Cor. 10:27	Accept the Offer to Eat Together
	1 Cor. 7:10	The Finality of Marriage
	1 Cor. 11:23–25	The Bread and the Cup
	Rom. 12:18; 1 Thess. 5:13	Live Peaceably
	Rom. 13:7	On Paying Taxes
	Rom. 14:13	Avoid Being a Stumbling Block
	Rom. 14:14	Nothing Is Unclean

judgment on others, being humble, and compensating congregational workers. Paul took from Q the law of love that extends even beyond the congregation to those who persecute the new faith.[9] Nevertheless persecution is to be expected because the prophets were also killed. So the new life requires a wisdom that makes relative the standards of this world. Those in the new Jesus movement will need great faith, will act as a leaven in the Mediterranean society, and will expectantly seek the reign of God. That reign will not follow any human sense of time or calendar.

The Gospel of Thomas has a tendency to furnish basic theology to Paul. Divine creation is good and the light of God can be seen in the face of believers. In the community of these believers, a oneness is created and celebrated by breaking bread together, inequalities among men and women are eradicated. The conflict of the Two Ways, flesh and spirit, will have been mitigated. Circumcision, that has so separated Jews from non-Jews, will continue to be a mark of devotion to God, but will be a spiritual sign.

From the Gospel of Mark tradition Paul tends to extract more formal community matters. Not only does he commend the Lord's supper account from Mark, but he notes that eating questionable food with nonbelievers may make new community possible. After all the Lord himself declared all things clean. Nor should the disciples of Jesus ever put a stumbling block in the way of others. In terms of community ethics, the Jesus movement is not anarchical, so believers should pay taxes as appropriate. And though sometimes conversion may cause a split in a family, the believer should remember that marriage is a permanent union. And above all, the community should live at peace with one another.[10]

Paul passed these oral traditions on to the Celts of north Galatia. The sophisticated oral system of the Celts (Druids and bards) assimilated the oral Jesus tradition and carried it at least to Gaul and Galicia. From Gaul the Jesus tradition passed into the eastern isles. From Galicia it passed into the western isles. The Jesus tradition was the primary basis for the new faith. Although the Celts must have heard Paul's teaching on apocalypticism, sin, guilt, justification by faith, the righteousness of God, death and resurrection, it must not have entered their tradition. The theology of Paul did not reach the islands. Both islands resisted Pauline theology and, at the same time, any romanization of the faith. Because Great Britain was occupied by the Romans for four centuries, romanization did occur. But that did not happen in Ireland. An example of the original, oral Jesus tradition exists in Ireland, collected before it could have been written, entering a completely oral culture, essentially out of touch with the Greco-Roman world. The resulting Christianity does not resemble its Roman counterpart.

Notes

1. Jonathan L. Reed, "The Social Map of Q," in *Conflict and Invention: Literary, Rhetorical, and Social Studies on the Sayings Gospel Q,* ed. John Kloppenborg (Philadelphia: Trinity Press International, 1995), 17–36. For a critique and evaluation see William E. Arnal, *Jesus and the Village Scribes: Galilean Conflicts and the Setting of Q* (Minneapolis: Fortress Press, 2001), 159–72.

2. Dieter Betz lists those elements of the Sermon on the Mount (Matthew) and the Sermon on the Plain (Luke) that appear in the letters of Paul (Betz, *The Sermon on the Mount* [Minneapolis: Fortress Press, 1995], 6 n. 12). Helmut Koester in *Ancient Christian Gospels: Their History and Development* (Philadelphia: Trinity Press International, 1990), 53, offers a more complete list of Q references in Paul. For a thorough analysis of the use of Q and Mark (sans the Gospel of Thomas), see Dale Allison, "The Pauline Epistles and the Synoptic Gospels: The Pattern of the Parallels," *NTS* 28 (1982): 1–32, and especially the list on p. 20.

3. Jonathan L. Reed, *Archaeology and the Galilean Jesus: A Re-examination of the Evidence* (Harrisburg, Pa.: Trinity Press International, 2000), 134–36.

4. Kloppenborg Verbin, *Excavating Q,* 72–80; Mack, *The Lost Gospel,* 59, 159.

5. Dale C. Allison, *The Jesus Tradition in Q* (Valley Forge, Pa.: Trinity Press International, 1997), 49–54. His point is well taken if indeed QS 34 should be taken as later Q. Likewise the discussion of 1 Corinthians 1–2 by Peter Richardson would indicate later Q (10:21–24) was available to Paul when the Corinthian correspondence was written. See Richardson, "The Thunderbolt in Q and the Wise Man in Corinth," in *From Jesus to Paul: Studies in Honour of Francis Wright Beare,* ed. Peter Richardson and John C. Hurd (Waterloo, Ontario: Wilfrid Laurier University Press, 1984), 91–111. Our argument here depends on the availability of Q to Paul before he made the visit to Galatia. In the long run it does not matter what level of Q that is. We are using all Q, all Gospel of Thomas, and all Gospel of Mark we discern in the authentic letters of Paul.

6. Mack, *The Lost Gospel,* 81–102.

7. Koester, *Ancient Christian Gospels,* 55–63.

8. I have listed possible Q parallels along with the Gospel of Thomas. In my opinion Paul more likely had access to the Thomas form than the Q.

9. For the use of the law of love in the New Testament, see Victor Furnish, *The Love Command in the New Testament* (Nashville: Abingdon Press, 1972), 25–185. As it affected attitudes toward those who persecuted the first Christians, see Klassen, *Love of Enemies,* 91–118.

10. Andreas Lindemann, "Die Funktion der Herrenworte in der ethischen Argumentation des Paulus im Ersten Korintherbrief," in *The Four Gospels: Festschrift Frans Neirynck,* ed. F. Van Segbroeck et al. (Leuven: University Press, 1992), 2:677–88.

Bibliography

Adcock, Gwenda. "Theory of Interlace and Interlace Types in Anglican Sculpture." In *Anglo-Saxon and Viking Age Sculpture and Its Context,* ed. James Lang, 36–45. BAR British Series 49. Oxford: British Archaeological Reports, 1978.

Adomnán of Iona. *Life of St. Columba.* Translated by Richard Sharpe. London: Penguin, 1995.

Allen, J. Romilly. *Celtic Art in Pagan and Christian Times.* London: Whiting & Co., 1887; Bracken Books, 1993.

Allison, Dale. *The Jesus Tradition in Q.* Valley Forge, Pa.: Trinity Press International, 1997.

———. "The Pauline Epistles and the Synoptic Gospels: The Pattern of the Parallels." *NTS* 28 (1982): 1–32.

Ancient Laws of Ireland [Senchus Mor]. Dublin: Alexander Thom, 1869.

Anderson, Joseph. *Scotland in Early Christian Times.* Edinburgh: D. Douglas, 1881.

Anderson, Marjorie O. "Columba and Other Irish Saints in Ireland." *Historical Studies* 5 (1965): 26–36.

Arnal, William E. *Jesus and the Village Scribes: Galilean Conflicts and the Setting of Q.* Minneapolis: Fortress Press, 2001.

Audouze, Françoise, and Oliver Büchsenschütz. *Towns, Villages, and Countryside of Celtic Europe: From the Beginning of the Second Millennium to the End of the First Century B.C.* Translated by Henry Cleere. London: Batsford, 1992.

Aus, R. D. "Paul's Travel Plans to Spain and the 'Full Number of the Gentiles' of Rom XI 25." *NovT* 21 (1979): 244–46.

Bailey, K. E. "Informal Controlled Oral Tradition and the Synoptic Gospels." *Asia Journal of Theology* 5 (1991): 34–54; reprinted in *Themelios* 20, no. 2 (1995): 4–11.

Baroja, Julio Caro. *Los pueblos del norte de la península Ibérica.* Madrid: Burgos, 1943.

Batto, Bernard F. *Slaying the Dragon: Mythmaking in the Biblical Tradition.* Louisville, Ky.: Westminster/John Knox, 1992.

Betz, Hans Dieter. *Galatians.* Philadelphia: Fortress Press, 1979.

———. *The Sermon on the Mount.* Minneapolis: Fortress Press, 1995.

Bieler, Ludwig. *Ireland: Harbinger of the Middle Ages.* German ed., 1961. London: Oxford University Press, 1963

———. *The Works of St. Patrick.* London: Longmans, Green & Co., 1953.

Black, Matthew. *An Aramaic Approach to the Gospels and Acts.* Oxford: Clarendon, 1967.

Borgen, Peder. *Paul Preaches Circumcision and Pleases Men: and Other Essays on Christian Origins.* Trondheim: Tapir, 1983.

Bornkamm, Gunther, "The Stilling of the Storm." In *Tradition and Interpretation in Matthew,* ed. Bornkamm, G. Barth, and H. J. Held, 52–57. London: SCM, 1963.

Bosch-Gimpera, P. "Two Celtic Waves in Spain." In *Proceedings of the British Academy,* 25–148. London: Published for the British Academy, 1940.

Bowen, E. J. "The Cult of Saint Brigit." *Studia Celtic* 8 (1973): 33–47.

Bradley, Ian. *Celtic Christianity: Making Myths and Chasing Dreams.* Edinburgh: Edinburgh University Press, 1999.

Briggs, Daphne Nash. "Coinage." In *The Celtic World,* ed. Miranda J. Green, 144–253. London: Routledge, 1995.

Burton, Ernest de Witt. *The Epistles to the Galatians.* 1921. Edinburgh: T. & T. Clark, 1971.

Bury, John B. *The Life of St. Patrick and His Place in History.* 1905. Mineola, N.Y.: Dover Publications, 1998.

Byrne, Francis J. "The Ireland of St. Columba." *Historical Studies* 5 (1965): 37–58.

Cahill, Thomas. *How the Irish Saved Civilization: The Untold Story of Ireland's Heroic Role from the Fall of Rome to the Rise of Medieval Europe.* New York: Doubleday, 1995.

Casey, Maurice. *Aramaic Sources of Mark's Gospel.* Cambridge: Cambridge University Press, 1998.

Cassidy, Brendan, ed. *The Ruthwell Cross.* Princeton, N.J.: Princeton University Press, 1992.

Charles-Edwards, Thomas. *Christianity in Roman Britain.* London: Batsford, 1981.

———. *Early Christian Ireland.* Cambridge: Cambridge University Press, 2000.

———. "The Social Background to Irish Peregrinatio." *Studia Celtica* 11 (1976): 43–59.

Charlesworth, Martin Percival. *Five Men: Character Studies from the Roman Empire.* Cambridge: Harvard University Press, 1936.

Cherpillod, André. *La Langue Gauloise.* Courgenard: Autoédition, 1998.

Collis, John. "The First Towns." In *The Celtic World,* ed. Miranda J. Green, 159–75. London: Routledge, 1995.

———. *Oppida: Earliest Towns North of the Alps.* Sheffield, England: Department of Prehistory and Archaeology, 1984.

Condren, Mary. *The Serpent and the Goddess: Women, Religion, and Power in Celtic Ireland.* San Francisco: Harper and Row, 1989.

Cook, Albert S. *The Date of the Ruthwell and Bewcastle Crosses.* New Haven: Yale University Press, 1912.

Crossan, John Dominic. *The Historical Jesus: The Life of a Mediterranean Peasant.* San Francisco: HarperSanFrancisco, 1991.

Cruden, Stewart. *The Early Christian and Pictish Monuments of Scotland.* Edinburgh: Her Majesty's Stationery Office, 1964.

Cunliffe, Barry. *The Ancient Celts.* Oxford: Oxford University Press, 1997.

————. *Facing the Ocean: The Atlantic and Its People, 8000 B.C.–A.D. 1500.* Oxford: Oxford University Press, 2001.

Czarnowski, Stefan. *Le culte des héros et ses conditions sociales: Saint Patrick, héros national de l'Irlande.* 1919. New York: Arno Press, 1975.

Dahl, Nils Alstrup. *Jesus in the Memory of the Early Church.* Minneapolis: Augsburg, 1976.

Dandoy, Jeremiah R., Page Selinsky, and Mary M. Voight. "Celtic Sacrifice." *Archaeology* 55 (2002): 44–49.

Davies, Norman. *The Isles: A History.* Oxford: Oxford University Press, 1999.

Davies, Oliver, ed. and trans. *Celtic Spirituality.* Mahwah, N.J.: Paulist Press, 1999.

Davies, Stevan L. *Jesus the Healer: Possession, Trance, and the Origins of Christianity.* New York: Continuum, 1995.

Davies, W. D., and L. Finkelstein, eds. *The Cambridge History of Judaism,* vol. 2. Cambridge: Cambridge University Press, 1989.

de Bruyn, Theodore. *Pelagius's Commentary on St. Paul's Epistle to the Romans.* Oxford: Clarendon Press, 1993.

de Paor, Liam. "The Aggrandisement of Armagh." *Historical Studies* 8 (1971): 95–110.

————. *St. Patrick's World.* Dublin: Four Courts Press, 1993.

de Paor, Máire, ed. and trans. *Patrick the Pilgrim, Apostle of Ireland: St Patrick's Confessio and Epistola.* Dublin: Veritas Publications, 1998.

de Paor, Máire, and Liam de Paor. *Early Christian Ireland.* London: Thames and Hudson, 1958.

Dillon, Myles. *Celts and Aryans: Survivals of Indo-European Speech and Society.* Simla: Indian Institute of Advanced Studies, 1975.

Dinkler, E. "Die Petrus-Rom-Frage." *Theologische Rundschau* 25 (1959): 189–230, 289–335; 27 (1961): 33–64.

Dodd, C. H. *The Parables of the Kingdom.* 1935. London: Nisbet and Co., 1950.

Doherty, Charles. "The Monastic Town in Early Medieval Ireland." In *The Comparative History of Urban Origins in Non-Roman Europe,* BAR International Series 255, ed. Howard Clark and Anngret Simms, 45–75. Oxford: British Archaeological Reports, 1985.

Donfried, Karl. "Chronology." *ABD* 1:1021.

Duke, John A. *The Columban Church.* Oxford: Oxford University Press, 1932.

Dumville, D. "Some British Aspects of the Earliest Irish Christianity." In *Ireland and Europe,* ed. Ní Chatháin and M. Richter. Stuttgart: Klett-Cotta, 1984.

Dunn, J. D. G. *Jesus, Paul, and the Law: Studies in Mark and Galatians.* Louisville, Ky.: Westminster/John Knox, 1990.

Ebeling, Gerhard. *The Truth of the Gospel: An Exposition of Galatians.* Translated by David Green. 1981; Philadelphia: Fortress Press, 1985.

Edwards, Nancy. *The Archaeology of Early Medieval Ireland.* Philadelphia: University of Pennsylvania Press, 1990.

Elliott, John H. "Paul, Galatians, and the Evil Eye." *Currents in Theology and Mission* 17 (1990): 262–73.

Elliott, Susan Margaret. "Choose Your Mother, Choose Your Master: Galatians 4:21–5:1 in the Shadow of the Anatolian Mother of the Gods." *JBL* 118 (1999): 661–83.

Ellis, Earle. *The Making of the New Testament Documents*. Leiden: Brill, 1999.

Ellis, Peter Berresford. *The Ancient World of the Celts*. New York: Barnes and Noble, 1999.

———. *The Celtic Empire: The First Millennium of Celtic History c. 1000 B.C.– 51 A.D.* London: Constable, 1990.

Esler, Philip F. *Galatians*. New York: Routledge, 1998.

Finney, Paul Corby. *The Invisible God: The Earliest Christians on Art*. Oxford: Oxford University Press, 1994.

Flanagan, Laurence. *Ancient Ireland: Life Before the Celts*. New York: St. Martin's Press, 1998.

Freeman, Philip. *The Galatian Language: A Comprehensive Survey of the Language of the Ancient Celts in Greco-Roman Asia Minor*. Lewiston, N.Y.: Mellen Press, 2001.

———. *Ireland and the Classical World*. Austin: University of Texas Press, 2001.

Frend, W. H. C. "Romano-British Christianity and the West: Comparison and Contrast." In *The Early Church in Western Britain and Ireland,* ed. Susan M. Pearce, 5–11. BAR British Series 102. Oxford: British Archaeological Reports, 1982.

Funk, Robert W. *Honest to Jesus: Jesus for a New Millennium*. San Francisco: HarperSanFrancisco, 1996.

Furnish, Victor. *Jesus According to Paul*. Cambridge: Cambridge University Press, 1993.

———. *The Love Command in the New Testament*. Nashville: Abingdon Press, 1972.

Gager, John. *Kingdom and Community: The Social World of Early Christianity*. Englewood Cliffs, N.J.: Prentice-Hall, 1975.

Ginnell, Laurence. *The Brehon Laws: A Legal Handbook*. London: T. Fisher Unwin, 1894.

Grabar, André. *Christian Iconography: A Study of Its Origins*. Princeton, N.J.: Princeton University Press, 1968.

Green, Miranda J. *Animals in Celtic Life and Myth*. London: Routledge, 1992.

———. *Celtic Goddesses: Warriors, Virgins and Mothers*. New York: G. Braziller, 1996.

———, ed. *The Celtic World*. London: Routledge, 1995.

———. *Dictionary of Celtic Myth and Legend*. London: Thames and Hudson, 1992.

———. *The Gods of the Celts*. Gloucester: Alan Sutton, 1986.

———. *The Wheel as a Cult-Symbol in the Romano-Celtic World*. Bruxelles: Latomus Revue d'Etudes Latines, 1984.

Grosjean, Paul. "Notes d'Hagiographie Celtique, 4. Une Invocation des Saintes Brigides." *Analecta Bollandiana* 61 (1943): 103–5.

Hanson, R. P. C. *The Life and Writings of the Historical Saint Patrick*. New York: Seabury Press, 1983.

Harbison, Peter. *Guide to the National and Historic Monuments of Ireland.* Dublin: Gill and Macmillan, 1992.

———. *Irish High Crosses: With the Figure Sculptures Explained.* Syracuse, N.Y.: Syracuse University Press, 1994.

———. *Pilgrimage in Ireland: The Monuments and the People.* Syracuse, N.Y.: Syracuse University Press, 1991.

———. *Pre-Christian Ireland: From the First Settlers to the Early Celts.* London: Thames and Hudson, 1988.

Hardy, Philip Dixon. *The Holy Wells of Ireland.* Dublin: P. D. Hardy, etc., 1836.

Harnack, Adolf von. *The Mission and Expansion of Christianity.* Translated by James Moffatt. New York: G. P. Putnam, 1904.

Hawkes, C. F. H. "Cumulative Celticity in Pre-Roman Britain." *Études Celtiques* 13, no. 2 (1973): 607–28.

Hennecke, Edgar. *New Testament Apocrypha.* Translated by R. McL. Wilson et al. Vol. 2. Philadelphia: Westminster Press, 1965.

Henry, Françoise. *Irish Art in the Early Christian Period (to 800 A.D.).* Ithaca, N.Y.: Cornell University Press, 1965.

———. *Studies in Early Christian and Medieval Art.* Vol. III. Architecture and Sculpture. London: Pindar Press, 1985.

Herbert, Máire. "The Legacy of Colum Cille and His Monastic Community." In *The Cultures of Europe: The Irish Contribution,* ed. James P. Mackey, 9–20. Belfast: Institute of Irish Studies, 1994.

Herm, Gerhard. *The Celts: The People Who Came Out of the Darkness.* New York: St. Martin's Press, 1977.

Hill, Emmeline W., Mark A. Jobling, and Daniel G. Bradley. "Y-chromosome Variation and Irish Origins." *Nature* 404 (2000): 351–52.

Hughes, Kathleen. *The Church in Early Irish Society.* London: Methuen, 1980.

Hughes, Kathleen, and Ann Hamlin. *The Modern Traveller to the Early Irish Church.* Dublin: Four Courts Press, 1997.

Hurley, Vincent. "The Early Church in the South-West of Ireland: Settlement and Organisation." In *The Early Church in Western Britain and Ireland,* ed. Susan M. Pearce, 297–332. Oxford: BAR 102, 1982.

Jackson, Kenneth H. *A Celtic Miscellany.* London: Routledge and Kegan Paul, 1967.

James, Simon. *The Atlantic Celts: Ancient Peoples or Modern Invention.* London: British Museum Press, 1999.

———. *Exploring the World of the Celts.* London: Thames and Hudson, 1993.

Jensen, Robin. *Understanding Early Christian Art.* London: Routledge, 2000.

Jeremias, Joachim. *The Prayers of Jesus.* Philadelphia: Fortress Press, 1975.

Jewett, Robert. *A Chronology of Paul's Life.* Philadelphia: Fortress Press, 1979.

Johnston, George. " 'Kingdom of God' Sayings in Paul's Letters." In *From Jesus to Paul: Studies in Honour of Francis Wright Beare,* ed. Peter Richardson and John C. Hurd, 143–56. Waterloo, Ontario: Wilfrid Laurier University Press, 1984.

Jonas. *Life of St. Columban.* Edited by Dana Carleton Munro. Felinfach: Llanerch, 1993.

Joyce, Timothy J. *Celtic Christianity: A Sacred Tradition, a Vision of Hope.* Maryknoll, N.Y.: Orbis Books, 1998.

Kee, Howard Clark. "From the Jesus Movement Toward Institutional Church." In *Conversion to Christianity: Historical and Anthropological Perspectives on a Great Transformation,* ed. Robert W. Hefner, 47–63. Berkeley: University of California Press, 1993.

Kerr, William Shaw. *The Independence of the Celtic Church in Ireland.* London: SPCK, 1931.

Kim, Seyoon. *Paul and the New Perspective: Second Thoughts on the Origin of Paul's Gospel.* Grand Rapids, Mich.: Eerdmans, 2002.

King, John. *Kingdoms of the Celts: A History and a Guide.* London: Blandford, 1998.

Klassen, William. *Love of Enemies: The Way to Peace.* Philadelphia: Fortress Press, 1984.

Kloppenborg Verbin, John S. *Excavating Q: The History and Setting of the Sayings Gospel.* Edinburgh: T. & T. Clark, 2000.

Koester, Helmut. *Ancient Christian Gospels: Their History and Development.* Philadelphia: Trinity Press International, 1990.

LaGrand, James. *The Earliest Christian Mission to "All Nations" in the Light of Matthew's Gospel.* Grand Rapids, Mich.: Eerdmans, 1999.

Laing, Lloyd, and Jennifer Laing. *Celtic Britain and Ireland: Art and Society.* New York: St. Martin's Press, 1995.

Lambert, Pierre-Yves. *La langue gauloise: Description linguistique, commentaire d'inscriptions choises.* Paris: Editions Errance, 1995.

Lehane, Brendan. *Early Celtic Christianity.* London: Constable, 1994.

Lindemann, Andreas. "Die Funktion der Herrenworte in der ethischen Argumentation des Paulus im Ersten Korintherbrief." In F. Van Segbroeck et al., eds. *The Four Gospels: Festschrift Frans Neirynck,* 2:677–88. Leuven: University Press, 1992.

Lives of the Saints. Translated and with an introduction by J. F. Webb. Baltimore: Penguin Books, 1965.

Lüdemann, Gerd. *Paul, Apostle to the Gentiles.* Philadelphia: Fortress Press, 1984.

Lührmann, Dieter. *Der Brief an die Galater.* Zürich: Theologische Verlag, 1978.

———. "Tage, Monate, Jahreszeiten, Jahre (Gal 4:10)." In *Wirken und Werden des Alten Testament,* ed. R. Albertz et al. Göttingen: Vandenhoeck and Ruprecht, 1980, 430–31.

Mac Airt, Seán, and Gearóid Mac Niocaill, eds. *The Annals of Ulster (to A.D. 1131).* Part 1. Dublin: Institute for Advanced Studies, 1983.

MacCana, Proinsias. *Celtic Mythology.* London: Hamlyn Publishing, 1970.

Macaulay, Donald. *The Celtic Languages.* Cambridge: Cambridge University Press, 1992.

McCone, Kim. "An Introduction to Early Irish Saints' Lives." *Maynooth Review* 11 (1986): 26–59.

Mac Eoin, Gearóid. "Irish." In *The Celtic Languages,* ed. Martin J. Ball with James Fife, 101–44. London: Routledge, 1993.

Mack, Burton L. *The Lost Gospel: The Book of Q and Christian Origins.* San Francisco: HarperSanFrancisco, 1993.

MacKendrick, Paul. *The Iberian Stones Speak: Archaeology in Spain and Portugal.* New York: Funk and Wagnalls, 1969.

Mackey, James P., ed. *The Cultures of Europe: The Irish Contribution.* Belfast: The Institute of Irish Studies, 1994.

———, ed. *An Introduction to Celtic Christianity.* Edinburgh: T. & T. Clark, 1989.

McManus, Damian. *A Guide to Ogam.* Maynooth: An Sagart, 1991.

Mac Mathúna, Séamas. *Immram Brain, Bran's Journey to the Land of the Women.* Tübingen: M. Niemeyer, 1985.

MacMullen, Ramsay. *Romanization in the Time of Augustus.* New Haven: Yale University Press, 2000.

McNeill, John Thomas. *The Celtic Churches: A History A.D. 200 to 1200.* Chicago: University of Chicago Press, 1974.

Mac Niocaill, Gearóid. "Christian Influence in Early Irish Law." In *Irland und Europa,* ed. Próinseás Ní Chatháin and Michel Richter, 151–56. Stuttgart: Klett-Cotta, 1984.

Madden, Patrick. *Jesus' Walking on the Sea: An Investigation of the Origin of the Narrative Account.* New York: de Gruyter, 1997; Beihefte zur NTW, 81.

Malbon, Elizabeth. *The Iconography of the Sarcophagus of Junius Bassus.* Princeton, N.J.: Princeton University Press, 1990.

Malina, Bruce J. *The Social Gospel of Jesus: The Kingdom of God in Mediterranean Perspective.* Minneapolis: Fortress Press, 2001.

Martin, Troy. *By Philosophy and Empty Deceit: Colossians as Response to a Cynic Critique.* Sheffield: Sheffield Academic Press, 1996.

———. "Pagan and Judeo-Christian Time-Keeping Schemes in Gal. 4:10 and Col. 2:16." *NTS* 42 (1996): 111–19.

Martyn, J. Louis. *Galatians.* New York: Doubleday, 1997.

Meier, John P. *A Marginal Jew: Rethinking the Historical Jesus,* vol. 1. New York: Doubleday, 1991.

Meyrick, Frederick. *The Church in Spain.* London: Wells Gardner, Darton & Co. 1892.

Milburn, Robert. *Early Christian Art and Architecture.* Berkeley: University of California Press, 1988.

Mitchell, Stephen. *Anatolia: Land, Men and Gods in Asia Minor.* Oxford: Clarendon Press, 1993.

Mohrmann, Christine. *The Latin of St. Patrick: Four Lectures.* Dublin: Dublin Institute of Advanced Studies, 1961.

Mugambi, J. N. K. *African Heritage and Contemporary Christianity.* Nairobi: Longman Kenya, 1989.

Mytum, Harold. *The Origins of Early Christian Ireland.* London: Routledge, 1992.

Nanos, Mark. *The Irony of Galatians: Paul's Letter in First-Century Context.* Minneapolis: Fortress Press, 2002.

Neirynck, Frans, "Paul and the Sayings of Jesus." In *L'Apôtre Paul: person-nalité, style et conception du ministère*, ed. Albert Vanhoye, 265–321. Leuven: Leuven University Press, 1986.

Nicholson, M. Forthhomme. "Celtic Theology: Pelagius." In *An Introduction to Celtic Christianity*, ed. James P. Mackey, 386–413. Edinburgh: T. & T. Clark, 1989.

Nordenfalk, Carl. *Celtic and Anglo-Saxon Painting: Book Illumination in the British Isles 600–800*. 1977; New York: George Braziller, 1995.

Ó Briain, Felim. "Irish Hagiography: Historiography and Method." In *Measgra I Gcuimhne Mhichíl Uí Chleirigh*, ed. Sylvester O'Brien, 199–31. Dublin: Assisi Press, 1944.

Ó Cathasaigh, D. "The Cult of Brigid: A Study of Pagan-Christian Syncretism." In *Mother Worship*, ed. James L. Preston. Chapel Hill: University of North Carolina Press, 1982.

O'Donoghue, N. D. "St. Patrick's Breastplate." In *An Introduction to Celtic Christianity*, ed. James P. Mackey. Edinburgh: T. & T. Clark, 1989.

Ó Fiaich, Tomás. "Irish Monks on the Continent." In *An Introduction to Celtic Christianity*, ed. James P. Mackey, 108–10. Edinburgh: T. & T. Clark, 1989.

O'Hanlon, John. *Lives of Irish Saints*. Dublin: James Duffy, 1875–1903.

O'Laoghaire, Diarmuid. "Irish Spirituality." In *Ireland and Europe*, ed. Ní Chatháin and M. Richter. Stuttgart: Klett-Cotta, 1984.

O'Neill, John C. "New Testament Monasteries." In *Common Life in the Early Church: Essays Honoring Graydon F. Snyder*, ed. Julian V. Hills, 118–32. Harrisburg, Pa.: Trinity Press International, 1998.

O'Rahilly, T. F. *The Two Patricks*. 1942; Dublin: DIAS, 1957.

Osiek, Carolyn. *Shepherd of Hermas*. Minneapolis: Fortress Press, 1999.

Pearce, Susan M., ed. *The Early Church in Western Britain and Ireland*. Oxford: BAR 102, 1982.

Perkins, Pheme. *Abraham's Divided Children*. Harrisburg, Pa.: Trinity Press International, 2001.

Phipps, William E. *Was Jesus Married? The Distortion of Sexuality in the Christian Tradition*. New York: Harper and Row, 1973.

Porter, Arthur Kingsley. *The Crosses and Culture of Ireland*. New Haven: Yale University Press, 1931.

Price, Glanville. *Ireland and the Celtic Connection*. Gerrards Cross: Colin Smythe, 1987.

Raftery, Barry. "Ireland: A World Without the Romans." In *The Celtic World*, ed. Miranda J. Green, 636–53. London: Routledge, 1995.

Rankin, David. "The Celts Through Classical Eyes." In *The Celtic World*, ed. Miranda J. Green, 21–33. London: Routledge, 1995.

Redknap, Mark. "Early Christianity and Its Monuments." In *The Celtic World*, ed. Miranda J. Green, 737–78. London: Routledge, 1995.

Reed, Jonathan L. *Archaeology and the Galilean Jesus: A Re-examination of the Evidence*. Harrisburg, Pa.: Trinity Press International, 2000.

———. "The Social Map of Q." In *Conflict and Invention: Literary, Rhetorical, and Social Studies on the Sayings Gospel Q*, ed. John Kloppenborg, 17–36. Philadelphia: Trinity Press International, 1995.

Rees, B. R. *Pelagius: Life and Letters.* Woodbridge: Boydell Press, 1998.

Reymond, Philippe. *L'eau, sa vie, et sa signification dans l'ancien testament.* Leiden: Brill, 1958.

Richardson, Peter. "The Thunderbolt in Q and the Wise Man in Corinth. In *From Jesus to Paul: Studies in Honour of Francis Wright Beare*, ed. Peter Richardson and John C. Hurd, 91–111. Waterloo, Ontario: Wilfrid Laurier University Press, 1984.

Roe, Helen M. *The High Crosses of Kells.* Meath Archaeological and Historical Society, 1966.

Salisbury, Joyce E. *Iberian Popular Religion, 600 B.C. to 700 A.D.: Celts, Romans, and Visigoths.* New York: E. Mellen Press, 1985.

Sanders, E. P. *Paul and Palestinian Judaism.* Philadelphia: Fortress Press, 1977.

Schwartz, Daniel. "The End of the GH (Acts 1:8): Beginning or End of the Christian Vision?" *JBL* 105 (1986): 669–76.

Sexton, Eric H. L. *Irish Figure Sculptures of the Early Christian Period.* Portland, Me.: Southworth-Anthoensen Press, 1946.

Simón, Francisco Marco. *Die Religion im keltischen Hispanien.* Budapest: Archaeolingua Alapítváry, 1998.

Snyder, Graydon F. "The Aesthetic Origins of Early Christian Architecture." In *Text and Artifact: Judaism and Christianity in the Ancient Mediterranean World*, ed. Stephen G. Wilson and Michel Desjardins, 289–307. Waterloo, Ontario: Wilfrid Laurier University Press, 2000.

———. *Ante Pacem: Archaeological Evidence of Church Life Before Constantine.* Macon, Ga.: Mercer University Press, 1985.

———. "The Historical Jesus in the Letters of Ignatius of Antioch." *Biblical Research* 8 (1963): 3–12.

———. *Inculturation of the Jesus Tradition: The Impact of Jesus on Jewish and Roman Cultures.* Harrisburg, Pa.: Trinity Press International, 1999.

———. "The Ironic Dialogues in John." In *Putting Body and Soul Together*, ed. V. Wiles, A. Brown, and G. F. Snyder, 3–23. Valley Forge: Trinity Press, 1997.

———. "John 13:16 and the Anti-Petrinism of the Johannine Tradition." *Biblical Research* 16 (1971): 1–11.

———. "Sea Monsters in Early Christian Art." *Biblical Research* 44 (2000): 7–21.

———. "Survey and 'New' Thesis on the Bones of Peter." *The Biblical Archaeologist Reader*, vol. 3, ed. Edward F. Campbell Jr. and David Noel Freedman, 405–24. Garden City, N.Y.: Doubleday, 1970.

———. "The *Tobspruch* in the New Testament." *New Testament Studies* 23 (1976–77): 117–20.

Stark, Rodney. *The Rise of Christianity.* San Francisco: HarperSanFrancisco, 1997.

Stevenson, James. *The Catacombs: Life and Death in Early Christianity.* Nashville: Thomas Nelson, 1985.

Strabo, Walahfrid. *The Life of St. Gall.* Edited by Maud Joynt. London: SPCK, 1927.

Stuhlmacher, Peter. *Paul's Letter to the Romans: A Commentary.* Translated by S. J. Hafemann. Louisville, Ky.: Westminster/John Knox, 1994.

Theissen, Gerd. *The Social Setting of Pauline Christianity.* Philadelphia: Fortress, 1982.

————. "The Wandering Radicals: Light Shed by the Sociology of Literature on the Early Transmission of Jesus' Sayings." In *Social Reality and the Early Christians: Theology, Ethics, and the World of the New Testament,* trans. M. Kohl, 33–59. 1973; Minneapolis: Fortress Press, 1992.

Theissen, Gerd, and Annette Merz. *The Historical Jesus: A Comprehensive Guide.* Translated by John Bowden. Minneapolis: Fortress Press, 1998.

Thompson, E. A. *Who Was Saint Patrick?* New York: St. Martin's Press, 1985.

Thompson, James. *Preaching Like Paul.* Louisville, Ky.: Westminster, 2000.

Tranoy, Alain. *La Galice romaine.* Paris: de Boccard, 1981.

Troeltsch, Ernst. *The Social Teaching of the Christian Churches,* vol. 1, trans. Olive Wyon. New York: Macmillan, 1931.

Ulmer, Rivka. *The Evil Eye in the Bible and in Rabbinic Literature.* Hoboken, N.J.: KTAV Publishing House, 1994.

van Hamel, A. G., ed. *Immrama.* Dublin: The Stationery Office, 1941.

Villares, Ramón. *História da Galiza.* Lisbon: Livros Horizonte, 1991.

Weisweiler, Josef. "Die Stellung der Frau bei den Kelten und das Problem des Keltischen 'Mutter-rechts.' " *Zeitschrift für Celtische Philologie* 21, no. 2 (1939): 205–79.

Wells, Peter S. "Resources and Industry." In *The Celtic World,* ed. Miranda J. Green, 213–29. London: Routledge, 1995.

Whitehouse, Harvey. *Arguments and Icons: Divergent Modes of Religiosity.* Oxford: Oxford University Press, 2000.

Wilken, Robert L. *The Christians as the Romans Saw Them.* New Haven: Yale University Press, 1984.

————. *The Myth of Christian Beginnings: History's Impact on Belief.* Garden City, N.Y.: Doubleday, 1971.

Wilson, Stephen G. "Early Christian Music." In *Common Life in the Early Church: Essays Honoring Graydon F. Snyder,* ed. Julian V. Hills, 390–401. Harrisburg, Pa.: Trinity Press International, 1998.

Zaczek, Iain. *Book of Irish Legends.* Chicago: Contemporary Books, 1998.

Zimmer, Heinrich. *Pelagius in Irland.* Berlin: Weidmann, 1901.

Index of Texts

Index of Authors

Index of Subjects

274.15
S6753 280

LINCOLN CHRISTIAN COLLEGE AND SEMINARY 10463/

3 4711 00169 5305